Managing and maintaining compliance

MANAGING AND MAINTAINING COMPLIANCE

Edited by

HENK ELFFERS
Netherlands Institute for the Study of Crime and Law Enforcement, NSCR

PETER VERBOON
Department of Marketing and Research,
Dutch Tax and Customs Administration

WIM HUISMAN
Department of Criminology, Leiden University

Boom Legal publishers
The Hague
2006

This publication was realized with the cooperation of the Ministry of Justice, the Dutch Tax and Customs Administration and Leiden University.

ISBN-10: 90-5454-767-7
ISBN-13: 978-90-5454-767-9

NUR: 820

www.bju.nl

PREFACE

Henk Elffers, Peter Verboon and Wim Huisman[1]

Modern society is riddled with laws and rules that should be obeyed. However, for many people and many organizations that are supposed to follow those rules it does not go without saying that they will indeed comply with those rules. Non-compliance with certain rules may well be an attractive option for some or many of them, in some or even many circumstances. For that reason many of the rule systems in place are being controlled by enforcing agencies, which may investigate whether rules are complied with and, if not, those agencies are invested with the power to punish the non-complier. In principle such a situation is simple: when the probabilities of being controlled are high enough and the then following sanctions are severe enough, every rational person or organization has an interest in complying: the cost of rule transgression is too high. However, law enforcement has its price as well, and it may well be that reaching a level of punishment threat high enough to guarantee compliance is simply out of reach, either for reasons of direct costs: enforcement costs too much money, or for reasons of indirect cost: it would frustrate the normal flow of affairs in a given regulatory domain, obstructing the functioning of the rule addressees by imposing too much control on them. Therefore, law enforcement agencies are interested in ways of enhancing compliance other than by strict control-and-punishment. Is it possible to seduce people or organizations to comply with rules voluntarily, by means of positive incentives, or through norm reinforcement, or otherwise? How can

1. Elffers is senior-researcher at the Netherlands Institute for the Study of Crime and Law Enforcement NSCR Leiden, (HElffers@nscr.nl) and professor of psychology and law at Antwerp University; Verboon is researcher at the Department of Marketing and Research B/CPP of the Dutch Tax and Customs Administration, Utrecht (p.verboon@belastingdienst.nl) and assistant professor at Open University Netherlands; Huisman served as associate professor of criminology at Leiden University when editing this book; he is now associate professor of criminology at Free University Amsterdam (w.huisman@rechten.vu.nl).

an enforcement agency manage an optimal mix of deterrence and positive incentives in order to maintain compliance at a satisfactory level without constructing a smooth functioning of the rule addressees?

Such questions formed the topic of an international conference in Leiden, the Netherlands, in April 2006, organized by the Dutch Tax and Customs Administration in cooperation with the Dutch Justice Department and experts from the academic world, under the title *Managing and Maintaining Compliance*. The objective of the conference was to bring together an audience of scientists and policy makers, in order to discuss latest research developments on compliance and confront new insights with experiences from policy and practice of law enforcement. The conference aimed at mapping out an eventual gap between scientists and practitioners in the field of rule enforcement and compliance in order to make it possible to close that gap through discussion and exchange of ideas and experiences.

The current volume presents the expanded version of the conference papers as presented by the speakers, revised in the light of the discussion between speakers and the audience during the conference sessions, the interchange of ideas was enhanced and stimulated by the reviewers that opened the discussion.

Compliance

Why people do or do not comply with the law is an important question for enforcement agencies. Understanding the reasons or motives underlying compliant or non-compliant behaviour can be used as a starting point for enforcement activities. The literature on compliance with or evasion of laws has been dominated by the perspective of economic deterrence. That is, people weigh the expected profits of evasion against the (perceived) chances of getting caught and the penalties imposed when evasion is being detected. These economic or instrumental models of criminal behaviour appear to form the main basis for policies developed by enforcement agencies to stimulate compliance and reduce evasion. Enforcement agencies seem to rely to a large extent on principles of deterrence in order to persuade people to comply with the law. However, economic models of criminal behaviour have several drawbacks. For instance, these models would predict much higher levels of evasion than observed in reality, for example in the case of tax evasion. In the social sciences literature alternative models of compliant behaviour have been developed as a response; this has become known as the normative view on compliance. This perspective emphasises that people are not solely motivated by self-interest and do not act as a result of cost-benefit analyses only. Rather, people's personal convictions about the way one should or should not behave and the anticipated reactions from their social environment are important motives for compliant or non-compliant behaviour. Although the normative view of compliance suggests that effective law enforcement should not only rely on deterrence, in practice few alternative enforcement strategies are used by enforcement agencies.

The present volume starts with a general outline of the above contraposition of the deterrent versus the normative approach to compliance, in the context of income tax laws, by the Viennese economic psychologists *Erich Kirchler* and *Erik Hölzl*. They present a general framework on the individual motives for compliance and its consequences for law enforcement. They emphasize the importance of the interaction processes between law enforcers and citizens. In their conceptual model, they differentiate between what they call the *cops and robbers* climate versus the *service for clients* climate. Once a cops and robbers climate has been established, law enforcement will be extremely difficult. Kirchler and Hölzl argue that it will be much easier for authorities to act within a climate of service for clients.

Many other papers can be seen as expanding on the question how law enforcement can fruitfully use a normative or positive, non-deterrence approach in its relation to those who have to follow those rules. Papers are presented on *rewarding* compliers, on *communication* methods as a means of influencing them, on *re-integrative shaming* as a way of letting non-compliers reconsider their choices henceforth and on ways of reallotting the responsibility of rule obeying to the rule addressees (*responsive regulation, self-regulation*). While there is a certain emphasis on examples from the tax field, several authors discuss various other rule domains as well.

Communication

With respect to addressing the rule subjects' willingness to obey the law, it is often suggested that public campaigns may and should be used for influencing citizens by issuing a general normative message. In this respect, *Lennart Wittberg*, who is employed by the Swedish Tax Agency, discusses a communication campaign initiated by the Swedish tax authorities, aimed at influencing the attitudes of young people. Young people are an important target group for communication strategies because attitudes acquired in younger years may last a lifetime. The campaign described by Wittberg was successful because it resulted in positive changes in attitudes towards tax compliance.

Rewards

Normative messages are not only given by negative reactions to non-compliance, but also by generating positive incentives. The economists *Lars Feld, Bruno Frey* and *Benno Torgler* (who cooperate within the Swiss CREMA – Center for Research in Economics, Management and the Arts), propose to use rewards as a tool for enhancing compliance and discuss the literature on this subject. In general, rewards may be more effective for motivating desired behaviour than punishment. Rewarding, as the counterpart of punishing, is a possible tool for authorities to enforce the law. However, there may be quite a few problems and unwanted side effects to applying the instrument of rewards. It is clear that more research is necessary on the effects of rewarding before it can be applied as an instrument by authorities. In their paper, Feld, Frey and Torgler make a plea for the use of field experiments to study the effect of rewards on compliance.

Responsive regulation

A distinction similar to Kirchler and Hölzl's model is used by the Maryland criminologist *Sally Simpson* in her study of safety regulation of corporations. Although formal sanctions may be effective in particular situations, it is also important to enhance the morality of certain behaviour. Besides normative and instrumental motives to comply with regulations, the complexity and quality of regulations may be another source for undesired behaviour. This may be especially true for corporations. Simpson uses a case study of two recent mining disasters in the United States and new data from her own research on corporate crime to study the influence of the quality of regulation on regulatory compliance, the importance of regulation compared to other instruments of social control and the risks of shortcomings of regulation. She concludes that inconsistencies in and failed implementation of regulatory strategy increase the risk of non-compliance. While the U.S. Mine Safety and Health Administration follows a non-formal, compliance oriented enforcement strategy, the mining disasters have led to new legislation increasing fines and penalties against violators. Furthermore, Simpson stresses the importance of the perception of the legitimacy of regulation. Compliance is better when the law, sanctions and regulatory procedures are perceived as legitimate and fair. This means that interventions should aim at familiarizing managers better with the law and should communicate the normative message of the reprehensibility of non-compliance. In this way, both the moral evaluations as well as the outcome expectancies might be influenced by formal sanctions.

Finally, the results from Simpson's studies might indicate the effectiveness of self-regulation. She finds that profitable corporations report fewer violations and suggests that these companies are more apt to have working management-systems in place that effectively monitor the corporations' level of compliance.

Self-regulation

It is exactly on the point of self-regulation that the Tilburg environmental law scholar *Rob van Gestel* takes the argument a bit further. Van Gestel uses the particular case of certification in the field of the health and welfare of domestic animals in the Netherlands to highlight the dangers of replacing public law with self-regulation. These dangers occur when legislators and policy-makers develop a tunnel vision while looking for regulatory relief. In the Dutch case, policymakers were biased by the semi-official ideology of deregulation and self-regulation without a proper investigation of the self-regulatory potential of the sector. They were overemphasizing the benefits of self-regulation, such as commitment and flexibility, without realizing that some of these will be lost by transforming it into a public policy instrument. Furthermore, Van Gestel claims that the sector of domestic animal health and welfare protection lacks basic conditions for a certification mechanism.

Reintegrative shaming and regulatory enforcement

Reintegrative shaming is a special way of handling the detection of non-compliance, not necessarily in the form of punishment, but instead by providing an opportunity for non-compliers to reconsider their non-compliant choices and change their behavioural choices henceforth. The Canberra psychologist *Valerie Braithwaite* discusses whether reintegrative shaming is a relevant tool for fighting tax evasion. Feelings of shame may confront people with the realization of their failing, which in turn may be a drive to change behaviour. However, shame must be managed carefully by the enforcing authorities, taking into account the social environment of the non-complier. If not, chances are that shame is displaced and results in a larger social distance between the shamed citizen and the authorities, which subsequently leads to resistance and a dismissive stance, in line with the antagonistic cops and robbers model.

The effect of shaming public figures

The Tilburg fiscal law researcher *Richard Happé* discusses a special case in which shaming is used, but more from the point of view of its effects on others, especially when non-compliance of well-known people and the consequences for them is published. By shaming VIPs, the instrument can serve as a strong tool of deterrence for themselves as well as, more importantly, for others. Legal aspects of this special treatment are discussed by Happé. In some situations other instruments may be more effective, like for instance persuasion. To publicly persuade people to voluntary disclose information to the authorities in exchange for not being punished may yield positive results. The special case of a tax amnesty is discussed. However, all consequences of such public campaigns should be carefully considered. If authorities fail to detect and punish those who do not disclose voluntarily, such campaigns may backfire by sending the message that crime pays after all.

Changing enforcement style and the position of enforcing staff

Many of these normative approaches to deterrence have been discussed by the previous authors from the point of view of their effectiveness with respect to the rule addressees. However, a major change in enforcement style also has its effect on enforcement officers. Can they cope with such a culture change in their organization? When authorities choose to change their regulation style from command-and-control to a more persuasive and responsive one, they are confronted with problems such as the tension between responsiveness and meeting legal objectives. The Australian tax researchers *Jenny Job, Andrew Stout* and *Rachael Smith* review what kind of culture changes are necessary in an enforcement organization in order to operate successfully in a responsive regulation style, confronting their model with data on actual change in several tax enforcement departments.

The various papers brought together in this volume show that on the topic of managing and maintaining compliance the model of normative enforcement is a promising one, for which various successes have been demonstrated. The idea, however, that a deep gap would become visible between, on the one hand, proponents of these ideas from the academia and on the other hand, reluctantly opposing practitioners did not come true at all. Indeed, both in the papers in this volume as well as in the discussion on the conference, academics as well as practitioners are well aware of the chances that this approach to enhancing compliance is offering, and both groups seem likewise aware of the many difficulties to be addressed and problems to be solved.

Utrecht, Leiden, August 2006

TABLE OF CONTENTS

1 | MODELLING TAXPAYERS' BEHAVIOUR AS A FUNCTION OF INTERACTION BETWEEN TAX AUTHORITIES AND TAXPAYERS

Erich Kirchler and Erik Hoelzl[1]

1.   INTRODUCTION

Tax non-compliance is a universal phenomenon. It takes place in all societies, in all social strata, in all professions, in all industries, in all religions and in virtually all economic systems. Scholars as far back as Plato wrote about the phenomenon, and the 15th century Ducal Palace of Venice features a drop box through which people could inform the Republic about tax evaders (Adams, 1993; Tanzi & Shome, 1994). Governments as far back as ancient Egypt have struggled to maintain compliance with tax laws (Erard, 1997). It is therefore surprising how little scientific attention this phenomenon had received until recent years. Only during the past 25 years has the subject of tax compliance come into its own as a research area within economics and economic psychology. Since then, studies on tax behaviour have significantly increased, and methods and techniques to study evasion have become manifold. This, however, is also an issue of concern since the results obtained in different studies are heterogeneous.

In the present article, we argue that some heterogeneity in results can be reconciled by considering the relationship between the authorities and the taxpayer. The interaction climate between them can range on a continuum between a *cops and robbers* climate and a *service for clients* climate. It can be characterized by mutual distrust on the one end and mutual trust on the

1.   Erich Kirchler, Erik Hoelzl, Faculty of Psychology, University of Vienna, Universitaetsstrasse 7, A-1010 Vienna, Austria (e-mail: erich.kirchler@univie.ac.at; erik.hoelzl@univie.ac.at).

other. In a climate of distrust, the power of the authority to control taxpayers becomes a matter of enforcing tax compliance through audits and fines. In a climate of trust, voluntary tax compliance is a matter of social representation, including tax mentality, personal and social norms and fairness perceptions.

The remainder of this article is structured as follows: first, economic-psychological tax research is briefly summarized. Then the interaction between tax authorities and taxpayers and resulting tax climates are described. After that a model of tax climate and tax compliance is presented, which can serve both as a conceptual tool to integrate research findings and as an operational tool to develop strategies of interaction with taxpayers. Next, results on tax decisions and representation of taxation are presented. Finally, methodological caveats are discussed, and conclusions are drawn.

2.   Tax behaviour research

Studies on tax behaviour have identified manifold determinants of compliance. By the late 1970s, the U.S. Internal Revenue Service (IRS) already identified more than 60 factors likely to determine taxpayer behaviour. Yet, important recent additions like gain and loss framing of tax dues and withholding phenomena were not included (IRS, 1978, quoted in Chang & Schulz, 1990). Table 1 shows a list of variables determining tax compliance which have been categorized into variables concerning social representation and decision making, with special attention to self-employed tax behaviour, and interaction style between tax authorities and taxpayers (It should be mentioned here that tax behaviour of self-employed people has received much attention in research but is not explicitly considered in this contribution).

The field has seen several literature reviews (e.g. Andreoni, Erard, & Feinstein, 1998; Brandstätter, 1994; Franzoni, 2000; Hasseldine & Bebbington, 1991; Hasseldine & Li, 1999; Jackson & Milliron, 1986; James & Alley, 2002; Lewis, 1982; Milliron & Toy, 1988; Richardson & Sawyer, 2001; Slemrod, Blumenthal & Christian, 2001; Torgler, 2002; Webley et al., 1991; Weigel, Hessing & Elffers, 1987), as well as collections of research in taxation such as the annual publication *Advances in Taxation*, edited by Thomas M. Porcano, and, since 2004, Suzanne Luttman, or special journal issues (e.g. *Journal of Economic Psychology*, 1992, edited by Paul Webley and Dick J. Hessing). This accumulated knowledge provides insight into taxpaying behaviour and is of practical relevance for fiscal policy. However, integration into a comprehensive model of taxpayer behaviour is missing. Thus, the fast growing evidence on tax behaviour and the still widely neglected psychological determinants of tax behaviour in economic models call for a review that integrates the most recent findings in social sciences.

Table 1   Classification of determinants of tax compliance

Political perspective (fiscal policy)
Tax system (complexity, tax rates, etc.)
Social psychological perspective
Mental (social) representations
Tax knowledge and mental concepts
Attitudes: beliefs and evaluations
Norms:
Personal norms; tax ethics
Social norms and identity
Societal norms
Perceived opportunity to evade
Fairness perceptions:
Distributive fairness
Procedural fairness
Retributive fairness
Motivation to comply
Motivational postures
Tax morale
Decision making perspective
Rational decision making
Audit probability, fines, tax rate and income
Psychological aspects of decision making
Sequence of audits: learning processes
Heuristics, biases, frames
Withholding phenomena
Self-employment (paying out of pocket)
Interaction between tax authorities and taxpayers
(*"Cops against robbers"* versus *"service for clients" perspective*)

Tax behaviour has been investigated from a political perspective, mainly focusing on tax law complexity and shadow economy, and from an economic perspective, with the focus on rational decision-making and the impact of tax audits, fines, tax rates and income on compliance. Tax behaviour research from a behavioural economic and economic psychological perspective has focused on various attitudinal variables, norms and fairness and decision anomalies. Taking all of this into account, the present work classifies this research into two main thematic fields: social representations of taxation and decisions to comply. It is assumed that, depending on the *tax climate*, those variables identified as determinants of tax non-compliance operate differently.

The crucial variable that determines tax climate is assumed to be the way tax authorities interact with taxpayers. Tax authorities who perceive taxpayers as *robbers* rather than *clients* are likely to establish a *command and control* climate with taxpayers engaging in escaping the authorities by taking extensive (rational) decisions. Tax authorities who perceive taxpayers as *clients* and governments committed to responsive regulation are likely to establish a climate of cooperation and trust. In the former case compliance can be enforced if the authorities have the power to control tax behaviour and to fine evasion; in the latter case compliance is expected to be the result of spontaneous cooperation. It is assumed that a *cops against robbers* climate favours selfish decision-making, and that taxpayers who engage in extensive decisions predominantly consider the probability of detection and fines. Thus, in a *cops against robbers* climate, tax behaviour should depend on audit probability and fines. On the other hand, if the climate favours cooperation, voluntary compliance is expected to depend on the taxpayers' social representations of taxation.

3.   INTERACTION BETWEEN TAX AUTHORITIES AND TAXPAYERS

With regard to interaction between taxpayers and tax authorities, two approaches have been distinguished: (a) a *cops against robbers* approach, based on the assumption that taxpayers are unwilling to pay their tax share, and try to avoid taxes legally whenever possible or illegally if it pays; (b) a *service for clients* approach, which assumes taxpayers to be cooperative citizens who are willing to comply if they understand tax laws and perceive the law and the procedures of tax paying to be fair (Kirchler, 2006). We assume that taxpayers react differently depending on the approach taken by the tax authorities. They either comply voluntarily or as the result of enforcement. As long as interaction is based on a positive, trusting foundation, as argued in procedural justice theories (Tyler, 1990), it can be hypothesized that taxpayers are willing to comply voluntarily, without considering what alternative provides the best individual profit. A *cops against robbers* relationship, on the other hand, is likely to provoke more *rational*, selfish behaviour, or at least an attempt to behave rationally in terms of personal profit maximization. When taxpayers start thinking about incentives for evading, they face an explicit decision with the options to comply or to take the risk to evade taxes with the possibility of saving money or, in the case of detection and fines, to lose money. It can be hypothesized that determinants of compliance, collected under the heading *decision-making* or under the title *social representations*, assume different importance. In the case of voluntary compliance, subjective tax knowledge, attitudes, norms and fairness may play a major role, whereas in the case of enforced compliance, audits and fines may prove useful to oblige citizens to pay their share. Before elaborating on which variables might influence tax behaviour under different tax authorities' perspectives and interaction approaches, we will briefly summarize the interaction styles which should be perceived as two end-poles of a continuum.

3.1.   Cops against robbers versus service for clients

Administration of the tax system is costly and audits are a relevant cost factor. Therefore, effective audit schemes are a necessity, and only those that are efficient in identifying evaders should be applied. Many strategies approach evasion detection with a *cops against robbers* orientation, with taxpayers as the thieves and tax inspectors as the cops trying to catch them. From such a perspective, it is important to detect individuals with identities and characteristics shrouded in mystery, the so-called *ghosts*; unknown to the tax agency, who is therefore unable to track them down through audit strategies based on reported income. It is also relevant to increase the effectiveness of tax audits by selecting those cases for audits which are most likely to be non-compliant and by awarding a bonus to informants and to tax inspectors. The *cops against robbers* approach is not only costly and of doubtful effect, it also raises the question of how to control the controllers. Moreover, this approach may seem useful in limiting tax evasion by constraining taxpayers to follow the letter of the law, but it is surely not adequate to limit tax avoidance and to motivate taxpayers to voluntarily follow the spirit of the law. Statistics on tax evasion and avoidance leave no doubt that avoidance is by far a greater problem than evasion, so another approach to tax enforcement is clearly necessary.

It is important to take into account that the perception of taxpayers and the resulting style of interaction determine the relationship between tax authorities and taxpayers. From an exchange perspective, the style of interaction determines the *psychological contractual relationship* between the involved parties, which shapes tax morale and consequently willingness to comply. If tax authorities treat taxpayers as fair partners rather than inferior people who are unwilling to pay their share – especially in a relationship where tax authorities have legal power – mutual respect, honesty and trust are likely to be the result.

With the emergence of New Public Management, tax authorities have also become aware of the necessity to consider taxpayers as customers. Instead of using control and unreasonable severity, which provokes a *cops against robbers* mentality, an approach characterized by education and support is more promising in the endeavour to persuade taxpayers to comply. Tax authorities of various countries are redesigning their approaches to taxpayers by treating them as clients and addressing their needs and improving fiscal consciousness. James, Hasseldine, Hite and Toumi (2003) report strategies to promote voluntary compliance, including: training of tax officers; improved public relations; simplification of tax laws and procedural fairness; organizational improvement to facilitate taxpayers' consultation, resolve problems at a single point of contact, and assist in taxpayer compliance; and improving citizens' awareness with regard to their tax responsibilities.

In 1992, Ayres and Braithwaite proposed a new approach to ensure business compliance with regulatory rules. Their approach of responsive regulation is presented in the form of a pyramid with cooperative strategies of self-regulation at the bottom and severe sanctions and incapacitating of wrongdoing at the top. The model recognizes that legal sanctions are not sufficient to enforce compliance. It rather focuses on education, persuasion and dialogue as strategies to gain and maintain compliance of most taxpayers. However, in the case of voluntary and repeated non-cooperation, severe economic and legal sanctions come into operation.

Introducing a new approach is not easy and resistance to change in organizations is likely to result. The proposed new culture of a customer relations orientation is, however, more promising in enhancing cooperation, creating a cooperative tax climate and increasing voluntary compliance than the traditional perception of taxpayers as egoistic utility abusers.

Tax authorities who adopt a *cops against robbers* perspective, who exert sharp undifferentiated control, and who apply severe punishment in cases of filing mistakes and evasion, are likely to contribute to the creation of a climate in which taxpayers are perceived as *enemies* whose illegal behaviour requires prosecution. On the other hand, taxpayers may themselves assume the role of the hunted. Rather than looking at tax authorities as accomplishing a relevant task for the welfare of the community, they may perceive them as hunters, whom taxpayers want to escape from. Perceived peril of persecution and prosecution is likely to corrupt taxpayers' willingness to comply voluntarily. Rather than perceiving interaction processes with the authorities as supportive and fair, and authorities as trustworthy, taxpayers may consider possibilities to legally avoid paying taxes, or, if it pays, to evade. It might be assumed that under these circumstances, taxpayers try to make a (rational) decision and will choose the option that promises the highest individual profit, rather than considering their tax share as a fair contribution to the public good. If this assumption is correct, tax behaviour can best be explained as the outcome of a decision process. Variables described in the decision-making chapter below may best describe compliance, whereas social norms and fairness judgments may serve as arguments for rationalizing ones behaviour rather than determining ones behaviour. Indeed, it is not voluntary cooperation that requires audits and punishment, but rather endeavours of individual profit maximization. Tax policy must consider when and how often to control taxpayers, and how to frame taxes in order to reduce taxpayers' perception of loss and reluctance to pay their share. While a *cops against robbers* climate might make the losses from paying taxes more salient, evoking thoughts on possible gains from evasion and a (rational) decision on these two prospects, a *service for clients* approach emphasizes the gains from paying taxes for the collective as a whole. Moreover, the latter establishes a relationship built on trust and cooperation, which leads to voluntary cooperation. The change of focus from the individual to collective welfare makes egoistic utility maximizing less likely. A *service for clients* atmosphere may be based on and lead to completely different attitudes of taxpayers. Taxpayers should be cooperative and willing to comply, as directed by their (social) representations of the government and of taxation: when the tax law is clearly understandable to be followed correctly, when the government policy meets citizens' acceptance, when tax mentality is positive, when personal and social norms favour cooperation, and when distribution of taxes is perceived to be fair and procedures are just, then taxpayers should be motivated to pay taxes correctly. Compliance due to fair treatment of taxpayers and a trusting climate in general may, in turn, stabilize favourable (social) representations and stabilize voluntary compliance. It should be mentioned that rational choices are not necessarily associated with an antagonistic climate only. Also in a cooperating climate, taxpayers can engage in extensive decision-making and their behaviour can be described as rational if besides short-term (possible) financial gains and losses the value of a trustworthy, friendly and cooperative climate is considered as well as a decision criterion. Voluntary compliance should depend and be based on those variables summarized under *social representations*. If taxpayers are treated as equal partners, if they understand tax law and agree with the government activities in general and with fiscal policy in particular, if taxes are perceived as fair and tax collection procedures are transparent and perceived as just, it can be assumed that taxpayers behave as cooperative citizens, and intrusive audits and severe punishments in case of unintentional filing errors would undermine their voluntary cooperation instead of stimulating them to file correctly. Indeed, it is assumed that a *cops against robbers* perspective can easily destabilize and corrupt a climate characterized by trust and cooperation.

3.2.   *Trust and voluntary compliance versus enforced compliance*

Tax authorities' orientation towards taxpayers and their interaction style create a tax climate which either favours taxpayers' cooperation and voluntary compliance or fosters resistance and individual profit maximization. Whereas a *cops against robbers* approach stimulates a climate of persecution and prosecution, and consequently one of unwillingness to cooperate and individual profit considerations, a *service for clients* approach seems likely to stimulate a climate of cooperation. Interaction processes based on transparency and neutrality of the procedures, trustworthiness of tax institutions and tax authorities, and respectful, polite and dignified treatment of taxpayers are likely to enhance voluntary compliance. Voluntary compliance is assumed to be related to taxpayers' social representations in particular. A climate of cooperation is likely if government policy is accepted, personal and social norms are favourable to cooperation and tax burden and tax procedures are perceived as fair.

If the climate is hostile, compliance can be enforced if government institutions, such as tax authorities, have the power to enforce compliance. Taxpayers who are unwilling to pay their taxes, but are threatened by audits and fines, need to carefully consider what option to choose: the safe option to pay their tax share, accepting the loss of some money, or the risky option with the possibility of saving on taxes or being detected and fined. Under such circumstances, extensive decision-making processes are likely to occur, with taxpayers carefully considering the value of their options. Audit probability, fines, tax rates, income effects, strategies assumed to be applied by tax authorities and chances to escape them, framing effects and withholding phenomena, etc., are likely to be meticulously considered in deciding how to deal with one's income and with tax authorities. People with many opportunities to evade or to avoid their taxes are likely to cut their share if it pays, that is, if the power of tax authorities is weak. In the case of strong power to enforce tax payments, that is, high audit rates, high detection probability and severe fines, and unequivocal tax laws forbidding tax avoidance, taxpayers are constrained to comply. It can be expected that the weights of determinants of compliance differ depending on tax climate. Hence, empirical studies should reveal different determinants in operating depending on the predominate climate of the society or laboratory environment. This would explain why empirical studies sometimes confirm a strong deterring effect of audits and fines, while these effects are low or even reversed in other circumstances (Andreoni et al., 1998).

If the climate is friendly and taxpayers trust the authorities, compliance is likely to occur voluntarily, independent of tax authorities' power. Taxpayers may perceive paying taxes as a civil duty and cooperate with government institutions to the benefit of the community. In a climate of mutual trust, audits and sanctions are likely to have no effect or they can even corrupt cooperation. A *service for clients* approach is characterized by clear and understandable regulations, transparency of procedures, neutrality, respect and politeness with regard to taxpayer treatment as well as support. Rather than deciding what option promises the highest individual profit, subjective understanding of tax law, attitudes towards the government, personal and social norms, perceptions of distributive fairness and procedural justice are likely to affect taxpayers' motivation to meet tax requirements. On the aggregate level, high tax morale and a strong sense of civic duty ensure citizens' willingness to cooperate with the state voluntarily.

Figure 1 displays these assumptions graphically in a three-dimensional space with the power of authorities to control and to fine taxpayers, trust in authorities, and compliance as dimensions. It is assumed that compliance can result under the condition of strong power of the state as well as under the condition of trust in authorities. On one hand, if tax authorities have the power to enforce compliance and if taxpayers, deciding how to increase their individual profit, come to the conclusion that it does not pay to evade, enforced compliance is high. If trust in authorities is low and if power of authorities is weak, it is likely that citizens seek opportunities to avoid or evade taxes. On the other hand, voluntary compliance is high if interaction with authorities is trustful and if citizens understand the law and perceive taxes as distributed fairly and procedures as just, if they hold positive attitudes towards the government and have developed favourable personal and social norms, that is, they have favourable social representations about taxation. The power of the state, expressed by audit frequency and the power to sanction non-cooperation, is ineffectual if trust is high.

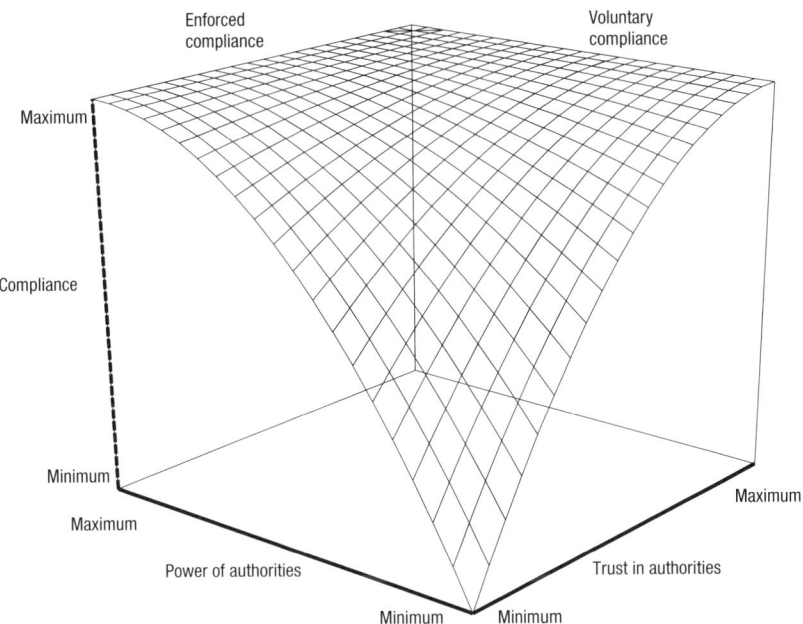

Figure 1   **Enforced compliance versus voluntary compliance depending on the power of the state and trust in the authorities.**

The model presented in Figure 1 can be used both as a conceptual tool and as an operational tool. As a conceptual tool it may serve to understand the importance of determinants of tax behaviour and the ambivalent effects reported in empirical research. In other words, it is expected that variables considered in decision-making approaches operate best if the tax climate is rather antagonistic, whereas variables considered in studies on social representations operate if the climate is characterized by trust. As an operational tool, the model can be used to develop strategies of effectual interaction between tax authorities and taxpayers. In a climate of distrust however, authorities need to exert audits and fines to enforce compliance, strategies leading to favourable social representations and trust may favour voluntary compliance. In the case of high trust, *cops against robbers* strategies may not only be ineffectual but may even corrupt the cooperative climate.

3.3.   *Distrusting climate and the importance of profit maximization*

If the tax climate is perceived as non-cooperative and if taxes are not paid voluntarily, taxpayers are likely to face a social dilemma situation. The optimal strategy for rational individuals is to evade. Such rational behaviour leads to the worst outcome for the commons and ultimately for each individual. Therefore, taxpayers need to be forced to cooperate by control mechanisms and severe fines in case of non-cooperation. The neoclassical economic approach to tax behaviour starts from this assumption. In their seminal works, Allingham and Sandmo (1972) and Srinivasan (1973) start with the assumption that taxpayers can choose between two main strategies: (a) a taxpayer may declare the actual income, or (b) declare less than the actual income. When deciding the latter strategy, the payoff will depend on whether or not the taxpayer is investigated by the tax authorities. If taxpayers are not investigated, they are clearly better off than under the first strategy. If they are investigated and evasion is detected, they are worse off. Taxpayers are assumed to engage in maximizing income by making a decision under uncertainty. Audits and sanctions in cases of evasion are perceived as the dominant instruments to ensure cooperative behaviour.

Studies on the impact of audits on compliance found that they are not strongly related. With regard to objective audit probabilities and subjectively perceived probabilities, Andreoni and colleagues conclude their 1998 review stating that audit probabilities have little effect on compliance and perhaps the effect of subjective audit and detection probabilities is mediated via psychological variables, such as moral obligations. 'The studies discussed ... indicate that individuals generally make poor predictions of the probability of audit and magnitude of fines from tax evasion. Moreover, there is consistency between their sense of a moral obligation to be honest and the tendency to overestimate the chance of being caught. Perhaps as a consequence, a high subjective probability of detection is associated with significantly more compliant behaviour' (p. 846).

The authors conclude their discussion on prior audits by emphasizing the importance of considering why audits have very little specific deterrent value: 'One possible explanation is that audits may not turn out as badly as taxpayers initially fear. For example, if an audit fails to uncover existing non-compliance or if a substantial penalty is not applied to discovered non-compliance, a taxpayer may conclude that it pays to cheat. Alternatively, perhaps taxpayers do find audits to be a negative experience, but the impact of this experience is to make them want to evade by more in the future in an attempt to "get back" at the tax agency' (Andreoni et al., p. 844).

With regard to fines, theoretical economic analyses of the effect of audits and fines suggest unequivocally a positive relationship between audit probability and fines on evasion. The empirical research, on the other hand, did not create a clear picture of the results. Fischer et al. (1992) conclude their review on the experimental literature on the relationship between audit and detection probabilities and taxpayer compliance by emphasizing the inconsistency of findings: some experiments failed to detect a significant positive relationship, other studies, attempting to determine the relative effectiveness of increased detection probability versus fines, provide weak evidence that fines are more effective, but other studies conclude that detection probability is more effective. Despite mixed results, the most common results seem to suggest a positive relationship between detection probability and compliance.

There are many reasons that can explain why probability of audits and fines do not have the predicted large effect on tax compliance. First of all, the assumption that taxpayers are trying to avoid taxes whenever it pays must be doubted, especially if taxpayers trust the government and tax authorities, and if the tax climate is favourable. Many studies show that a vast majority of citizens are willing to pay taxes and do not seem to undertake economic decisions under uncertainty in order to maximize income. Most taxpayers seem to take the legitimacy of the tax system and its overarching objectives for granted, and are probably not engaged in decision-making if the tax climate is characterized by mutual trust, but pay their share without considering possibilities to avoid or to evade taxes.

Rational models of decision-making assume perfect information processing. However, studies in behavioural economics, economic psychology and cognitive psychology present convincing evidence that the information processing capabilities of individuals are limited. The more complex a situation is, the more decision makers deviate from what the rational model predicts and the more inconsistent decisions are likely to be. People use heuristics and are vulnerable to biases. Due to limited understanding of tax issues and lack of interest in the issue, individuals were sometimes found to be inconsistent with regard to their preferences for specific types of tax, i.e., regressive, flat or progressive tax systems. Depending on the metric, individuals seem to prefer progressive tax if their judgments are based on probabilities, but they like flat tax in situations where tax is presented in absolute amounts of money.

Most research on decision-making biases is related to the prospect theory, and the tendency to seek risk in situations in which one loses and to avoid risk in situations in which one gains. If taxpayers pay a lump sum of income tax when filing their taxes, they have either paid too much or not enough and either a refund or a balance will be due. Those taxpayers who have a refund seem to perceive their tax refund as a gain, whereas those whose tax liability actually paid is lower than the liability determined by the tax office (and thus owe an additional tax payment), seem to perceive the taxes due as a loss and try to repair it by not reporting income or by overstating expenditures. Studies on advance tax payments and refunds or additional taxes due at the time of tax reporting, show that compliance is more likely to occur and involves larger amounts of money among participants who are confronted with the prospect of a tax refund. Also, in the case that withholding leads to a tax refund at the end of the year, fairness judgments are more favourable.

Prospect theory seems to be able to explain, at least in part, decisions to comply or not to comply in view of a taxpayer's current cash position and expected payments or refunds due. However, the impact of current cash position and expected outcomes on tax decisions is complex and seems to vary between taxpayer groups, depending on their experiences. Moreover, predictions of prospect theory and framing effects differ with regard to taxpayers' tax ethics. Taxpayers who strongly agree that tax evasion is morally wrong seem not to be influenced by the withholding frame, while those with low tax ethics may not declare the full income when additional taxes are due at filing (e.g., Cox & Plumley, 1988; Webley et al., 1991).

3.4. *Trusting climate and the importance of social representations*

Individual and social representations of taxation refer to the knowledge, thoughts and beliefs, feelings and evaluations, norms, fairness perceptions, motivational tendencies and, in general, citizens' tax morale. Although empirical studies lack findings of a strong relationship between individual and social representations and tax behaviour, we do not doubt Schmölders's 1960 claim that '... the state is mirrored in citizens' minds', an idea key to understanding what citizens approve and disapprove of in tax politics and which arguments lead to acceptance of tax non-compliance, to acceptance of noncooperation between citizens and the community, and opposition to prosecution of evasion. In everyday life taxes might not be a hotly disputed issue. Nevertheless, people periodically try to make sense of their contributions to the community, namely when taxes are due, when government spending is contested or when new taxes are introduced. Moreover, the public discussion of taxation issues leads individuals to evaluate fiscal policy, tax rates and the use of taxes for the provision of public goods, as well as the interaction between themselves as taxpayers and tax authorities. Eventually, motivation to comply or not to comply develops and respective behaviour follows.

Tax law is complex. Most people are neither interested in nor do they have a proper understanding of the law. They often only have vague ideas about the taxes they pay. Poor understanding or misunderstanding breeds distrust and opposition. Traditional assumptions link low tax knowledge with non-compliance. It was, however, also argued that lack of knowledge leads to uncertainty and people's risk aversion may increase in situations of uncertainty. Indeed, Beck, Davis and Jung (1991) found that income uncertainty can increase reported income. Snow and Warren (2005) showed that an increase in taxpayer uncertainty about the amount of tax evasion an audit can detect, increases compliance of prudent taxpayers. Caballe and Panades (2005) conclude that effects of uncertainty about audit costs are generally ambiguous. Nevertheless, it can be generalized that most survey studies confirmed a positive relationship between tax knowledge, subjective understanding and tax attitudes.

People's attitudes, judgments and behaviour intentions are more affected by what they think than what actually is (Lewis, 1978). Since tax laws are criticized as being too complex to be fully understood by ordinary taxpayers, representations and evaluations of taxes are mainly a product of myth. Unsurprisingly, associations with taxes are often negative. However, representations about taxation are different in different taxpayer groups: while most people recognize the need for contributing to the public budget and are aware of public goods, taxes are either perceived as a loss of personal freedom to decide how to invest one's own money, as contributions without a fair return, or as a repeated request by the government to plug the gaps in the state's finances which are caused by inefficient management by politicians.

Studies on tax psychology often focus on attitudes and tax compliance. Within the frame of the theory of planned behaviour (Fishbein & Ajzen, 1975) and the theory of reasoned action (Ajzen, 1991), attitudes are – among norms and perceived control of behaviour or perceived opportunities of avoidance – determinants of intentions of behaviour. Often attitudes towards tax evasion are quite positive. People avoiding their tax payments were frequently judged rather positively, as quite intelligent and hard working. This result is not surprising, since work and achievement are fundamental values in societies with Christian tradition and wealth is perceived as a consequence of hard work and discipline. Some types of shadow work might be perceived as a virtue rather than a vice, especially if it is hard work, and keeping what one has earned may not be judged as criminal behaviour. On the other hand, taking advantage of public goods to which one is not entitled is condemned and judged as incorrect.

Besides attitudes as combined beliefs about an entity and evaluations of these beliefs, norms and control determine behaviour intentions. Like attitudes, norms have received considerable attention in tax research. However, the conceptualization and use of norms as predictors of tax compliance is mixed. There is considerable overlap between perceived personal norms, values and a person's tax ethics, defined as the belief that there is a moral imperative that one should deliberately comply, and social norms, usually defined as prevalence or acceptance of tax evasion among a reference group (Wenzel, 2005). Personal norms reflect a taxpayer's tax ethics and are related to moral reasoning, authoritarianism and Machiavellianism, egoism, norm dependency and values. If someone's moral conscience is more developed, he is more honest and less egoistical or Machiavellian. His social values will be more pronounced and harmonious, the religious beliefs will be stronger, and therefore he is more likely to feel shame and guilt when misbehaving, and is more likely to comply with the law.

Social norms are a function of an individual's perceived expectation that one or more relevant referents would approve of a particular behaviour and the extent to which the individual will be motivated to comply with such a referent's beliefs. The relevance of social norms is generally supported in empirical studies on tax evasion. If taxpayers believe that non-compliance is widespread and socially accepted behaviour, then it is more likely that they too will not comply. The relationship between social norms and tax compliance intentions is complex, however. Wenzel (2004) argues that social norms should elicit concurring behaviour when taxpayers identify with the group to whom the norms are ascribed. Taxpayers then internalize the social norms and act accordingly. However, when identification is weak, social norms are ineffective or even counterproductive.

Norms are conceived as behaviour standards on three levels: the individual, social reference group, and national level. On the individual level, norms define internalized standards on how to behave; in one's social setting, norms determine the behaviour of a social group, e.g. friends, acquaintances or vocational group. Finally, on the national level, norms become cultural standards, often mirrored in the actual law. Research on tax compliance has focused on personal ethics and subjective perception of behavioural habits in taxpayers' reference groups. On the cultural level, norms have been addressed mainly under the terms tax morale (Schmölders, 1960) and civic duty (Frey, 1997), and also under the term cultural norms. Also, cultural norms and societal institutions are perceived as important in determining tax compliance.

When citizens are asked what they think about the tax system, most often fairness concerns are communicated. Consequently, Andreoni et al. (1998) claim that incorporating morals and social dynamics in economic theory is essential. The most frequent differentiation in tax compliance research referred to exchange equity with the government and to equity of one's contributions relative to the contributions of other taxpayers. Wenzel (2003) provided a conceptual framework for justice and fairness considerations based on conceptual distinctions made in social psychological justice research. In social psychology, three areas of justice are differentiated: (a) distributive justice refers to the exchange of resources, both benefits and costs, (b) procedural justice refers to the processes of resource distribution, and (c) retributive justice refers to perceived appropriateness of sanctions in cases of norm breaking. The central questions refer to attributions of responsibility to wrongdoers, the restoration of damages of wrong behaviour and the punishment a norm-breaker deserves.

With regard to distributive justice, comparisons are made on different levels. At an individual level, research on horizontal fairness considers the distribution of resources between taxpayers of comparable income groups. If an individual's perceived tax burden is heavier than that of comparable others, tax evasion is likely to increase. Besides horizontal fairness, vertical fairness and exchange fairness are of taxpayers' major concern. If taxpayers disapprove of government spending and perceive the exchange with the government as unjust, tax evasion is likely to increase. At the societal level, taxpayers may evaluate the fairness of the tax system. There is evidence that suggests that the structure of taxes has an influence on people's willingness to comply. On the societal level, especially questions regarding progressive, regressive or flat tax are important.

In tax research, procedural justice is of inestimable importance. On the individual level, procedural justice refers to the quality of treatment in interaction between taxpayers and authorities, the degree of quality of information provided by tax authorities, and to compliance and administration costs as well as dynamics of allocation of revenues. Access to and provision of information related to the tax law and explanations for a tax law change can increase fairness perceptions. It seems that information which reduces the complexity of the tax law and makes it more accessible leads to perceptions of greater fairness. Efficiency of interactions between taxpayers and tax authorities, length of queues at information desks, and satisfaction with audit treatment all seem to determine perceptions of procedural justice. At the individual level, fair treatment of individual taxpayers and the culture of interaction are relevant aspects of the perceptions of fairness and justice and creating a trustworthy relationship. On the group and societal level, procedural fairness concerns the neutrality of tax officers regarding cohorts such as occupational groups or income groups. The perception that certain groups of people have more liberty leads to the perception of unfair treatment. If tax authorities and officers treat taxpayers equally, in a respectful and responsible way, trust in the institution and cooperation is likely to increase on individual, group and societal levels. Tax non-compliance can be the result of disapproval of government policy. Experimental work by Alm, Jackson and

McKee (1990) also provides similar evidence: tax compliance tends to be higher when taxpayers are aware of a direct link between their tax payments and the provision of a desirable public good. Considerable sociological work suggests that taxpayers are more likely to report honestly if they feel that they are being treated courteously and respectfully by the tax agency. Consistent with this perspective, Frey (1992) argued that tight monitoring and heavy punishment on non-compliant citizens can crowd out tax morale and ultimately result in greater non-compliance.

Similar to procedural justice, retributive justice has rarely been investigated in the field of tax compliance. Moreover, retributive justice is closely related to the interaction between tax authorities and taxpayers as well as to procedural justice. Retributive justice regards the rigidity of audits and the responsibility for wrongdoing, the restoration process and appropriateness of penalties in case of norm breaking. Unreasonable and intrusive audits and unfair penalties lead to negative attitudes toward the tax office and taxes in general. Also, tax amnesties are an issue of retributive justice, if amnesties are perceived as legalising illegal behaviour and favouring the wealthy who resisted compliance.

Justice research has not always yielded consistent evidence for the impact of justice perceptions on tax compliance. The cause is mainly that different aspects of justice and fairness were investigated; making justice operational and the measurement of justice are heterogeneous and inter-individual while situational differences, such as the tax climate, were largely neglected. As Wenzel (2002) shows, fairness judgments are not stable but depend on the object of comparison and on taxpayers' identification with a social group or category to which justice refers. Justice concerns seem to be especially strong if taxpayers identify with their nation and the tax collecting government.

Subjective construction of tax phenomena and collective sense making are based on subjective tax knowledge, myths and legends, on subjective constructs and evaluations in terms of attitudes, on perceived and internalized norms, perceived opportunities not to comply, and on fairness perceptions. The condensation of knowledge, attitudes, norms, opportunities and fairness considerations yields the motivation and drive of taxpayers to behave honestly. V. Braithwaite (2003) refers to the aggregation of subjective constructs and socially shared beliefs and evaluations as motivational postures. The concept of motivational postures as *interconnected beliefs and attitudes that are consciously held and openly shared with others* includes individuals' attitudes toward the government, the tax system, other taxpayers, and individual and social norms (V. Braithwaite, 2003). On the level of the society and nation, the aggregate of citizens' beliefs and evaluations of the state, taxation, and non-compliance yield tax morale and civic duty. On the individual level, motivational postures are the driving factor of compliance and non-compliance, whereas at the national level, tax morale and civic duty are the motivational forces leading to or deterring from engagement in the shadow economy, tax evasion and avoidance.

The integration of taxpayers' beliefs and evaluations as well as expectations relative to the tax authority, their actions in response to their beliefs, evaluations and expectations are labelled *motivational postures*. Motivational postures determine the way taxpayers position themselves in relation to tax authorities. They determine cooperation and non-compliance and justification processes. Five motivational postures were identified (V. Braithwaite, 2003; V. Braithwaite, J. Braithwaite, Gibson & Makkai, 1994). Commitment and capitulation reflect an overall positive orientation towards tax authorities, whereas resistance, disengagement and game playing reflect a negative orientation. V. Braithwaite (2003) found that different motivational postures can be held simultaneously, they are not stable individual characteristics, allowing taxpayers to shift between them. Commitment and capitulation were the most frequent motivational postures in surveys conducted in Australia. Resistance, game playing, and disengagement were found less frequently. Moreover, commitment and capitulation were negatively related to evasion and tax avoidance, whereas the other three postures were positively related.

On the aggregate societal level, tax knowledge, attitudes, norms, perceived opportunity, fairness considerations and motivational postures are forming tax morale. Tax morale implies the intrinsic motivation to comply. The term *tax morale* was coined in 1960 by Schmölders, who defined it as 'attitude of a group or the whole population of taxpayers regarding the question of accomplishment or neglect of their tax duties; it is anchored in citizens' tax mentality and in their consciousness to be citizens, which is the base of their inner acceptance of tax duties and acknowledgment of the sovereignty of the state' (pp. 97f). The importance of tax morale and its impact on shadow economy in general and tax non-compliance in particular has been widely supported by empirical research (Alm & Torgler, 2006).

3.5.   *Methodological caveats*

We started from the fact that results in tax research are heterogeneous. This is not only due to different approaches of *cops against robbers* or *service for clients*, or simply due to the fact that tax evasion is difficult to measure because 'individuals often undertake substantial efforts to conceal their evasion' (Andreoni et al., 1998, p. 836), but also has a methodological aspect.

Results depend on the definitions of the concepts, the way ideas are made operational and the methods that are applied. Not surprisingly, the arsenal of methods, sampling techniques, getting the variables to work and the differ-

ences between self-reported and observed tax non-compliance have been discussed extensively (e.g., Fischer, Wartick & Mark, 1992; Groenland, 1992;
Torgler, 2002; Webley, Robben, Elffers & Hessing, 1991). In their review of the
literature on detection probability and compliance, Fischer et al. (1992) sum-
marise insights stemming from analytic studies in the field of microeconomic
decision theory, which develop mathematical models of tax evasion, predominantly examining the impact of audit probability, fines in cases of evasion,
tax rate and income. The models are highly stylised analyses that neglect
many facets of taxpayers' realities. Although mathematical models provide
valuable insights in compliance behaviour and may be highly sophisticated,
they reduce taxpayers to people who are motivated solely by financial profit.

The difficulty of obtaining *hard* empirical data on tax compliance has led
researchers to collect data via surveys and experimental simulation (Baldry,
1987). Economic psychological approaches particularly rely on surveys. In
surveys, taxpayers are asked to self-report their evasion activities. Although
surveys are usually an economical way of collecting data, they have several
shortcomings which limit the generalization of findings (e.g. Wilson & Sheffrin, 2005). Reliability and validity of measures, especially construct validity,
constitute major problems with the approach. Hessing, Kinsey, Elffers &
Weigel (1988) explored the limitations of self-reports as substitutes for observation of tax evasion behaviour and found negligible correspondence
between respondents' self-reports of tax evasion and officially documented
behaviour. Insignificant correlations were obtained despite the fact that all
government claims against the respondents had been settled, without pro-
test, before the study began and despite the respondents' awareness that the
accuracy of their self-reports could be checked against their tax records. The
results of the study suggest that different explanatory variables may be correlated with each type of behavioural measure: attitudes toward the tax non-
compliance measures and subjective norm measures exhibited significant
correlations with the self-report data but not with officially documented
behaviour, and measures of more broadly focused personal dispositions predicted actual behaviour but not self-reports.

Having observed a lack of association between self-reported evasion
behaviour and officers' classifications, Elffers, Weigel and Hessing (1987)
studied data generated from self-reports, tax officers' classifications and
experimental methods on the same sample of taxpayers. Not only was the
lack of association between self-reported behaviour and officers' classifications replicated, but also the evasion in the experiment did not correlate with
either. The authors conclude that tax evasion consists of at least three concep-
tually independent aspects that need to be assessed by three independent
measures, which leads to the conclusion that self-reported tax evasion is not a
proxy of observed evasion.

Problems of measurement originate from different sources. First, it is not always clear what is understood as non-compliance, evasion or avoidance. While non-compliance represents the most inclusive conceptualization and refers to the failure to meet tax obligations whether or not that failure is intentional, evasion and cheating refer to a deliberate act of non-compliance that results in the payment of fewer taxes than actually owed, whether or not the behaviour eventuates in subsequent conviction for tax fraud. Secondly, tax officials may not always be able to correctly detect intentional and unintentional acts and, thus, be unable to distinguish between fraud and taxpayers' errors. In the third place, variables that influence intentional evasion behaviour may be quite irrelevant for explaining inadvertent non-compliance, and with respect to income taxes, evasion in the form of deliberately underreporting income may depend on variables different from those that determine unwarranted deductions being claimed.

In economics, experiments increasingly become accepted methods to test theoretical predictions in a controlled field (Davis & Holt, 1993). From these experiments, causality conclusions are drawn. Experimental approaches have often been criticized as lacking validity. With regard to internal validity, inferences about a causal relationship between independent and dependent variables must be accurate; investigated higher-order constructs must be made operational appropriately so that they are reflected in the experimental treatments; and external validity, that is, the generalisation of causal relationships, must be assured (Fischer et al., 1992).

Besides methodological concerns, it should be noted that most findings originate from studies that were conducted in the US, which limits the generalisation of results. Few studies focus on cultural differences and differences between tax systems have rarely been addressed. As we have argued above, the tax climate as transmitted through the tax system and the demeanour of tax authorities could be an important factor for tax compliance.

4.   CONCLUSIONS

Several countries (e.g. Austria, Australia, France) have put particular effort in simplifying tax law for the self-employed and small business owners, and in establishing a *service for clients* approach. With the emergence of New Public Management (Andrews, 2003; Gruening, 2001; Horton, 2003), tax authorities have become aware of the necessity to consider taxpayers as customers. Instead of control and unreasonable severity, an approach leading to a *cops against robbers* mentality, an approach characterized by education and support is more promising in the endeavour to persuade taxpayers to comply with the spirit of the law. Tax advisors and tax officers play a key role in securing overall compliance. Should they develop an adversarial relationship through a *cops against robbers* mentality, characterized by poor communication skills, lack of technical and legal knowledge, and inconsistency in punishment, current and future tax compliance may decrease (Hansford & Hasseldine, 2002).

We developed a model based on the assumption that a *cops against robbers* climate favours taxpayers' engagement in (rational) decision-making, aiming at maximizing their individual profit. Under such circumstances we further assume that audit rate, fines and the marginal tax rate are relevant variables that determine (enforced) compliance. If the climate favours mutual cooperation, voluntary compliance is likely to be the result. Voluntary compliance is assumed to depend on taxpayers' social representation of taxation. Subjective knowledge, attitudes, personal, social and societal norms, and fairness perceptions are likely to determine motivation to comply at the individual level, and high tax morale at the aggregate national level. At present, the tax compliance model is based on theoretical reflections. Further research may show whether it holds its promises to serve as a conceptual tool for integrating the manifold findings in tax research, and as an operational tool to develop strategies which enforce and stabilize a trustworthy tax climate which favours voluntary compliance.

References

Adams, C. (1993). For good and evil: The impact of taxes on the course of civilization. Lanham, MD: Madison Books.

Ajzen, I. (1991). The theory of planned behavior. *Organizational Behavior and Human Decision Processes*, 50(2), pp. 179-211.

Allingham, M. and A. Sandmo (1972). Income tax evasion: A theoretical analysis. *Journal of Public Economics*, 1(3-4), pp. 323-338.

Alm, J. and B. Torgler (2006). Culture differences and tax morale in the United States and in Europe. *Journal of Economic Psychology*, 27(2), pp. 224-246.

Alm, J., B.R. Jackson and M. McKee (1990). *Alternative government approaches for increasing tax compliance* (Mimeo). Bolder: University of Colorado, Department of Economics.

Andreoni, J., B. Erard and J.S. Feinstein (1998). Tax compliance. *Journal of Economic Literature*, 36(2), pp. 818-860.

Andrews, M. (2003). New public management and democratic participation: Complementary or competing reforms? A South African study. *International Journal of Public Administration*, 26(8-9), pp. 991-1016.

Ayres, I. and J. Braithwaite (1992). *Responsive regulation: Transcending the deregulation debate*. New York, NY: Oxford University Press.

Baldry, J.C. (1987). Income tax evasion and the tax schedule: Some experimental results. *Public Finance*, 42(3), pp. 357-383.

Beck, P.J., J.S. Davis and W.-O. Jung (1991). Experimental evidence on taxpayer reporting under uncertainty. *Accounting Review*, 66(3), pp. 535-558.

Braithwaite, V. (2003). Dancing with tax authorities: Motivational postures and noncompliant actions. In: *Taxing democracy. Understanding tax avoidance and tax evasion*, V. Braithwaite (ed.). Aldershot, UK: Ashgate, pp. 15-40.

Braithwaite, V., J. Braithwaite, D. Gibson and T. Makkai (1994). Regulatory styles, motivational postures and nursing home compliance. *Law & Policy*, 16(4), pp. 363-394.

Brandstätter, H. (1994). Determinanten der Steuerhinterziehung: Ergebnisse der experimentellen Psychologie. In: *Stand und Entwicklung der Finanzpsychologie*, C. Smekal and E. Theurl (eds.). Baden-Baden, D: Nomos, pp. 213-245.

Caballe, J. and J. Panades (2005). Cost uncertainty and taxpayer compliance. *International Tax and Public Finance*, 12(3), p. 239.

Chang, O.H. and J.J.J. Schulz (1990). The income tax withholding phenomenon: Evidence from TCMP data. *The Journal of the American Taxation Association*, 12(1), pp. 88-93.

Cox, D. and A. Plumley (1988). *Analyses of voluntary compliance rates for different income source classes*. Washington, DC: International Revenue Service, Research Division.

Davis, D.D. and C.A. Holt (1993). *Experimental economics*. Princeton, NJ: Princeton University Press.

Elffers, H., R.H. Weigel and D.J. Hessing (1987). The consequences of different strategies for measuring tax evasion behaviour. *Journal of Economic Psychology*, 8(3), pp. 311-337.

Erard, B. (1997). Self-selection with measurement errors – A microeconometric analysis of the decision to seek tax assistance and its implications for tax compliance. *Journal of Econometrics*, 81(2), pp. 319-356.

Fischer, C.M., M. Wartick and M.M. Mark (1992). Detection probability and taxpayer compliance: A review of the literature. *Journal of Accounting Literature*, 11(1), pp. 1-46.

Fishbein, M. and I. Ajzen (1975). Belief, attitude, intention and behavior: An introduction to theory and research. Reading, MA: Addison-Wesley.

Franzoni, L.A. (2000). Tax evasion and tax compliance. In: *Encyclopedia of Law and Economics*, B. Bouckaert and G. de Geest (eds.). Cheltenham, UK: Edward Elgar, Vol. 4, pp. 51-94.

Frey, B.S. (1992). Tertium Datur – Pricing, Regulating and Intrinsic Motivation. *Kyklos*, 45(2), pp. 161-184.

Frey, B.S. (1997). Not just for the money: An economic theory of personal motivation. Cheltenham, UK: Edward Elgar.

Groenland, E.A. (1992). Developing a dynamic research strategy for the economic psychological study of taxation. *Journal of Economic Psychology*, 13(4), pp. 589-596.

Gruening, G. (2001). Origin and theoretical basis of New Public Management. *International Public Management Journal*, 4(1), pp. 1-25.

Hansford, A. and J.D. Hasseldine (2002). Best practice in tax administration. *Public Money & Management*, 22(1), pp. 5-6.

Hasseldine, J.D. and K.J. Bebbington (1991). Blending economic deterrence and fiscal psychology models in the design of responses to tax evasion: The New Zealand experience. *Journal of Economic Psychology*, 12(2), pp. 299-324.

Hasseldine, J.D. and Z. Li (1999). More tax evasion research required in new millennium. *Crime Law and Social Change*, 31(2), pp. 91-104.

Hessing, D.J., K.A. Kinsey, H. Elffers and R.H. Weigel (1988). Tax evasion research: Measurement strategies and theoretical models. In: *Handbook of economic psychology*, W.F. van Raaij, G.M. van Veldhoven and K.E. Warneryd (eds.). Dordrecht, NL: Kluwer Academic Publishers, pp. 516-537.

Horton, S. (2003). Guest editorial: Participation and involvement – The democratisation of new public management? *International Journal of Public Sector Management*, 16(6), pp. 403-411.

IRS (1978). *A dictionary of compliance factors*. Washington DC: Government Publishing Office.

Jackson, B.R. and V. Milliron (1986). Tax compliance research: Findings, problems, and prospects. *Journal of Accounting Literature*, 5(1), pp. 125-165.

James, S. and C. Alley (2002). Tax compliance, self-assessment and tax administration. *Journal of Finance and Management in Public Services*, 2(2), pp. 27-42.

James, S., J.D. Hasseldine, P.A. Hite and M. Toumi (2003, December). *Tax compliance policy: An international comparison and new evidence on normative appeals and auditing*. Paper presented at the ESRC Future Governance Workshop, Institute for Advanced Studies, Vienna, Austria.

Kirchler, E. (2006). Tax Compliance: A Literature Review of Economic-Psychological Research. Unpublished paper at the University of Vienna. Austria.

Lewis, A. (1982). *The psychology of taxation*. Oxford, UK: Martin Robertson.

Milliron, V. and D. Toy (1988). Tax compliance: An investigation of key features. *Journal of the American Taxation Association*, 9(2), pp. 84-104.

Richardson, M. and A. Sawyer (2001). A taxonomy of the tax compliance literature: Further findings, problems and prospects. *Australian Tax Forum*, 16(2), pp. 137-320.

Schmölders, G. (1960). *Das Irrationale in der öffentlichen Finanzwirtschaft*. Frankfurt am Main, D: Suhrkamp.

Slemrod, J., M. Blumenthal and C. Christian (2001). Taxpayer response to an increased probability of audit: Evidence from a controlled experiment in Minnesota. *Journal of Public Economics*, 79(3), pp. 455-483.

Srinivasan, T.N. (1973). Tax evasion: A model. *Journal of Public Economics*, 2(4), pp. 339-346.

Tanzi, V. and P. Shome (1994). A primer on tax evasion. *International Bureau of Fiscal Documentation*, 48(6-7), pp. 328-337.

Torgler, B. (2002). Speaking to theorists and searching for facts: Tax morale and tax compliance in experiments. *Journal of Economic Surveys*, 16(5), pp. 657-683.

Tyler, T.R. (1990). Why people obey the law: Procedural justice, legitimacy, and compliance. New Haven, CT: Yale University Press.

Webley, P., H.S.J. Robben, H. Elffers and D.J. Hessing (1991). *Tax evasion: An experimental approach*. Cambridge, UK: Cambridge University Press.

Weigel, R.H., D.J. Hessing and H. Elffers (1987). Tax evasion research: A critical appraisal and theoretical model. *Journal of Economic Psychology*, 8(2), pp. 215-235.

Wenzel, M. (2002). The impact of outcome orientation and justice concerns on tax compliance: The role of Taxpayers' identity. *Journal of Applied Psychology*, 87(4), pp. 629-645.

Wenzel, M. (2003). Tax compliance and the psychology of justice: Mapping the field. In: *Taxing democracy: Understanding tax avoidance and evasion*, V. Braithwaite (ed.) Hants, UK: Ashgate, pp. 41-69.

Wenzel, M. (2004). An analysis of norm processes in tax compliance. *Journal of Economic Psychology*, 25(2), pp. 213-228.

Wenzel, M. (2005). Motivation or rationalisation? Causal relations between ethics, norms and tax compliance. *Journal of Economic Psychology*, 26(4), pp. 491-508.

Wilson, J.L.F. and S. Sheffrin (2005). Understanding surveys of taxpayer honesty. *Finanzarchiv*, 61(2), p. 256.

2 | CAN COMMUNICATION ACTIVITIES IMPROVE COMPLIANCE?

Lennart Wittberg[1]

1. INTRODUCTION

Communication with the public is an important task for any tax administration. In most cases, the purpose of communication is to inform the public. It can be about providing information on new legislation and rules, or on the work of the tax administration. In this respect, communication is mostly a tool for improving compliance amongst the honest taxpayers – those who want to do it right but do not always succeed. An interesting question is therefore whether it is possible to improve overall compliance, including eliminating some kinds of the intentional evasion. Communication can never be the only tool for improving compliance, and neither can enforcement activities. It would be of great benefit to any tax administration if communications activities were to be used in a broader perspective.

Like most tax administrations, the Swedish Tax Agency is always trying to improve its performance and develop new approaches. During 2002–2005, three parallel lines of developments were connected to communications activities and the improvement of overall performance.

1.1. *Understanding behaviour by studying research*

In order to apply the right form of treatment, we must be aware of the underlying causes of non-compliance. Why do some people avoid paying taxes? Why do most people pay taxes as expected? These questions were the start-

---

1. Swedish Tax Agency, (e-mail: lennart.wittberg@skatteverket.se).

ing point for studying research. The Swedish Tax Agency did not conduct any research of its own but instead tried to learn from research conducted by others. A great deal of research in the field exists, mostly in the academic world. This big dive into the ocean of research had a much broader scope than just communication activities, but the findings proved to be very important for all types of communication strategy. A brief description of some of these findings is provided in Section 2.

1.2.   *Influencing the attitudes of young people*

A three-year campaign started in 2002 with the purpose of influencing the attitudes of young people regarding tax evasion. The campaign was based on two vital assumptions: 1) it is possible to influence attitudes and 2) attitudes affect behaviour. The design of the campaign and its results are described in Section 3.

1.3.   *The attitude of the tax administration*

Communication always includes at least two parties – a sender and a receiver. The result of the communication is not only affected by the message and the receiver. The behaviour of the sender can also affect how the receivers perceive the message. In order to gain a better understanding of this, the Swedish Tax Agency commissioned a study with the aim of finding out more about how taxpayers perceive the attitude of the tax administration and how this attitude can affect their behaviour. The results are briefly described in Section 4.

These three lines of developments represent a journey that the Swedish Tax Agency has embarked on, and which continues today. It has turned out to be very educational but also a somewhat bumpy ride. The findings and activities have caused debate and discussions both within the Agency and externally. Some overall conclusions are presented in Section 5.

2.   UNDERSTANDING BEHAVIOUR BY STUDYING RESEARCH

2.1.   *Background*

'Nothing is certain in this world except death and taxes,' is a famous quotation attributed to Benjamin Franklin. It implies that taxes – and therefore tax evasion and the fight to combat it – have existed for a very long time. It may thus seem strange that we are puzzled today about the problem of taxpayers' behaviour as though it were a completely new phenomenon.

The fact is, however, that we do not know enough about how common the various errors made by the taxpayer are, or about the reasons behind them. Nor do we know enough about how to deal best with different types of errors, nor about the underlying explanations for taxpayers' behaviour.

In order to improve knowledge and the strategies for reducing the tax gap,[2] the Swedish Tax Agency decided to study existing research on tax compliance. A great deal of research exists, the bulk of which has been produced during the last 10 years. The findings were described in a report.[3] The research described in this report has been obtained from a number of different sources, both government bodies and academic institutions, and from well-known and lesser-known researchers. While internal material from the Swedish Tax Agency itself is used, most is from institutions and researchers outside Sweden. It contains material from researchers such as Valerie Braithwaite, Robert B. Cialdini, Antonio Damasio, Ernst Fehr, Lars Feld, Natalie Taylor, Tom R. Tyler, Paul Webley, Michael Wenzel and many others. The findings described below are facts and conclusions from the report.

2.2.   *The research*

Research into tax compliance and taxpayers' behaviour started to attract attention in 1972 as a result of the research conducted by Allingham and Sandmo.[4] They presented a model which, in simplified terms, posited that tax evasion was a product of the risk of detection and punishment in the form of tax penalties.

This was a purely economic approach based on economic rationality, defined simply as a calculus of pleasure and pain expressed in monetary terms. In its extreme form, this narrow approach does not take into account any moral or social aspects of tax evasion but regards it as a purely economic decision. One gains if the evasion is successful and pays in terms of penalties if it fails.

Taxpayers all over the world evade taxes less than these models predict. Therefore there must be other explanations for this behaviour. With regard to risk of detection and punishment, there should theoretically be no difference whether the risk of detection is increased or the punishment is increased: both measures should result in increased compliance. Empirical evidence

---

2.   The 'tax gap' represents the shortfall between theoretically correct revenue and the actual revenue collected, attributable to non-compliance with tax laws.

3.   The whole report is available on the Swedish Tax Agency's website, www.skatteverket.se, under 'International', 'English' and 'brochures'. The report also includes a complete list of references.

4.   Allingham, M., G., Sandmo, A. 1972, Income Tax Evasion: A Theoretical Analysis. University of Pennsylvania, Philadelphia, USA and The Norwegian School of Economics and Business Administration, Bergen, Norway.

does, however, suggest that the risk of detection is more important than the punishment.

There is not one single answer to the question why some people evade tax. A number of different factors influence taxpayers' behaviour. These include:

– Opportunity
– Knowledge of taxation and the tax system
– Individual differences
– Equal and fair treatment
– Social norms
– Risk of detection
– Extent of punishment

Most of the research points in the same direction: the fear of feelings of guilt and the risk of social stigmatisation, i.e. personal and social norms, have a considerably greater effect on the decision to pay tax than pure economic self-interest.[5]

Social norms can be seen as the values of a certain social group. Personal norms are the individual's own ethical values and moral convictions. But the difference is not always important. Social norms can be transformed into personal norms when norms are internalized by the individual and become a real part of his or her values.[6]

Research distinguishes between two different kinds of norms: prescriptive and descriptive. *Prescriptive*, or moral, norms indicate which behaviours are socially acceptable or unacceptable. *Descriptive* norms indicate which behaviours actually occur. Research indicates that both norm types influence human behaviour; we tend to do what is both socially accepted and what is popular.[7]

This means that tax compliance is no different from other human behaviour, which is largely governed by norms. The prescriptive and descriptive norms mean that people do what other people do and that they avoid doing things that can lead to social disapproval. Cialdini says that one of the strongest norms governing human behaviour is reciprocity. This means that people *repay* a certain kind of behaviour. An individual will choose to cooperate and

5. Taylor, N. 2001 a, Understanding Taxpayer Attitudes Through Understanding Taxpayer Identities. Centre for Tax System Integrity, The Australian National University. Working Paper No. 14.
6. Wenzel, M. 2002 a, An Analysis of Norm Processes in Tax Compliance. Centre for Tax System Integrity, The Australian National University. Working Paper No. 33.
7. Robert B. Cialdini has done a lot of work regarding norms and influence:
    2001, Influence Science and Practice, 4th ed., Allyn & Bacon, Boston.
    1989, Social Motivations to Comply: Norms, Values, and Principles. Taxpayer Compliance, Vol. 2, Edited by Roth, J. A., Scholz, J.T., University of Pennsylvania.

to contribute to the common good if others are doing the same. Another part of our norm-based behaviour is our profound dislike of unfairness and injustice. We tend to react very strongly to even minor injustices inflicted on us.

Norms regulate behaviour and are more important factors than risk of detection and punishment when it comes to explaining compliant or non-compliant behaviour. Does this mean that risk of detection and punishment are of very little value? Repressive actions have played the leading role in most tax administration strategies.

Research shows, however, that enforcement activities are of decisive importance for maintaining and strengthening norms. Voluntary compliance can work if audits are made of, and sanctions taken against, those who try to evade. This norm-reinforcing effect is much more significant than the deterrent effect of audits.

Most people are prepared to follow norms as long as there is an expectation that other people will do so too. If an individual does not consider others to be honest, he will not expect them to comply. For this reason, the individual will choose not to comply. In this context, enforcement activities are of decisive importance. The reason why an individual complies is not the threat of detection and punishment but that the individual expects that the threat of detection and punishment will get *other* individuals to comply. Their expected behaviour should thus be that they comply – then the individual will comply too.

The most important aspect of the risk of detection and punishment is therefore its norm-reinforcing function by virtue of it being perceived as deterring *other people* from cheating. Norms govern behaviour directly, in general, enforcement activities maintain the norms. Naturally there will always be individuals who are more or less immune to norms and for whom the direct deterrent power of enforcement activities has an effect.

We now know that norms regulate behaviour and that they can be reinforced through risk of detection and punishment. It is important to be aware of this when producing any kind of communication strategy. But it could also be beneficial to gain a better understanding of where the norms come from and how they are formed. Or, to put it differently: who decides which norms apply in different situations?

Not all researchers share the same opinions when it comes to the origins of norms and moral values. The reason behind the existence of cooperation and generosity in all forms has been a hard nut to crack for scientists throughout history. When Charles Darwin introduced the theory of natural selection in the second half of the 19th century, generous and altruistic behaviour became even more difficult to explain.

It is not only a matter of biological evolution, however; it is also about social evolution. Social norms arise through an evolutionary process in which individuals rationally imitate the behaviour of others. These norms are then based on a cost-benefit analysis – a balancing act between the benefits of complying with a norm and the discomfort of deviating from other people's actual or expected behaviour. If a social norm is beneficial to the species, it is in everyone's interest that it is developed and maintained. Darwin's theories are also true for the development of social norms.

Antonio Damasio, professor of neurology, has described the link between emotion and rationality. Social stigmatisation makes people feel uncomforta-ble, and gives them a guilty conscience. Being popular or generous can give rise to positive feelings. These feelings play an important role in our behav-iour. From an evolutionary perspective, emotions cannot be viewed as some luxury accessory. Evolution would not have created emotions if they were not beneficial for survival. There is probably a link between basic innate drives and the most elevated ethical rules and conventions, quite simply because it contributes to the survival of the species.

The human brain is equipped with drives and instincts that not only include a set of physiological control mechanisms, but also the basic tools needed to adapt to a social context. These are influenced and developed by external cultural conditions during childhood and adolescence. The combina-tion of innate instinct and acquired survival strategies creates something that is presumably unique to humans: a moral sense which in certain contexts can enable the individual to disregard the immediate interests of his or her own group.[8]

Not all researchers share the view that moral norms are something benefi-cial that has been developed through evolution. The objections to this theory generally include a description of benefit-based moral norms as an indication of a negative outlook on human beings, or it includes the claim that humans are far, far more than this.

Other researchers claim that ethics can either be expected to contribute to something as simple as benefit or else maintain the distance to trivial reality and assist with thoughts of a more ideal world. Visions that one has hoped to influence in the *right* direction, but whose effects have frequently been destructive in practice. Is it not questionable to judge ethics so much accord-ing to ambition and so little according to result?[9]

What can we learn from this? We learn that norms are beneficial and that humans, to some extent, are programmed to apply certain norms. This may be good news for anyone trying to influence behaviour, as explained below.

---

8. Damasio, A., R., 2003, Descartes Misstag (Descartes' Error). Bokförlaget Natur och Kultur, Stockholm.
9. Tullberg, J. Moral Compliance and the Concealed Charm of Prudence and Replik om evolutio-nens konsekvenser för etiken (Rejoinder on the consequences of evolution for ethics). Filo-sofisk tidskrift, Vol. 18, No. 2, pp. 46-56.

2.3.   *Conclusions on communication activities*

The research described above is of vital importance when designing a communication strategy. Norms regulate behaviour, but how can communication influence behaviour? It can, if the communication strategy works *with* the norms, not *against* them.

On a general level there are two basic norms:
– People do what other people do
– People do what is perceived as right

More specific norms are:
– People *repay* a certain kind of behaviour (reciprocity)
– People strongly dislike unfairness and injustice

Most people follow these norms to some extent. They are therefore very difficult to change or influence, but there is in fact no need to do so. What people actually do and the behaviour perceived to be right can differ widely from one place to another and from one time to another. This means that it is actually possible to influence the perceived images of *what people do* and *the right thing to do.*

This influence should not be exerted through deception, but rather by telling the truth. An example can illustrate this. The Swedish Tax Agency's own surveys show that people in general believe that tax evasion is more widespread than it actually is. In these surveys, 5% of respondents in 2004 agreed with the statement: 'I personally think it's okay for people to cheat on their taxes if they get the chance'. This shows people's personal point of view, and the vast majority quite clearly does not accept tax evasion. Questions on what people think about other people's tax evasion produce a different picture. Only 22% of respondents agreed with the statement: 'In Sweden everybody or almost everybody pays the correct amount of tax'.

People's own personal opinion is that tax evasion is not acceptable, but they do not believe that other people share that view. There is a difference between what people themselves think is right and what they think other people will do. This misunderstanding is not unique to Sweden; the same discrepancy occurs in many countries. To inform people that they have misunderstood other people's behaviour can directly lead to an increase in voluntary compliance.

One conclusion as regards communication is that descriptive and prescriptive norms should be placed on a par with each another, instead of pitted against each another. Therefore, when trying to change undesirable behaviour, one should be careful not to dramatize the negative effects of the behaviour by describing it as normal. If a tax administration only talks about the problem of tax evasion and *only* focuses on the evaders, this can give the impression that most people evade taxes. This impression, true or false, will only further increase evasion.

Communication should instead focus on the fact that most people think it is acceptable to pay taxes and that most people actually do it honestly. The tax evasion that actually occurs should not be kept a secret. Telling the truth is usually a good move to make, and the truth in this case is that tax evasion is an exception to the rule, not the rule itself. Telling the truth is of course valid even if non-compliance is widespread. To communicate that non-compliance is very common is, however, not in the administration's interest and it should not be done actively, nor should it be kept a secret. In this respect, the level of non-compliance will have an impact on the communication strategies.

What effect would it then have to publish the names of tax evaders (naming and shaming)? It could be effective if the tax evader is a well-known or prominent person. It gets more attention and the responses perhaps have a higher level of moral outrage, sending a very strong (prescriptive) signal that the behaviour is wrong. On the other hand, the ordinary taxpayer will have more objections towards famous people evading taxes and it could lead to provocation. 'If they evade taxes, then I can too', is how the taxpayer might argue. The problem is that the naming sends mixed messages. This is reason enough to be very careful about publishing names of tax evaders. Another reason is the expected effect on the evader's behaviour. If the evader feels that naming and shaming is unjustified, it will turn him against the accuser (which could be the whole society). Treating people like criminals can make them precisely that. The trick is to apply sanctions that will have a positive effect on the behaviour of the individual as well as on the public in general. To sacrifice the rehabilitating effect of the individual in order to set an example is morally questionable and most likely counterproductive.[10]

Knowledge about norms tells us that it is not very effective to try to intimidate people into obedience by communicating a risk of detection. Most people are compliant because other people are compliant and because it is the right thing to do – not because they are afraid of being caught. Honest people who are threatened by risk of detection can react in a counterproductive way; they feel accused and may turn against the accuser.

Communicating risk of detection can, however, still be very effective. But it has to be done in a way that works with the norms, not against them. The risk of detection should be aimed at *other people*. If *other people* perceive a

---

10. Naming and shaming could also have a negative impact on the public trust in the tax administration and thus lead to lower compliance. This is outside the scope of this paper but the reader is encouraged to study the report (2005:1B, Right From The Start, Research and Strategies) mentioned earlier to find more research about the importance of trust in the regulator.

greater risk of detection, it will convince the honest taxpayer that more people will be compliant and thus reinforce the willingness to be compliant.

There is a huge difference between the risk of detection that people themselves perceive and the risk of detection they think is applicable to others. In most cases, people think that they are exposed to a larger risk of being caught than others, i.e. people tend to think: 'it's me they're after – they just ignore the real crooks'. According to the Agency's survey from 2004, 42% of the taxpayers believe that they would be caught if they cheated on their taxes. But only 20% thinks that the tax agency is good at detecting evasion in a more general sense.

Publishing the result of successful audit activities is a good way to create a perception that the evaders are caught. The purpose of the communication should be to show that *real* tax evaders are being caught and at the same time make clear that evasion is the exception and not the rule. This will reinforce both the prescriptive and descriptive norms. There is no need for publishing the names of the evaders in order to achieve this; on the contrary, it is better if names are left out (according to the reasons mentioned above).

In short, the lessons learned regarding communication activities are as follows:
– Communicate the message that the majority of taxpayers is honest (but always tell the truth)
– Align descriptive and prescriptive norms
– Do not communicate the message that everybody cheats
– Communicate the risk of detection for others
– Be careful about publishing names of tax evaders

3. INFLUENCING THE ATTITUDES OF YOUNG PEOPLE

3.1. *Background*

The Swedish Tax Agency conducts taxpayer surveys on a regular basis. The results from the 2001 survey showed signs of a potential future risk. One statement in the survey was: 'I personally think it's okay for people to cheat on their taxes if they get the chance'. The number of people who agreed with the statement was as follows:

	Age 18-24	Total population
1998:	7%	7%
2001:	12%	7%

In the age group 16-20, 25% agreed with the statement in 2001.

The surveys showed a change in attitude among young people. Should this be considered a major risk? It could be a temporary phenomenon, since their attitude may change as they grow older. Even if it is a risk, is it possible to influence their attitudes? And if they can be influenced, will this lead to any change in behaviour? The tax administration was faced with a number of questions and had to make a decision.

It is a known fact that illicit work in general represents about 60% of the total tax gap and that young people, mostly students, are often employed in the cash sector (such as restaurants). In the long-term, if young people establish a habit that they maintain as they grow older, this could mean that the tax gap may increase in the future, which would be a major problem. It is probably too late to undertake any proactive measures if and when that happens. It is therefore better to be safe than sorry and any attempt to influence the attitudes of young people is considered a sensible measure. The attempt would not do any harm even if the attitudes of young people changed anyway as they got older. But if their attitudes would not change, and no attempts were made, the tax administration would find itself in a less desirable situation. A decision was made to take action in this area.

3.2.   *Can attitudes be influenced and could this have any effect on behaviour?*

Before any attempt at influencing attitudes can be made, it is necessary to have some understanding of the ways to achieve this. After all, there is a difference between *selling* taxes and selling diapers or detergent: attitudes towards tax evasion are more closely connected with basic values and therefore more difficult to influence.

The Swedish Tax Agency's decision to try to influence the attitudes of young people was based on two vital assumptions: 1) it is possible to influence attitudes and 2) attitudes affect behaviour. These are assumptions because there was not enough knowledge available in order to be sure about this. The tax administration, however, had to make a decision.

As the campaign on attitudes went on, more insight was gained about the importance of attitudes. The Swedish Tax Agency commissioned a study of long-term attitude changes.[11] The purpose was to find out if people change their attitudes as they grow older. The result suggests that people tend to maintain the attitudes established during their youth throughout life. The graph below (see Figure 1) shows the percentage of respondents from each generation that agrees with the statement: 'Combating tax evasion is an absolute necessity'. Each line on the graph represents one generation (based on the year of birth).

---

11. Source: Kairos Future (results of a study commissioned by the Swedish Tax Agency).

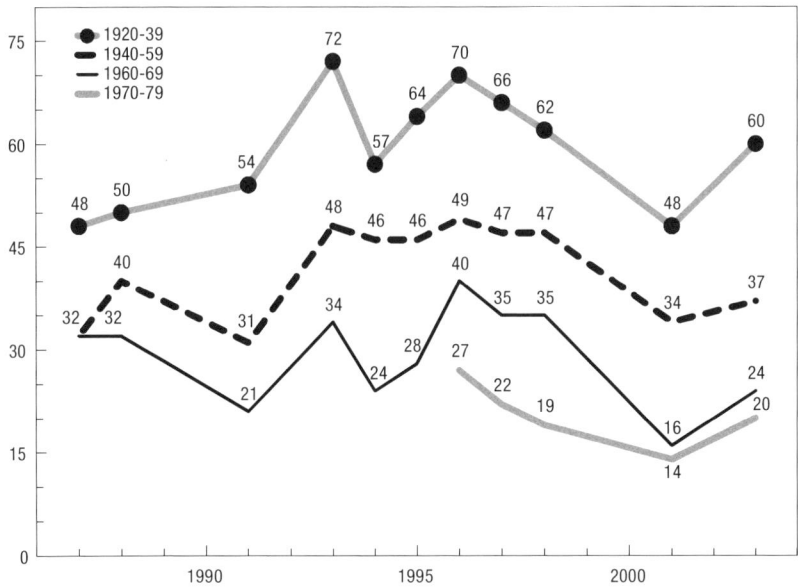

Figure 1   Attitudes among different generations. Percentage who agree with the statement: 'Combating tax evasion is an absolute necessity'.

Even if attitudes have changed somewhat from 1987 to 2003 within each generation, the difference between generations is mostly unchanged. Each generation has its own values and they tend to maintain them over time. This graph is based on a single question in a survey and cannot be regarded as conclusive evidence, but it gives cause for concern.

One conclusion in the report mentioned in the previous section was that moral values, in the sense of biologically inherited and socially learned norms, are underestimated as an explanatory component in behaviour. Therefore, moral values could also be underestimated as regards their effect on influencing behaviour. This means that behaviour can be influenced by influencing attitudes. The psychologist Cialdini[12] says that most people have a desire to be and look consistent within their words, beliefs, attitudes and deeds. In order to have an impact on behaviour one must make people take a stand or position. These kinds of commitment are most effective when they are active, public, effortful and viewed as internally motivated, that is they do not have to be coerced. This suggests that it could be possible to influence behaviour by influencing attitudes but it is extremely important that it is done in the right way, propaganda alone will not work. It is necessary to invoke a personal judgment and moral position.

12. 2001, Influence Science and Practice, 4th ed., Allyn & Bacon, Boston.

3.3.   *The campaign*

It was clear that influencing attitudes could not be done through *normal* activities like auditing or service/education. It would require direct communication with the young people themselves. Thus the decision was made to launch a special campaign with the purpose to change the attitude of the young.

The campaign started in 2002, and its goal was to influence young people's attitudes towards a lower acceptance of tax evasion. The purpose of the campaign was not to spread moral propaganda, to say 'you should pay your taxes'; it was to encourage young people to talk and think about taxes so that they could make their own decisions about what was morally right or wrong. There was, of course, a risk attached to this approach: the young people might decide not to pay tax. However, most people are willing to do the right thing if they are given a fair chance.

The campaign was to run for three years with different activities each year and to target young people aged 16-20 (approximately 500,000). The aim was to build on their knowledge of taxes and communicate on their terms, which meant no lecturing. An advertising agency was used to help design the campaign. Changing young people's attitudes towards a subject like taxes was generally regarded as very difficult. Some advertising agencies did not want to take on the assignment as they considered it to be too difficult.

Different activities were planned for each year of the campaign. The political parties were informed in advance. It was important for the campaign not to be seen as political, especially since it was launched during an election year. The campaign was only to assert that taxes should be paid; it was not to say anything about how high taxes should be. A first important step was to explain what taxes are spent on. A survey carried out at the beginning of the campaign showed that 24% of young people believed that most of the taxes were spent on salaries for politicians and bureaucrats. The following activities were carried out during the first year of the campaign (2002):
–   A film was produced and shown in cinemas and on television. The purpose was to illustrate what taxes are used for and what a society without taxes would look like.
–   Information material was provided to schools, including a tray cloth (to be used in the school canteen) with a picture of a city with public goods and services highlighted.
–   A letter was sent from the Director-General to everyone in the target group.
–   A website was built with information on taxes.
–   Mass media debate was encouraged through press releases and articles.

The advertising film attracted the most attention, even outside the target group (16-20 years old); 51% of the target group saw the film, on average five times; 78% wanted to see it again. The film was even more effective for people aged

21-25; 62% of that group saw the film and 77% wanted to see it again. Young adults liked the film, and said it created a positive image of tax issues and the Tax Agency. The film did not contain any spoken or written messages, except for a short text at the end. It attempted to show a society without taxes, in which no public services functioned. The short text at the end said: 'Or you can pay tax', followed by the logotype of the Swedish Tax Agency. Nothing in the film indicated that it was about taxes until the very end.

The following activities were carried out in the second year of the campaign (2003):

- A new film was shown in cinemas. The purpose was to illustrate a society in which only those people who have paid the correct tax would be entitled to public benefits.
- Small stickers with the message 'Paid for by you' were sent to the municipalities to put on park benches, waste bins, schools and similar objects that have been paid for through taxes. Postcards were sent to everyone in the target group with the same message.

The second film also attracted a lot of attention. The film showed a society in which it is impossible for some people to use public services. The film used the same concept as the first one, with no spoken message. There was merely a short text at the end saying: 'Imagine if only honest taxpayers could use public services'.

Another activity was carried out during the third year of the campaign (2004). A longer film (40 mins) was produced about some young people wondering about how to get a job during the summer. It was to be used in schools with the aim of encouraging a discussion on taxes. The teachers were given material for a role-playing activity to use with students. Some students were asked to argue in favour of tax evasion and others against. This educational package was given the name *The Black Box.*

The campaign was discussed a great deal in the media (mostly in editorials). Although the campaign was designed not to be political, a lot of media attention and debate was focused on political issues. Some newspapers accused the Tax Agency of spreading propaganda in favour of a high-tax society. The issue became the subject of a parliamentary debate. It was, however, reassuring that young people did not find the message political. It was mostly writers of editorials that were of this opinion, a group that was not part of the target group of the campaign.

3.4.   *The results*

The campaign itself and the results regarding changes in attitudes were evaluated. Some results concerning the campaign were that:

- 90% noticed the campaign.
- 50% discussed taxes with friends or parents.

As regards the outcome of the campaign, surveys indicated positive developments.

One statement in the survey was: 'I personally think it's okay for people to cheat on their taxes if they get the chance'. The number of people who agreed with the statement was as follows:

	Age 18-24	Total population
1998	7%	7%
2001	12%	7%
2002	7%	7%
2004	5%	5%

In the 16-20 age group, 21% agreed with the statement in 2002 compared to 25% in 2001.

It was clear that attitudes among young people had changed during the campaign period. It is also interesting to note that the attitude towards tax evasion in general has changed throughout the population. The campaign cannot take all the credit; other activities carried out by the Tax Agency may also have contributed as well as changes taking place in society in general.

Another statement presented to the 16-20 age group was: 'It is okay that people work in the informal sector'. The results are shown in the diagram below.

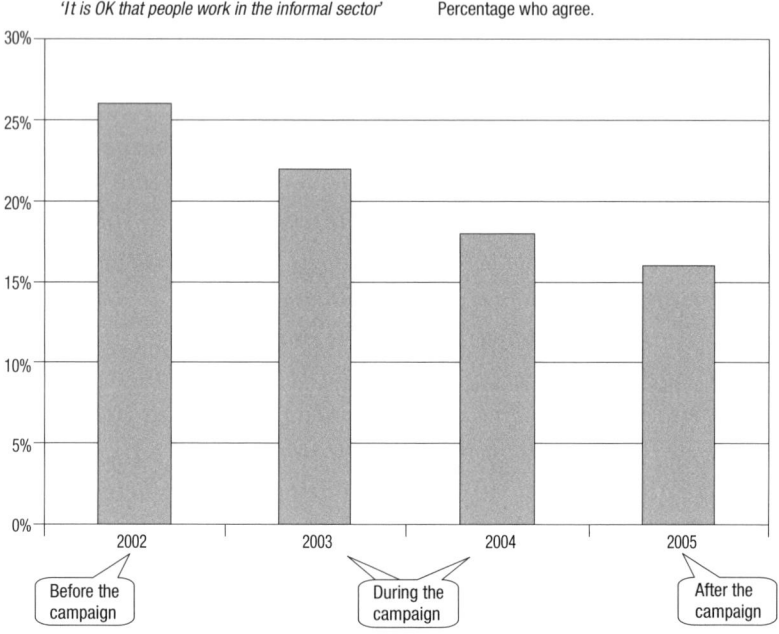

Figure 2   Attitudes of young people aged 16-20. Survey commissioned by the Swedish Tax Agency and conducted by GFK Sverige AB.

The University of Linköping also evaluated the campaign.[13] They concluded that it had been successful and that attitude-changing campaigns are something that authorities can and should undertake. The reason for its success is that the public in Sweden has a high level of confidence in the Tax Agency. According to the Tax Agency's survey in 2004, 51%[14] had confidence in the Tax Agency and 9% did not. Such confidence is essential if this kind of campaign is to be successful. The message must come from an authority that is regarded as trustworthy and reliable.

The conclusion drawn by the Swedish Tax Agency was that the campaign had been successful, and that campaigns can be a useful tool for influencing attitudes with the purpose of influencing behaviour. Attitudes can be measured but it is of course more difficult to establish the real impact on behaviour from this kind of campaign.

4.   PUBLIC PERCEPTION OF THE ATTITUDES OF THE TAX
        ADMINISTRATION

4.1.   *Background*

In 2003/2004, the Swedish Tax Agency commissioned a study[15] with the purpose of finding out more about how taxpayers perceive the attitudes of the tax administration and how this attitude can affect the behaviour of taxpayers. The aim was also to survey the attitudes people wished to encounter from officials and the attitudes that created trust in the Tax Agency.

A broad definition of attitude was used. Attitude encompasses emotion, thought and action as well as behaviour. The study focused on measuring how citizens perceive the officials' attitudes. The perceived attitude may be different from the actual attitude, but it is the perceived attitude that counts and the taxpayer judges just that. The study looked at different kinds of encounters with taxpayers – telephone contacts, written correspondence and face-to-face meetings. The results were to be used as a basis for various activities to improve public confidence in the Tax Agency and thus improve compliance.

As the Agency's surveys show, public confidence in the Tax Agency is an important factor in improving compliance. One of the statements in the survey was: 'I personally think it's OK for people to cheat on their taxes if they get the chance'. The number of people who agreed with the statement was

---

13. Mååg, C., Sunehag, L. 2003, 'Myndigheter och attitydförändrande kampanjer'. Linköping University, Sweden.
14. 36% had confidence in authorities in general.
15. The study was carried out by NFO Infratest.

5% in 2004. This figure applies to the whole population, but in the group of taxpayers who have confidence in the Tax Agency, only 3% agreed with the statement. The percentage is much higher in the group that does not have confidence in the Tax Agency: 14% in that group agreed with the statement. If the behaviour of the Tax Agency has a direct impact on the confidence of the public, this in turn will mean that it has an impact on compliance.

4.2.   *The study*

The study included both a qualitative and a quantitative section. The qualitative section involved in-depth interviews with people in nine different segments consisting of both private individuals and businesses. The segments were:
−   New businesses
−   Well-established businesses
−   Tax agents
−   Businesses with tax debts (subject to actions from the Enforcement Service)
−   Immigrants
−   Young people (aged 18-24)
−   Pensioners (aged 65+)
−   Individuals with tax debts (subject to actions from the Enforcement Service)
−   Other individuals (aged 25-64)

The purpose of segmentation was to find out if there were any major differences between different groups of citizens and businesses. The total number of interviews conducted was 84. Each interview took approximately one hour. The qualitative study provided information on the segments' perceptions of attitudes that exist among the Tax Agency's staff. The quantitative study was carried out through telephone interviews with 503 individuals and businesses. The target groups were:
−   Businesses in general
−   Businesses with tax debts
    (subject to actions from the Enforcement Service)
−   Individuals in general (aged 18-80)
−   Individuals with tax debts
    (subject to actions from the Enforcement Service)

The qualitative study was carried out before the quantitative and the results from the qualitative study (outlined below) clearly indicated that it was not necessary to have different segments for the quantitative study. However, individuals and businesses with tax debts are of special interest to the Tax

Agency, since it is responsible for the Enforcement Service. The quantitative study provided information on how common various attitudes were.

4.3. *The results*

The citizens and businesses surveyed encountered three different attitudes from the officials. These were designated A, B and C.

Attitude A is characterized by behaviour from the official that is perceived as arrogant, accusatory and insensitive. This attitude communicates the view that the individual cannot be trusted (i.e. will cheat).

Attitude B is characterized by the official's behaviour being formal and rule-bound. The official is governed entirely by rules and regulations and appears strict and impersonal. This attitude communicates the view that the individual is merely a case that is to be treated fairly and correctly, but also that the citizen should know the law.

Attitude C is characterized by the official being open, and taking time to listen and explain. The individual perceives the official as sensitive, educating and cooperative. This attitude communicates the view that most individuals are honest but that they perhaps do not understand the rules and therefore may need some help.

The differences between the nine segments in regard of the perceived attitudes were not bigger than the differences between subjects within a segment. This information – that all individuals and businesses perceived the same attitudes from the officials – was very valuable. It was irrelevant whether the person in question was a young person from another country or an older, established businessperson – they all encountered the same attitudes from the Tax Agency.

The quantitative study showed that 20% of private individuals and businesses agreed that they had encountered an official with attitude A, 50% with attitude B, and 60% with attitude C. The fact that people had encountered a particular attitude does not preclude them from also having encountered one or both of the other attitudes (which explains why the total sum exceeds 100%).

Since the quantitative study included questions about confidence in the Tax Agency, it was possible to find correlations between perceived attitude and confidence. Attitude A has a strong negative effect on confidence in the Tax Agency, attitude B has a slightly less negative effect on confidence, and attitude C has a strongly positive effect on confidence. The negative effect on confidence that is triggered by being treated badly is greater than the positive effect on confidence that is triggered from being treated well. It is therefore very important to avoid giving people a bad perception.

It was also interesting to learn that all the attitudes were linked to the perception that the officials behaved correctly and complied with laws and rules. This perception was, however, more strongly linked to attitude C. The main difference lies in *how* the officials behave and communicate the rules that apply, not the fact *that* the rules apply.

The attitude that individuals and businesses wish to encounter at the Tax Agency is identical to attitude C. This attitude increases confidence in the Tax Agency and thus voluntary compliance.

One conclusion is that communication activities are not only about what to communicate, it is also about *how* to do it. Communication activities will only have an effect if the public perceive the sender as trustworthy and credible. That will only happen if the tax administration adopts an open and cooperative attitude (the C-attitude described above) towards the taxpayers in various forms of communication. Perhaps more important is the insight that attitudes *are* communication. The attitude of the tax administration sends very clear signals. If the tax administration treats the taxpayer as untrustworthy and with disrespect, it will lead to the taxpayer repaying (according to the norm of reciprocity) the behaviour by treating the tax administration in the same way.

5.   Conclusions

It is extremely important for a tax administration to understand the huge impact norms and moral values have on behaviour. There are several reasons for tax avoidance and tax evasion. However, research clearly shows that financial incentives, as well as the risk of detection and punishment, are less important than the influence of norms and moral values. To achieve voluntary compliance, one cannot rely on deterrents. But this does not mean that audit activities and punishment are of less value; on the contrary, they are of vital importance. Their importance does not lie in their deterrent function, however, but in the fact that they can be used to strengthen and support existing norms.

People do what other people do. Audit activity and penalties can help convince people that other people are complying with rules. Norms govern behaviour, but audit activity and penalties ensure that the norms are upheld.

Moral values, in the sense of biologically inherited and socially learned norms, are underestimated as an explanatory component in behaviour. Moral values are also underestimated as regards their effect on influencing behaviour. Communication strategies can therefore be of vital importance in improving compliance.

Compliance can be influenced through campaigns but also through an authority's approach to its day-to-day operations. The way in which taxpayers are treated, attitudes of officials, how brochures and forms are worded, processing times and several other factors influence taxpayers' behaviour and thus also the tax gap. It also means that everyone who works for the Tax Agency can have an impact on the tax gap.

An individual will more readily accept a negative decision if the action of the authority was perceived as fair. The feeling of trust and of being treated fairly is influenced by the attitude adopted by the authority. Citizens who feel they are treated with respect and understanding and who are given the help they need, will have more confidence in the authority. The importance of a high degree of trust and confidence in the tax administration cannot be over-estimated.

Communication in a broad sense, special campaigns, and all forms of contact between the Tax Agency and the taxpayers can be actively used in order to improve compliance.

3 | REWARDING HONEST TAXPAYERS

Lars P. Feld, Bruno S. Frey and Benno Torgler[1]

1. INTRODUCTION

Why do people pay taxes? This question has attracted increased attention in the tax compliance literature over the last few years. Allingham and Sandmo (1972) presented a formal model, showing that the extent of tax evasion is negatively correlated with the probability of detection and the degree of punishment. However, this seminal model has been criticized by many authors (see e.g., Graetz and Wilde 1985; Alm, McClelland and Schulze 1992; Frey and Feld 2002). An important point connected to the empirical and experimental findings is that these deterrence models predict far too little compliance and far too much tax evasion (for an overview, see Alm 1999 and Torgler 2002). In many countries the level of deterrence is too low to explain the high degree of tax compliance. Moreover, there is a big gap between the amount of risk aversion that is required to guarantee such compliance and the effectively reported degree of risk aversion. For the United States, the estimated Arrow-Pratt measure of risk aversion is between one and two, but only a value of 30 would explain the observed compliance rate (see Graetz and Wilde 1985; Alm, McClelland and Schulze 1992). Similarly, in Switzerland the

1. Lars P. Feld, Philipps-University of Marburg, Public Finance Group, Am Plan 2, D-35037 Marburg (Lahn), Germany, Feld@wiwi.uni-marburg.de; Bruno S. Frey, Institute for Empirical Research in Economics, University of Zurich. Bluemlisalpstrasse 10, CH-8006 Zürich, Switzerland, e-mail: bsfrey@iew.unizh.ch; Benno Torgler, The Whitney and Betty MacMillan Center for International and Area Studies at Yale, Leitner Program in International & Comparative Political Economy, New Haven, CT 06520 (USA), e-mail: benno.torgler@yale.edu. All three authors are also associated with CREMA – Center for Research in Economics, Management and the Arts, Switzerland. The authors have benefited from the comments of participants of the Conference on 'Managing and maintaining compliance', Leiden, 9-11 April 2006 (especially Henk Elffers, Erich Kirchler and Willy Rovers).

relative risk aversion varies between 1 and 2, but a value of 30.75 would be necessary to reach the observed level of tax compliance of 76.52% (see Frey and Feld 2002).[2]

Elffers (2000) shows that it is a long way before a person becomes a tax evader. He defines three steps in the staircase to tax evasion: (1) taxpayers have to have the will not to comply, (2) not everyone with the inclination to evade taxes is able to translate the intention into action, and (3) individuals inclined to evade taxes check for the opportunity to do so. In the third step, standard economic theory comes into play and individuals evaluate the expected value of evasion. Similarly, other researchers argue that many individuals do not even think of tax evasion. Pyle (1991) criticizes the assumption that individuals are amoral: 'Casual observation suggests that not all individuals think quite like that. Indeed, it seems that whilst the odds are heavily in favor of evaders getting away with it, the vast majority of taxpayers behave honestly' (p. 173). Frey (1999) uses the expression *ipsative possibility set* (p. 196) and shows that there are taxpayers who do not even search for ways to cheat on taxes. Long and Swingen (1991, p. 130) argue that 'some individuals are simply predisposed *not* to evade'. Experiments indicate that there are individuals who always comply, that is, a certain compliance exists even without (low) penalties and audits (Feld and Tyran 2002).

In general, Elffers (2000) suggests reducing the significance of coercive instruments to resolve the social dilemma of tax payments. His conclusion (policy advice) is to try to prevent people from reaching the final step of the staircase. Thus, the instrument of deterrence is not the only instrument to make individuals comply. The theoretical models of individual choice, using the economics of crime approach, are too simple. There are numerous factors that affect the reporting decision of individuals. The Internal Revenue Service (1978) listed 64 potential factors that could affect tax compliance. Governments and tax administrations have an incentive to search for tax policy strategies that generate additional revenues, especially in times with large and persistent deficits. There is a persistent theme in the tax compliance literature in the last few years to move away from deterring non-compliance toward positive encouragement for compliance and therefore emphasizing 'the *carrot* for compliance rather than the *stick* for non-compliance... This insight is especially important because, from the tax collection standpoint, it is extraordinarily expensive to arrange an enforcement regime so that, from a strict cost-benefit calculus, non-compliance does not appear attractive to many citizens' (Slemrod 1992, p. 7).

---

2. Risk aversion can be defined as the reluctance to accept a bargain with an uncertain payoff to one with a more certain but possibly lower expected payoff. A common measure of risk aversion has been introduced by Pratt (1964) and Arrow (1965), asking the question: What payment would a risk-averse agent make to avoid or accept a fair gamble?

This paper focuses on rewards, which may influence individuals' compliance behaviour like a *carrot*. Instead of raising the relative cost of not paying taxes, the instrument of rewards raises the benefits of paying taxes. Currently, there is limited amount of empirical and experimental evidence that investigates the impact of positive rewards on tax compliance in detail. Section 2 introduces the concept of positive rewards and provides an overview of the current literature. Section 3 discusses possible instruments that allow us to investigate the impact of rewards on tax compliance and Section 4 finishes with some concluding remarks.

2.   THE IMPORTANCE OF REWARDS

Under many circumstances in daily business activities, we can observe different kinds of prerogatives. People get special treatment, such as being given fast-lane treatment for having been a good customer in the past. Good clients often have the chance to obtain special and more flexible treatment. Businesses use such prerogatives to improve and cultivate their relationship with good clients.

However, it is a relatively novel approach to investigate the impact of rewards on tax compliance. Some previous studies have stressed the possibilities of indirect rewards through, for example, a system of discounts that are given if someone refrains from applying for deductions (see Elffers 1992; Elffers and Hessing 1997). There is also some anecdotal evidence about the implementation of rewards to enhance tax compliance, especially in Asian countries. For example, Japan offers the possibility of having your picture taken together with the Emperor if you were found to be honest. The Philippines put your name into a lottery if you were found to be compliant with the VAT. South Korea considers access to airport VIP rooms, certificates or awards, and discusses the possibility of free parking in public parking facilities.[3]

Instead of rewarding honest taxpayers, it's our observation that governments around the world use tax amnesties more and more often. Tax amnesties offer the opportunity of paying previously unpaid taxes without being subject to penalties. The idea is to get evaders 'back on the route to honesty'. However, the financial success of countries is very diverse and amnesty revenues are seldom more than a small percentage of total tax revenues. Honest taxpayers are informed about the existence of tax evasion, because of the probability that other taxpayers are less compliant (Alm and Beck 1993). Thus, previously honest taxpayers often view an amnesty as unfair, and feel less motivated to comply in the future. They interpret the amnesty as a signal

---

3.   We are thankful to Jim Alm and Hyung-Wook Kang for providing us with these anecdotes.

that tax evasion is a forgivable and insignificant *peccadillo* (Leonard and Zeck-hauser 1986). This might increase their feeling that they paid too much in the past, compared to other taxpayers. Therefore, the psychological costs of not complying are reduced when observing others' opportunistic behaviour, which results in a crowding out of the intrinsic motivation to comply (Torgler and Schaltegger 2005a). In many cases, the government expected higher reve-nue to be gained from tax amnesties. Furthermore, the long-run impacts of tax amnesties are often disregarded in the political process. The tax compli-ance literature indicates a tendency that no long-term tax revenue effects can be expected (see Torgler and Schaltegger 2005b).

Rewards could be more effective than punishments or allowing tax evaders to come *clean* by eliminating undesired behaviour or by motivating desired behaviour because it is perceived as supporting (see e.g. Nuttin and Greenwald 1968). Indeed, the role of rewards in shaping human and also animal behaviour has long been a topic among social psychologists (see e.g. Thorndike 1911, 1932; Postman 1947; Skinner 1953; Nuttin and Greenwald 1968). Early exchange theorists excluded punishment from the scope of social exchange relations (see e.g. Blau 1964; Homans 1974). Punishment seemed to be less effective than reinforcement (Estes 1944; Skinner 1938; Thorndike 1932).

Molm (1988) criticizes that these forms of power have been studied largely by separate scientific disciplines in such a way that little is known about how they interact with one another and what their strengths and weak-nesses are under equivalent conditions. Molm (1994) reports that in a series of experiments that compared reward-based power with punishment-based power in not negotiated exchange relations, in which all actors have the capacity to reward and punish their exchange partners, the effects of punish-ment-based power are consistently weak: 'The distribution of exchange is almost entirely a function of reward power; actors with greater power to punish do not receive increased benefits from their exchange partners' (p. 75). Sims (1980, p. 136) summarized the literature on punishment in organiza-tions focusing on cross-sectional and longitudinal psychometric research studies undertaken in both laboratory and field settings, stating that some preliminary conclusions indicate that, in most studies, rewarding behaviour tends to have a much stronger effect on subordinate performance. Several areas of psychology and organizational behaviour suggest an asymmetrical effect of rewards and punishment; they are therefore not equally efficient at influencing workers' behaviour, such as, for example, reducing loafing (see, George 1995). Such an asymmetrical effect of rewards and punishments is supported by neuroscience. Studies suggest that rewards and punishments are processed in different parts of the brain and therefore have differential effects on behaviour (Gray 1981, Larsen and Katelaar 1991).

To the authors' knowledge, there is only one detailed theoretical study in economics (Falkinger and Walther 1991) that analyzes the possibility of pecuniary rewards as an economic incentive for taxpayers to be honest. In their model, a taxpayer under investigation has to pay a penalty for the evaded tax and receives a reward for the paid tax. The authors show that, on the one hand, a mixed penalty-reward system improves the taxpayer's position and, on the other hand, does not lower the tax revenues of the government. Thus, introducing rewards, together with an increase in the penalty, constitutes a welfare improvement. This study shows that the analysis of rewards might be an important topic in the tax compliance literature. A rational choice approach would take the impact of both rewards and sanctions into consideration. However, investigations on illegal activities solely emphasize deterrence through sanctions. For example, it can be argued that sanctions can be problematic and damaging, even when dealing with terrorism (Frey 2004). It is highly relevant to consider the possible effects of rewards on tax compliance behaviour and thus move beyond standard theories of tax evasion.

In psychology and behavioural economics, *crowding out* and *crowding in* effects have received considerable attention (Frey 1997; Le Grand 2003; Bénabou and Tirole 2003; Fehr and Rockenbach 2003; Falk and Kosfeld 2006). On the one hand, the theory suggests that outside interventions that are perceived to be controlling, such as deterrence, tend to crowd-out intrinsic motivation. On the other hand, actions that are perceived to be supporting tend to crowd-in intrinsic motivation. Punishment for not acting as a *good* taxpayer is felt to be controlling, in particular if the charges brought do not fully apply (Feld and Frey 2002). Taxpayers who are falsely accused of cheating with their taxes may perceive the intervention by the tax office as controlling. Thus their tax morale lessens or is even completely erased. Similarly, by increasing monitoring and penalties for non-compliance, individuals notice that extrinsic motivation is increased, which in turn crowds out intrinsic motivation to comply with taxes. Thus, the net effect of a stricter tax policy is unclear. If intrinsic motivation is not recognized, taxpayers get the feeling that they can just as well be opportunistic. This places the relevance of policy instruments, which encourage or discourage intrinsic motivation, in the fore. Intrinsic motivation depends on the application of policy instruments. Tax morale is not expected to be crowded out if the honest taxpayers perceive the stricter policy to be directed against dishonest taxpayers. Regulations, which prevent free riding by others and establish fairness and equity, help preserve tax morale. In contrast, receiving certain types of rewards for being a good taxpayer may be perceived as supporting and tend to bolster and raise tax morale. This motivational effect thus works in the same direction as the relative price effect, and strengthens the attractiveness of rewarding *good* taxpayers. In the case of the punishment normally applied for failing to pay the taxes due, the relative price effect and the motivational crowding-out effect work in opposite directions. This may explain why the empirical evidence on the effect of punishment on tax evasion is inconclusive, and the respective econometrically estimated parameters are often not statistically significant, or are even the wrong sign. If the crowding-out effect is stronger than the relative price effect of punishment, tax evasion is raised rather than lowered.

According to standard economic theory, rewards are expected to change the relative prices in such a way that paying taxes becomes a more attractive alternative to evading taxes. However, this does not necessarily mean that the effect is big enough that it can be *identified empirically*. This applies even if the reward given is *small* in size. The tax administration faces a trade-off between the costs and benefits of giving rewards and the costs and benefits of other incentives, in particular the costs involved with punishment. To be cost effective, rewards must raise *net* tax revenues, i.e. the gross revenues after deducting the cost of rewards.

There are various ways of giving rewards for paying taxes. They may range from direct payments, like participating in a lottery offering a sizeable sum of money, to getting various kinds of gifts. It is to be expected that the reward structure systematically affects tax compliance. In general, a reward given for correctly fulfilling one's duty changes the relative prices in favour of paying taxes and against evading them. However, it requires that the income effect induced by a higher wealth position does not work in the opposite direction. In general, the effect of income on tax compliance is difficult to assess, as it depends, for example, on risk preferences and the progression of the income tax schedules. However, the reward is very small in relation to the tax liability, so that any possible income effect tends to be small.

Alm, Jackson and McKee (1992) investigated four different forms of positive inducements in their laboratory experiment. The lottery had the highest average compliance rate of all the sessions (0.513), followed by the fixed reward session (0.448) and the audit reduction session (0.369). In all cases, compliance was statistically significant and higher than the baseline case of 0.332. Interestingly enough, the lottery mechanism led to a higher compliance than the fixed reward session, even though their expected returns were identical. Two aspects are essential for rewarding taxpayers via random allocation, which induces the *chance* of getting rewarded and allows for relatively *high rewards*. Both factors can be encouraging. Uncertainty and unpredictable rewards are attention catching, which is enforced by the size of the rewards being larger. A large prize with low probability of success is more attractive than a smaller, more certain prize. Such an effect recently gained support in the form of evidence from neuroscience, showing that a reward schedule, in which subjects knew the outcome in advance, produced only modest dopamine transmissions (which are responsible for behavioural responses), while an unpredicted financial reward produced significant dopamine trans missions (see Zald et al. 2004).

We may also observe differences between direct payments and the non-financial rewards. Direct payments may be proportional to the size of the tax payment (i.e. a percentage rebate), or, at the other extreme, may be the same size for all *good* taxpayers. The relative price effect is larger in the first case, but this beneficial effect may easily be overcompensated by a crowding-out effect. A reward proportional to the tax payments is likely to be discounted by the taxpayer as a *claim*, and then does not positively influence tax compliance. In contrast, a reward deliberately separate from the taxes due tends to be perceived as a sign of acknowledgement. If this is indeed the case, it is even better to provide a reward in another form than the financial. The idea of a gift may emphasize the exchange relationship between taxpayers and the state, and thereby enhance reciprocity, which affects social exchanges in a positive way (e.g. Falk and Fischbacher 2006; Fehr and Gächter 2000). It is a sign of appreciation that may work more powerfully than a mere reduction in taxes. Gifts can take different forms, including better and cheaper access to public services (in the case of private taxpayers, it could be the receipt of a voucher for public transport), free entry to cultural activities in the neighbouring area, more favourable access to government services (entering public museums and similar institutions), free access to recreation areas, or food coupons for local festivities etc. The *way* rewards are handed out to *good* taxpayers is essential for their effect on taxpayer behaviour and therefore different treatments should be included in a field experiment.

However, rewards can induce strategic behaviour on the taxpayer's part. For example, if rewards are provided due to behavioural *changes* (e.g. depending on the reduction of evasive behaviour), it might be rational to increase tax evasion in a first step in order to reduce it in a second step in order to generate higher benefits from the rewards. Thus, it is relevant to make the rewards dependent on whether a taxpayer is completely honest or not. This would reduce the incentives for behaving strategically. On the one hand, it should be noted that rewards have the tendency to increase compliance primarily by altering the frequency of extreme behaviour, possibly shifting individuals from a very low to a very high compliance rate (Alm, Jackson and McKee 1992). On the other hand, there are taxpayers who do not look for ways to cheat on taxes. Their behaviour does not respond to changes in the tax policy parameters or to the relative price effect, and is therefore not subject to a marginal, but rather absolute evaluation (see Frey 1997 and Long and Swinger 1991). Thus, relative price changes as a reason for higher punishment or higher rewards are only considered by taxpayers with relatively low tax morale, who want to cheat the system.

A key aspect is to know how to recognize a *good taxpayer*. The use of a system of rewards depends strongly on the tax administration's assessment of a good taxpayer. The reputation of the tax administration may suffer, if (notorious) tax evaders are rewarded by mistake because of not being detected. A lack of adequate assessment therefore reduces the strength of a system of rewards.

3.   INSTRUMENTS TO INVESTIGATE THE IMPACT OF REWARDS

Whereas much work in the tax compliance literature has concentrated on standard factors, such as audit, penalty and tax rate, it is useful to evaluate alternative policy instruments. Laboratory and field experiments might be useful approaches to investigate the relevance of such instruments.

3.1.   Laboratory experiments

During the last 20 years, economists have increasingly used experiments to analyze various topics (for a survey see e.g. Roth 1995). More than 20 years ago, it could be argued that economics wasn't an experimental science. Now, experimental papers have been published in all the leading international economic journals. The Nobel Prize awarded to Vernon Smith indicates that experiments are an important instrument in economics and have acquired a significant degree of recognition and legitimation. The strong point of this approach is the possibility of controlling and manipulating the variables of interest. This allows the reduction of causality problems, and thus gives good information, not only about the relationship between two variables, but also about the direction of the effect.

Currently, two experiments have investigated the impact of rewards for tax compliance. To a certain extent, both allow for an analysis of the impact of positive rewards relative to other tax policy strategies. Both cases support the idea that rewards are a very powerful policy instrument to enhance tax compliance. Alm, Jackson and McKee (1992) use experiments to analyze the effects of positive inducements upon tax compliance behaviour. They designed: (1) a lottery treatment where those subjects who were checked and found to be fully compliant for the current and the previous four rounds, could take part in a lottery in which the chances of winning were 1 in 25, with a lottery prize roughly equal in size to the average earnings of a subject for the entire session (50 tokens), (2) a fixed reward session where those subjects, who were in full compliance, received a reward of 2 tokens, which was equal to the expected value of the lottery, (3) an audit reduction scheme, where individuals, who had been audited and found to be in compliance, would have their future probability of audit reduced from 0.04 to 0.027 the first time and from 0.027 to 0.013 the next time. In addition, they introduced a public good session, where the public good is determined by adding up the taxes collected from the group in a given period, multiplying this sum by 2 to reflect the consumers' surplus generated by the public good, and then dividing the amount equally among the five people in the group. The results indicate that positive inducements have a significant and positive impact on compliance. However, although (1) and (2) have the same expected value, the lottery session had the largest impact on compliance.

Torgler (2003a) conducted an experiment in Costa Rica with taxpayers, keeping traditional factors, such as the probability of detection and the fine rate, constant and thus analyzing to what extent other factors, such as fiscal exchange, moral suasion and positive rewards systematically influence tax compliance. The findings indicate that these factors increase the compliance rate ceteris paribus. In the positive reward session, a subject who was audited and found to be totally honest, received a monetary reward. Such a reward can also be seen as a compensation for the burden of investigation which the taxpayer has to pass if he or she is audited (see Falkinger and Walther 1991). Interestingly enough, the highest tax compliance rate was found in the positive reward session, followed by the moral suasion session and the fiscal exchange treatment. It seems that the norm of reciprocity in the degree of tax compliance is followed by taxpayers where the government creates positive rewards or a fiscal exchange. The more the governments provide public services corresponding to taxpayers' preferences in exchange for an adequate tax price, and the more they honour honesty, the more taxpayers are willing to comply. These results support the previous findings of Alm, Jackson and McKee (1992) that positive incentives seem to be a good instrument to enhance tax compliance.

In sum, laboratory experiments enable a good research design to continue the investigation on rewards for tax compliance. Alternatively, as we will discuss next, the research design of field experiments is also an interesting tool to investigate the impact of rewards on compliance.

3.2.   Field experiments

Using controlled field experiments has many advantages. Compared to laboratory experiments, real tax authorities instead of experimenters are involved, which evokes real processes in the usual environment outside of a laboratory setting. It helps provide a better test for the effects of different instruments on taxpayers in the real-life situation of filling out the tax form and paying taxes. This helps with formulating practical advice on tax policy, based on a scientific test. Certainly, compared to lab experiments, field experiments allow social and economic interactions, and are thus less controlled, but causality can be determined better in experimental studies than in other studies (see Burtless 1995, and Harrison and List 2004 about the advantages and disadvantages of field experiments).

There is no observable effect of an artificial experimental environment, as subjects were completely unaware of having taken part in the field experiment. The experiments are thus conducted in the usual environment where social and economic interactions occur (see Burtless 1995). This has the advantage that the subject pool is more representative than in laboratory experiments. The results have a strong policy implication and might be relevant for policymakers. However, it is surprising that there are hardly any field experiments in the tax compliance literature. The higher transaction costs involved in organizing cooperation between the tax administration and the researchers, compared to laboratory experiments, as well as the sensitivity of the tax filing data, according to privacy protection laws, might be valid reasons why field experiments are used less frequently. Field experiments use a great deal of real resources. First, cooperation between tax authorities must be established. It is difficult to develop and implement a treatment, as it has to be approved by the tax administration and other government authorities. Thus, it may be supposed that sensitive or unorthodox treatments cannot be developed. Secondly, compared to laboratory experiments, such experiments are costly in terms of time. The experiment has to be prepared before individuals receive their tax forms. It takes almost a year until all tax forms are returned to the tax administration and are then ready to be evaluated. Moreover, field experiments have a limited duration. While experiments can analyze inter-temporal aspects, field experiments are normally conducted only once. For some questions, it might be interesting to analyze to which extent a policy instrument works over time. A short-duration intervention might have an immediate effect, but long-term effects are unknown. Furthermore, questions as to what might happen if a policy instrument, such as moral suasion, was used regularly, remain unanswered.

To our knowledge, this instrument has only been used in a few studies. Slemrod, Blumenthal and Christian (2001) use a controlled field experiment in Minnesota to analyze taxpayer response to an increased probability of audit. Over 1,724 randomly selected taxpayers were informed by letter that the return they were about to file (state and federal) would be closely examined. They used 2 years' income return data from the same taxpayers, which enabled them to compare changes in reported income, deductions and tax liability between those taxpayers who received the treatments and similar groups of taxpayers who were not subject to any treatment. They found that the treatment effect varies according to income. In the treatment group, low and middle income taxpayers increased their reported income between 1993 and 1994 relative to the control group. The effect was much stronger for those with a higher opportunity to evade. In 1994, the reported income of high income taxpayers dropped dramatically in relation to the control group. According to the authors, the perception that tax evasion will not be detected and punished automatically, could be a reason for these results, and thus they propose that 'heightened audit threat should be carried out simultaneously with a rethinking of how the audits themselves are carried out' (p. 482). As the authors state, the analysis had a comparably small sample size of high-income taxpayers, which reduces the inference to be drawn. Follow-up experiments should start the field experiment at the beginning of the tax year to analyze avoidance behaviour as well.

Similarly, Blumenthal, Christian and Slemrod (2001) worked together with the Minnesota Department of Revenue to analyze the impact of moral suasion on voluntary income tax compliance in a field experiment. They used the difference-in-difference approach with data for the tax years 1993 and 1994. Compliance behaviour was measured by the income reported, or tax paid, and was compared with the reference group (no communication). They found that the average compliance rate of those in the treatment group was $220 higher compared to the control group (0.08% of average income). However, the coefficient was not statistically significant. Hence, this study did not find a significant effect of moral appeals. In a second step, Blumenthal et al. (2001) conducted a multiple regression, in which they used the treatments as dummy variables to check other variables. The results indicate that people with more opportunities to evade or avoid taxes (e.g. the self-employed) are less susceptible to normative appeals.

Using a similar approach, Torgler (2004) analyzes the effects of moral suasion, focusing on two different compliance variables: filling out the tax form and timely paying. In cooperation with a local tax administration in Switzerland, a controlled field experiment was undertaken, together with taxpayers. Contrary to the previous controlled experiment done by Blumenthal et al. (2001), which found little or no evidence of a positive effect of normative appeals on tax compliance, Torgler (2004) chose to cooperate with a *local* tax administration, because moral suasion efforts might be more effective at the lower government level. The results show that the moral suasion treatment group has a higher compliance rate than the reference group. The findings also indicate an increasing effect over time in the treatment groups. In general, the strongest treatment effect was observed for the variable that measured taxpayers' payment morality. However, the difference-in-differences approach and the multivariate regressions indicate that the treatment effect was not statistically significant. Thus, results are in line with the Blumenthal et al. (2001) findings, indicating that moral suasion hardly has any effect on taxpayers' compliance behaviour.

Compared to previous experiments, field experiments offer the great opportunity of observing taxpayers' behaviour in a natural environment, using a representative sample of taxpayers and working with relatively large samples. However, there are specific aspects that are challenging when the instrument of field experiments is used to investigate the impact of rewards. A field experiment requires cooperation between the tax administration and the researchers. Using a field experiment in the tax compliance area faces many restrictions. First of all, the sensitivity of the tax filing data reduces the incentives of the tax administration to cooperate in such a project. Contrary to a lab experiment, a field experiment has to be realistic. It is, for example, highly problematic to develop treatment designs that do not correspond to official (tax) law. This reduces the possibility of conducting experiments. Thus, traditional parameters, such as the tax rate, are hardly an instrument to investigate in a field experiment. However, alternative tax policy strategies, such as positive incentives, might be more attractive for a field experiment to investigate, as they are less affected by the restrictions the tax administration encounters. On the other hand, unequal treatments between different taxpayers (e.g. experimental and control group) is also against the law. Moreover, it is to be expected that taxpayers discuss this issue amongst themselves. Individuals in the control group may become quite emotional if they detect that they are not treated equally. Thus, compliance may decrease in the control group, which leads to biases when comparing the treatment group with the reference group (stronger reward effects).

Alm, Jackson and McKee (1992) stress that rewards must be both immediate and salient to have a quantitatively significant effect. The reward sessions indicate that compliance tends to decrease over time. Thus, long-term effects should be taken into account, which suggests the relevance of observing the panel of taxpayers over a certain time period. There is the danger that taxpayers will get used to the chance of obtaining rewards. A one period field experiment may catch a certain *surprise effect* that will disappear over time. Furthermore, a random audit selection system induces additional problems. If only a limited amount of good taxpayers are evaluated and rewarded, it is possible that previously rewarded taxpayers are not rewarded in the future. What sort of reaction can be expected from these taxpayers? Additionally, what happens if the reward system is not established after the controlled field experiment? Tax administrations could fear possible negative effects and oppose such a field experiment in advance. It is also interesting to check whether some sub-groups of taxpayers react differently across time.

4.   CONCLUSIONS

This paper analyzes the impact of rewards on tax compliance as an additional instrument to punishments. While social psychologists and neuroscientists have investigated the impact of rewards in detail, the topic is novel in the area of tax compliance. We suggest that experimental and field experiments are highly relevant to investigate a variety of strategies that governments and tax administrations can pursue to increase tax compliance. Rewards could be an effective tool to increase compliance. Two previous laboratory experiments show that compliance increases significantly when individuals who were found to be compliant are rewarded for their honesty. We propose to investigate the impact of rewards on compliance in field experiments as well.

Different subject groups may react differently to a reward system. Similar behavioural responses could be expected in firms, because individuals in firms also decide about the level of tax compliance (Fehr and List 2004). However, firms are subject to important additional constraints, due to the competitive environment they are acting in. This produces incentives among the individual decision makers to quickly discount a monetary reward into total tax liability. In such a case, only the relative price of rewards would work. Nevertheless, rewards other than the monetary ones may also be highly attractive to firms. It might be useful to generate a reward to the firm as a whole rather than to specific leaders. Especially in a complex firm structure, it is difficult to find an adequate reward system that considers the value of the individuals in a firm. Providing some with a relative advantage to others may lead to different kinds of emotions. One useful form of reward could be that the tax office issues a *certificate* indicating that the taxes, to the best of their knowledge, have been declared correctly, that the firm has been cooperative, and that the taxes due have been paid on time. Such a certificate demonstrates that the firm acts as a *good* taxpayer. The firm's reputation and image will increase. Shareholders may respond in a positive way by raising share prices; the firm may get more favourable conditions on the capital market; and the customers' trust in the firm's products may increase. Field experiments, for example, would allow for the generation of additional insights, as they have the advantage of differentiating between individual taxpayers and firms.

In sum, we believe that future tax compliance studies should pay more attention to the impact of rewards, taking tools such as laboratory and field experiments into account.

References

Allingham, M.G. and A. Sandmo (1972). Income Tax Evasion: A Theoretical Analysis. *Journal of Public Economics*, 1: pp. 323-338.

Alm, J. (1999). Tax Compliance and Administration. In: *Handbook on Taxation*, W. Bartley Hildreth and J.A. Richardson (eds.). New York: Marcel Dekker, pp. 741-768.

Alm, J., G.H. McClelland and W.D. Schulze (1992). Why Do People Pay Taxes? *Journal of Public Economic*, 48: pp. 21-48.

Alm, J. and W. Beck (1993). Tax Amnesties and Compliance in the Long Run: A Time Series Analysis. *National Tax Journal*, 46: pp. 53-60.

Alm, J., B. Jackson, and M. McKee (1992). Deterrence and Beyond: Toward a Kinder, Gentler IRS. In: *Why People Pay Taxes*, J. Slemrod (ed.). Ann Arbor: University of Michigan Press, pp. 311-329.

Alm, J., M.B. Cronshaw and M. McKee (1993). Tax Compliance with Endogenous Audit Selection Rules. *Kyklos*, 1: pp. 27-45.

Arrow, K.J. (1965). *Aspects of the Theory of Risk-Bearing*. Helsinki: Yrjö Hahnsson Foundation.

Bénabou, R. and J. Tirole (2003). Intrinsic and Extrinsic Motivation. *Review of Economic Studies*, 70: pp. 489-520.

Blau, P. (1964). *Exchange and Power in Social Life*. New York: Wiley.

Blumenthal, M., C. Christian and J. Slemrod (2001). Do Normative Appeals Affect Tax Compliance? Evidence from a Controlled Experiment in Minnesota. *National Tax Journal*, 54: pp. 125-138.

Burtless, G. (1995). The Case for Randomized Field Trials in Economic and Policy Research. *Journal of Economic Perspective*, 9: pp. 63-84.

Elffers, H. (1992). A Discount System for Voluntary Non-Itemizers. In: *IRS, A Tax System for the 21st century*. Document 7302 (Rev. 3-93), Catalogue No. 64956T, Washington, DC.

Elffers, H. and D.J. Hessing (1997). Influencing the Prospects of Tax Evasion. *Journal of Economic Psychology*, 18: pp. 289-304.

Elffers, H. (2000). But Taxpayers Do Cooperate! In: *Cooperation in Modern Society. Promoting the Welfare of Communities, States and Organizations*, M. Van Vught, M. Snyder, T.R. Tyler and A. Biel (eds.). London: Routledge, pp. 184-194.

Estes, W.K. (1944). *An Experimental Study of Punishment*. Psychological Monographs, No. 263.

Falk, A. and M. Kosfeld (2006). Distrust – The Hidden Cost of Control. *American Economic Review*. Forthcoming.

Falk, A. and U. Fischbacher (2006). A Theory of Reciprocity. *Games and Economic Behaviour*, 54: pp. 293-315.

Falkinger, J. and H. Walther (1991). Rewards versus Penalties: On a New Policy Against Tax Evasion. *Public Finance Quarterly*, 19: pp. 67-79.

Fehr, E. and S. Gaechter (2000). Fairness and Retaliation: The Economics of Retaliation. *Journal of Economic Perspectives*, 14: pp. 159-181.

Fehr, E. and J.A. List (2004). The Hidden Costs and Returns of Incentives – Trust and Trustworthiness among CEOs. *Journal of the European Economic Association*, 2: pp. 743-771.

Fehr, E. and B. Rockenbach (2003). Detrimental Effects of Sanctions on Human Behaviour. *Nature*, 422: pp. 137-140.

Feld, L.P. and B.S. Frey (2002). Trust Breeds Trust: How Taxpayers are Treated. *Economics of Governance*, 3: pp. 87-99.

Feld, L.P. and J.-R. Tyran (2002). Tax Evasion and Voting: An Experimental Analysis. *Kyklos*, 55: pp. 197-222.

Frey, B.S. (1997). *Not Just for Money. An Economic Theory of Personal Motivation*. Cheltenham, UK: Edward Elgar Publishing.

Frey, B.S. (1999). *Economics as a Science of Human Behaviour*. Boston/Dordrecht/London: Kluwer.

Frey, B.S. (2004). *Dealing with Terrorism – Stick or Carrot?* Cheltenham, UK: Edward Elgar.

Frey, B.S. and L.P. Feld (2002). *Deterrence and Morale in Taxation: An Empirical Analysis*. CESifo Working Paper, No. 760, August 2002.

George, J.M. (1995). Asymmetrical Effects of Rewards and Punishments: The Case of Social Loafing. *Journal of Occupational and Organizational Psychology*, 68: pp. 327-338.

Graetz, M.J. and L.L. Wilde (1985). The Economics of Tax Compliance: Facts and Fantasy. *National Tax Journal*, 38: pp. 355-363.

Gray, J.A. (1981). A Critique of Eysenck's Theory of Personality. In: A *Model for Personality*, H.J. Eysenck (ed.). New York: Springer, pp. 246-276.

Harrison, G.W. and J.A. List (2004). Field Experiments. *Journal of Economic Literature*, 42: pp. 1009-1055.

Homans, G.C. (1974). *Social Behaviour: Its Elementary Forms*. New York: Hartcourt Brace Jovanovich.

Internal Revenue Service (1978). A Dictionary of Compliance Factors. Washington: United States Department of the Treasury.

Larsen, R.J. and T. Katelaar (1991). Personality and Susceptibility to Positive and Negative Emotional States. *Journal of Personality and Social Psychology*, 61: pp. 132-140.

Le Grand, J. (2003). *Motivation, Agency, and Public Policy*. Of Knights and Knaves, Pawns and Queens. Oxford: Oxford University Press.

Leonard, H.B. and R.J. Zeckhauser (1986). *Amnesty, Enforcement and Tax Policy*. NBER Working Paper Series, No. 2096, National Bureau of Economic Research, Cambridge.

Long, S. and J. Swingen (1991). The Conduct of Tax-Evasion Experiments: Validation, Analytical Methods, and Experimental Realism. In: *Tax Evasion: An Experimental Approach*, P. Webley, H. Robben, H. Elffers and D. Hessing. Cambridge University Press, Cambridge, pp. 128-138.

Molm, L.D. (1988). The Structure and Use of Power: A Comparison of Reward and Punishment Power. *Social Psychology Quarterly*, 51: pp. 108-122.

Molm, L.D. (1994). Is Punishment Effective? Coercive Strategies in Social Exchanges. *Social Psychology Quarterly*, 57: pp. 77-94.

Nutin, J. and A.G. Greenwald (1968). *Reward and Punishment in Human Learning*. New York: Academic Press.

Pratt, W. (1964). Risk Aversion in the Small and in the Large. *Econometrica*, 32: pp. 122-136.

Pyle, D.J. (1991). The Economics of Taxpayer Compliance. *Journal of Economic Surveys*, 5: pp. 163-198.

Roth, A.E. (1995). Introduction to Experimental Economics. In: *The Handbook of Experimental Economics*, J.H. Kagel and A.E. Roth (eds.). Princeton: Princeton University Press, pp. 1-98.

Roth, J.A., J.T. Scholz and A.D. Witte (eds.) (1989). *Taxpayer Compliance*, Vol. 1 and Vol. 2. *Philadelphia*: University of Pennsylvania Press.

Sims, H.P. jr. (1980). Further Thoughts on Punishment in Organizations. *The Academy of Management Review*, 5: pp. 133-138.

Skinner, B.F. (1938). *The Behavior of Organism*. New York: Academic Press.

Skinner, B.F. (1953). *Science and Human Behavior*. New York: Macmillan.

Slemrod, J. (ed.). *Why People Pay Taxes. Tax Compliance and Enforcement*. Ann Arbor: University of Michigan Press, pp. 193-218.

Slemrod, J., M. Blumenthal and C. Christian (2001). Taxpayer Response to an Increased Probability of Audit: Evidence from a Controlled Experiment in Minnesota. *Journal of Public Economics*, 79: pp. 455-483.

Thorndike, E.L. (1911). *Animal Intelligence*. New York: Macmillan.

Thorndike, E.L. (1932). The Fundamentals of Learning. New York: Teachers College, Columbia University.

Torgler, B. (2002). Speaking to Theorists and Searching for Facts: Tax Morale and Tax Compliance in Experiments. *Journal of Economic Surveys*, 16: pp. 657-684.

Torgler, B. (2003a). Beyond Punishment: A Tax Compliance Experiment with Taxpayers in Costa Rica. *Revista de Análisis Económico*, 18: pp. 27-56.

Torgler, B. (2003b). *Tax Morale and Tax Evasion: Evidence from the United States*. WWZ-Discussion Paper 03/01, WWZ, Basel.

Torgler, B. (2004). Moral Suasion: An Alternative Tax Policy Strategy? Evidence from a Controlled Field Experiment in Switzerland. *Economics of Governance*, 5: pp. 235-253.

Torgler, B. and C.A. Schaltegger (2005a). Tax Amnesties and Political Participation. *Public Finance Review*, 33: pp. 403-431.

Torgler, B. and C.A. Schaltegger (2005b). Tax Amnesties in Switzerland and Around the World. *Tax Notes International*, 27 June, pp. 1193-1203.

Weck, H. (1983). *Schattenwirtschaft: Eine Möglichkeit zur Einschränkung der öffentlichen Verwaltung? Eine ökonomische Analyse*. Finanzwissenschaftliche Schriften 22, Peter Lang, Bern.

Zald, D.H., I. Boileau, W. El-Deardy, R. Gunn, F. McGlone, G.S. Dichter and A. Dagher (2004). Dopamine Transmissions in the Human Striatum during Monetary Reward Tasks. *Journal of Neuroscience*, 24: pp. 4105-4112.

4 | CORPORATE CRIME AND REGULATION

Sally S. Simpson[1]

1. INTRODUCTION

An explosion on January 2nd of this year [2006] in the Sago Mine near Tallmansville, West Virginia trapped 12 miners underground. By the time rescue workers could reach the men, 40 hours had passed. Only one miner was still alive.

Several weeks later, also in West Virginia, two minors were separated from their 12 person crew as they tried to escape a conveyer-belt fire in a mine owned by Massey Energy Company and operated by Aracoma Coal. The other members of the crew managed to escape the fire unharmed. The bodies of Don Bragg and Ellery Hatfield were recovered two days later.

These two incidents, so closely coupled in time and place, have re-focused public debate about regulatory policy in the United States. Media accounts of the accidents and their tragic outcomes have emphasized a number of regulatory factors that may have contributed to the loss of life. Because the regulatory record of the Mine Safety and Health Administration (both before and after the incidents) is illustrative of some of the key issues and concerns confronting corporate crime regulation today, I will use the West Virginia incidents and actions of the MSHA (both before and after the mine disasters) to highlight the broader regulatory debate and touch on critical questions that have emerged within this debate. Some of these questions include (but are not limited to): (1) How and to what extent does quality of regulation matter in shaping regulatory compliance? (2) How important is regulation compared to other incentives and mechanisms of social control, and how does it

1. Department of Criminology and Criminal Justice, University of Maryland, College Park, MD 20742, USA (e-mail: ssimpson@crim.umd.edu).

interact with those mechanisms? (3) How do the shortcomings of regulation (e.g. complexity, contradictory rules, and unreasonableness) increase the risk of non-compliance? In addition, how politics and scientific claims affect the context of regulation is woven throughout this discussion.

In the second part of the chapter, a brief review of the corporate crime regulation and control literature is presented. More quantitative studies, including descriptions of some of my own work in this area, dominate this part of the paper. Key findings (as they relate to the above questions of interest) and some main weaknesses of the regulation literature are emphasized in this section as well as in the concluding section of this chapter.

2.   MINING REGULATIONS IN THE UNITED STATES: A CASE STUDY

2.1.   The 2006 U.S. mine disasters: A failure of regulation?

Were the accidents in West Virginia preventable? Could regulatory agencies have done more? If yes, where did regulation fail? According to the U.S. Mine Safety and Health Administration, the mining deaths were aberrations amid a strong record of mining safety. The agency reports that the mining industry realized a 35% decrease in fatal accidents nationwide since 2000 (MSHA Fact Sheet, 2006) as MSHA pushed for cooperative health and safety partnerships with labour, mine operators, and industry associations coupled with strong *enforcement* against unsafe operators (MSHA Fact Sheet, 2006, 95-1).

Critics of the MSHA strategy argue that the disasters occurred precisely because of the cooperative tactic adopted by the agency. The MSHA pulled back from approximately 18 potential regulations since 2001 (Skrzycki, 14 February 2006), including mandatory supplies of oxygen tanks and breathing masks inside every coal mine, safety proposals to lessen the risk of conveyor belts catching fire (the cause of the Aracoma mine disaster), and expanding the number of mine rescue teams available to respond to disasters. Accompanying the change in regulatory strategy were substantial cuts to the agency's workforce and reductions in the number of criminal prosecutions and major fines when violations were detected (Warrick, 31 January 2006).

The MSHA, under the Bush Administration, ostensibly has adopted what Braithwaite (1985) has called a pyramid of enforcement – a regulatory strategy that merges cooperative with punitive interventions. Yet, the regulatory record demonstrates numerous instances of failed *implementation* – a problem not unique to the MSHA or to regulatory agencies in the United States. The Public Management Service (1995) of the Organization for Economic Cooperation and Development, for instance, identifies implementation failures in a variety of areas (including education, assistance, persuasion, promotion, economic incentives, monitoring, enforcement, and sanctions) throughout OECD countries. Instead, PMS asserts that regulatory processes in OECD countries tend to 'rely too much on ineffective punitive threats and too little on other kinds of incentives' (Public Management Service, 1995:10 cited in Sparrow, 2000:7).

If it is true that MSHA policies failed, how and why did this happen? On the surface, MSHA can point to supportive evidence that the change in enforcement strategies (from command and control to cooperative) was successful. For instance, at the same time that U.S. coal mine production reached its highest historical levels, mining fatality and injury rates were declining. Inspectors were logging more on-site inspection hours per mine over the past 5 years (evidence that the agency was *proactively* inspecting mining operations) and issuing a greater number of hazard complaints (the main tool for obtaining compliance). Inspectors were finding fewer significant and substantial hazards (MSHA Fact Sheet, 2006).

Miners and other regulatory critics, however, point to a blizzard of 'slap on the wrist' citations against the Sago mine, noting that 273 violations were recorded including 16 that were designated *unwarrantable failures* (the most serious infractions or those that were *repeat* violations). Although federal inspectors took action that forced the mine temporarily to suspend operations, the mine was allowed to resume operations after taking corrective steps to fix some of the problems. Many critics felt the mine was unsafe and should have been closed for a longer period of time, or permanently even (see MSHA Sago Mine Information, 2006 for more detail on the Sago citations). Fines brought against the mine owners (Anker West Virginia Mining Co. and later ICG), were modest – $24,000 over the two year period preceding the disaster, with an average fine of $150 (Warrick, 8 January 2006).

Collectively, these facts point to MSHA's *failure* to effectively step-up enforcement after cooperative interventions failed. As the mine became more unsafe and generally unresponsive to the MSHA, the blizzard of citations should have given way to substantial criminal penalties and mine closure. These deficiencies were noted in a 2003 GAO report in which MSHA was rebuked for is lack of follow-up when violations were discovered. Additionally, the GAO criticized MSHA leaders in Washington for not providing *adequate oversight* to ensure that inspectors were enforcing compliance (cited in Warrick, 8 January 2006).

Another implementation failure can be tied to the MSHA shift away from public scrutiny and oversight. Mine enforcement has become less transparent after 2000. MSHA eliminated or scaled back programmes that made mining records available to the public. The regulatory agency halted the release of notes (under FOIA) from mine inspections and accident investigation became a closed-door proceeding – even for relatively minor and commonplace accidents (Warrick, 8 January 2006). Thus, the opportunity to educate and promote compliance based on these cases was lost – in essence, another implementation failure.

Finally, it seems likely that the MSHA has been caught between regulatory styles. Under the Bush Administration, regulators rejected a more punitive style in favour of a *non-threatening* approach. Symbolically, this new style was apparent in the new titles created for inspectors, *compliance assistance specialists* (Warrick, 8 January 2006). In practice, however, MSHA inspectors adopted a *lenient* regulatory style that emphasized cooperative partnerships between miners, companies, and regulators that may have failed to condemn the violations. We know that there is an increased risk of non-compliance when cooperative intervention styles neglect also to embrace condemnation of the violation (Makkai and Braithwaite, 1994). The shift in regulatory style at MSHA may have sent the wrong signal and message to the industry.

So, we return to our original set of questions and ask: 'How and to what extent did quality of regulation matter in shaping regulatory compliance?' Using Sparrow's (2000:2) definition of quality (i.e. which law regulators choose to enforce and when; how they focus their efforts, structure discretion, and select their methods), one could easily conclude from this case study that *quality* mattered a great deal – that is to say a lack of *quality* regulation appears to have negatively affected compliance, potentially increasing the risk of non-compliance. The second question of interest (i.e. how does regulation fare in comparison to other incentives and mechanisms of control?) has less *direct* evidence in the case study. As noted, the Public Management Service has asserted that OECD countries (including the USA) rely more on punitive sanctions and less on other incentives and mechanisms of social control (e.g. education, ethics, morality, informal controls). Clearly, sanctions/citations played a major role in the administrative response to wrongdoing and health and safety failures in the mining industry. However, there is little information in this case about incentives or any alternative instruments utilized by the MSHA or the mine owners/operators. One could certainly argue from the facts of the case that regulators failed to *signal* the moral reprehensibility of certain behaviours (e.g. minor citations did not give way to criminal penalties, MSHA reopened the Sago mine when many felt it was still unsafe) and thus informal controls (education, ethics, morality, informal costs) were less apt to be triggered.[2] Similarly, the new secrecy surrounding accident investigation failed to educate owners/operators about wrongdoing and alternative strategies or incentives to promote compliance. Finally, regarding

2. A similar claim could be made about 'scientific' gamesmanship regarding the merits of MSHA policy (see hereafter).

the last question of interest, nothing in the official account and documentation of events indicates that an *oppressive* regulatory regime produced criminal defiance (Braithwaite, 1989; Sherman, 1993). The case study does, however, reveal the highly politicized context in which much regulatory policy is formed, framed, and implemented. Politicization also has important implications for the success and failure of regulatory policy.

2.2. *Politicizing regulatory enforcement*

Not surprisingly, the mining disasters produced some highly politicized reactions including the inevitable 'get tough on crime' call. Politicians must be (or at least give the appearance of being) responsive to highly publicized disasters and stakeholder/general public outrage. Consequently, much regulation is reactive instead of proactive. This often means that strategic and long-term regulatory goals are sacrificed in the interest of political expediency.

Regulation depends on setting desirable standards for society to achieve (e.g. ambient pollution standards) and then choosing the means of attainment (Portney, 2000) but as already noted, regulatory goals often are assessed within a politicized command and control framework. Too much attention is focused around punishments, fines, and other formal legal sanctions as indicators of regulatory *success* and toughness (bean counting) and not enough on the societal good (e.g. positive outcomes like cleaner water and air, better products, and safer working conditions) and alternative means to achieve these goals. Too much time is spent legislating short-term responses to disasters and not enough attention given to long-term threats and benefits (Skrzycki, 14 February 2006).

Given that policy makers favour efficient regulation, the usual tool for assessing whether regulation is efficient (or not) is cost-benefit analysis. However, this too is subject to politics. Politics conceivably can shape regulatory priorities by over-emphasizing costs (conservative) or benefits (liberal). Because it is often difficult to directly quantify and place a value on the long-term favourable effects of regulation (e.g. reduced mortality and morbidity), costs tend to be more readily identifiable and concrete – consequently, easier to politicize. As post 9-11 deficits sky-rocketed, for instance, Congress cut the annual budget at the Labor Department's Mine Safety and Health Administration. This cut resulted in the reduction of 183 safety inspectors and office staff (Blomberg News, 24 January 2006), potentially compromising the number, type, and thoroughness of inspections and oversight/follow-up in the interest of saving money.

Regulatory policy also appears to be mired increasingly in what might be called *the science game*. Pro- and anti-regulation forces engage in a battle of scientific wits, pitting one set of scientists against another. For instance, in a law suit filed by the Mining Awareness Resource Group Diesel Coalition (a coalition of mining companies with financial support from a mining trade group), a lawyer for the group described a Clinton era law controlling the effects on minors of diesel fumes and particulate matter as having 'no scientific basis' and 'unachievable from an engineering standpoint'. He characterized the law as a 'giant failed high school science project' (Skrzycki, 14 February 2006:D01). Citing this example does not mean to imply that scholarly challenges and policy evaluations are inappropriate (quite the contrary), but to highlight that regulation appears to be driven increasingly by scientific gamesmanship. Howard Silver (Executive Director of the Consortium of Social Science Associations), commenting on this phenomenon observes (*Footnotes*, February 2006):

'Sound science' has become part of the lexicon of Washington policy debates, but the 'sound' often becomes a cacophony of competing claims. ...a member of Congress once told a scientist testifying at a hearing: 'you've got your science, I have mine.'

If the science of regulation is viewed as a political game, then law will be seen by some in the industry as an opportunity for circumvention. This approach can produce (and reinforce) what McBarnett (2004) has called creative compliance and Bardach and Kagan (1982) describe as cultures of resistance. Because much of the regulatory arena is not black and white but shades of *grey*, companies seek out legal gaps to exploit in their favour. If law is perceived as illegitimate, unnecessarily restrictive or punitive, companies may *fight back*. One response might be to lobby and press to change regulatory policy (demonstrating a willingness to play within the *political* regulatory box). But another approach dismisses the legitimacy of law by active resistance: obstruction, lack of cooperation with authorities, and non-compliance. The latter response symbolizes an underlying attitude, among business leaders and managers, that law is a game that justifies creative compliance or, even worse, active resistance (McBarnett, 2004:11).

This last point highlights the impossibility of discussing regulation without bringing the regulated community into the discussion. The strengths and weaknesses of regulation should be discussed in the context of corporate behaviour – specifically what causes companies to offend (failure to comply with regulation) and what role, if any, does regulation along with other mechanisms of social control play in affecting firm behaviour? In the next section, I briefly summarize some of this literature before using my own research to take up the questions raised at the beginning of this chapter.

3   CORPORATE OFFENDING AND REGULATORY SANCTIONS

3.1.   *Firm characteristics, corporate crime, and legal sanctions*

One of the more common explanations for why companies violate the law is economic – firms violate the law because it is in their economic interests to do so (Asch and Seneca, 1975; Staw and Szwajkowski, 1975; Conklin, 1977, Clinard and Yeager, 1980; Simpson, 1986; 1987; Jamieson, 1994). Yet, research demonstrates that economic considerations represent only part (if any) of the picture (Jenkins and Braithwaite, 1993; Vaughan, 1996; Ermann and Rabe, 1997) and other company characteristics (e.g. structure, strategy, culture, offending history, internal programmes) may be more important predictors of corporate offending.

The relationship of organizational characteristics to offending and recidivism, however, is not well understood and findings are inconsistent and equivocal. This may be related to the fact that different offence types carry different costs and benefits. Importantly, variability may exist not only within broad classifications of crime types (e.g. antitrust, environmental, financial, securities), but within offence types and levels of seriousness (e.g. price-fixing versus unfair advertising; air emissions versus water; OSHA wilful versus repeat violations, see Simpson, 1986; Simpson and Schell, 2006). Therefore, it makes sense first to study offending outcomes within crime types (Becker, 1968; Cornish and Clarke, 1987; Cohen and Simpson, 1997).

Mixed findings in the empirical literature may also be due to potential reciprocal effects between firm characteristics, offending, and sanctions. For instance, smaller companies may be more likely to receive punitive sanctions because they are less apt to have the necessary resources to put into place a comprehensive compliance programme – which, according to the U.S. Sentencing guidelines, is a mitigating factor in punishment and thus minimizes the firm's culpability score and subsequent punishment (Joseph, 1998).

Research results are also equivocal because most studies of corporate offending use cross-sectional data and it is difficult to establish proper temporal ordering or, if data are longitudinal, the studies track a relatively short time horizon. Such designs make it difficult to explore the offending histories of firms and, importantly, to study the impact of sanctions (especially their deterrent effects) on company recidivism. Additional concerns about sanctions revolve around the source and target of sanctions. The evidence is far from conclusive regarding whether corporate violators should be criminally prosecuted or whether other justice systems (civil or administrative) produce higher levels of corporate compliance or if sanctions should be directed toward the company, responsible managers, or both (Coffee, 1980; 1981; Laufer, 1994; Paternoster and Simpson, 1997). Generally, these questions have generated more smoke than light because there is so little empirical research from which to draw firm conclusions.

3.2.   *Broadening the formal sanction model: The enforcement pyramid*

John Braithwaite (1985) believes that regulatory enforcement should resemble a pyramid in which formal legal sanctions are punitive elements within a broader crime control strategy. Because law is the most commanding and intrusive form of social control, it should be the intervention of last resort (and thus, located at the tip of the enforcement pyramid). And, because criminal law is more punitive than regulatory and (generally) civil law, regulatory interventions should be more frequent than formal sanctions located higher on the pyramid. Yet, from this regulatory perspective, *the first line of defence* against corporate violators is informal control based in normative beliefs about ethical conduct and the morality of law. Regulatory sanctions found in legal systems build on the normative pro-social components found among corporate managers and within corporate cultures.

Braithwaite's model (see also Ayres and Braithwaite, 1992) assumes that most actors want to comply with the law and are willing to obey legitimate rules. This suggests that morality, ethics, and informal constraints should play an important role in the enforcement equation. At the organizational level, companies will care about their good name, they will monitor the activities of their employees, officers will set a strong moral standard for the company, and firms will cooperate with regulators to move back into compliance should violations occur. At the regulatory level, a cooperative model of corporate crime control *first* assumes that firms are good citizens who are willing to comply. Thus, the initial contact between the firm and the regulator will stress more informal interventions. At the manager level, it means that decision-makers will care about their own good name (along with that of their company), the opinions of significant others, and meeting their own ethical standards.

Cooperative models of crime control provide some insight into why some companies consistently meet and/or exceed regulatory standards (Harrington, 1988; Magat and Viscusi, 1990). It is not fear of sanctions (the deterrent threat) that produce compliance and good citizenship, but rather moral habituation, high ethical standards, and the potential damage to reputation that non-compliance is apt to bring (Dowling and Kimball, 1982; Cahill and Kane, 1994). However, a cooperative system of crime control benefits from the availability, accessibility, and use of punitive interventions. While cooperative models assume that most actors will comply, the model also recognizes that others will act in an economically self-interested manner. In other words, some firms and managers will do the right thing only when they are forced to do so. With an eye toward these actors, Braithwaite's model couples what criminologists know from deterrence studies – that deterrence works best for those who are not morally habituated.

Currently, we know little about how deterrence and compliance strategies fit together in the compliance area and how organizational characteristics may influence outcomes of interest (i.e. offending, recidivism, sanction strategy). Moreover, we know even less about how managers think about corporate offending in the context of potential discovery and punishment risks and crime benefits. Several of my studies offer evidence regarding these regulatory puzzles. In particular: (1) vignette surveys have been used to estimate the conditions under which respondents are likely to engage in corporate offending; and (2) secondary data from the U.S. Environmental Protection Agency are used to assess whether and what type of regulation affects firm compliance and recidivism.

3.3. *Regulation and corporate compliance: evidence from two studies*

3.3.1. *Factorial (vignette) survey*

Explicit within rational choice theories of corporate crime (Paternoster and Simpson 1993) is the idea that a prospective offender weighs the benefits and costs of illegal behaviour, including assessments of the threat (certainty and severity) of perceived formal sanctions.[3] Nonetheless, research suggests that formal sanctions may not be perceived as very likely or consequential.[4] Indeed, this position is commonly taken in the corporate crime literature and is consistent with that taken by critics of the MSHA under the Bush Administration. At the Sago mine, over a 23 month period leading up to the disaster, several dozen miners had been injured in a string of accidents. In spite of 272 citations by the MSHA, regulators did not shut down the mine nor did they impose any criminal sanctions. The largest fine imposed during this period

---

3. Note that the objective likelihood of a corporation being subject to criminal sanction is low and may reflect more than the egregiousness of the illegal act, including such factors as political considerations of prosecutors, resource constraints, and evidentiary limitations. Because of such factors, there is a greater likelihood that criminal sanctions for white-collar crimes would be brought against individual managers rather than criminal sanctions for corporate wrongdoing (see, for example, Laufer, 1999 and Wells, 1993). Further, a firm generally is more likely to face civil or regulatory procedures than criminal prosecution as a result of an illegal act (Clinard and Yeager, 1980; Geis and Salinger, 1998). Our interest, however, is in managerial perceptions of sanction threats for themselves and the firm, which may not accord with the actual likelihood of sanctions being imposed.
4. For instance, Williams and Hawkins (1989) found that men in their study believed, on average, there was only a 36% likelihood of arrest for spousal assault. Similar results were found for Grasmick and Green (1980) and Grasmick and Bursik (1990) in their studies of perceived sanction risk for a variety of offense types.

was $440.00, approximately .0004% of the $110 million net profit reported in 2005 by International Coal Group, Inc. (Warrick, 8 January 2006).

The *failure* of corporate regulation, therefore, may be due to the fact that sanctions are rarely imposed for illegal conduct and, if a company is caught, the resulting punishment is no more than *a slap on the wrist*. Formal sanctions may not be seen by managers as highly likely and they may not directly inhibit corporate crime.

Formal sanctions may not be irrelevant, however. Instead, sanction threats may operate indirectly, mediated through other variables. Their existence may set expectations as to related outcomes, such as loss of respect of family and friends or as an important indicator of the morality of certain conduct and thus will influence the individual's evaluations of the ethics of the act as well as his or her perceptions of the judgments of others.

I have explored these ideas using a vignette survey of managers and MBA students. In this survey, respondents were asked whether they would behave like a hypothetical manager described in a scenario. The scenarios depict managers engaging in illegal *corporate* acts, such as price-fixing, bribery, accounting fraud and EPA violations. The context of the offences varied – with different company and manager characteristics randomly assigned. So, for instance, a company might be described in the scenario as small, medium, or large; the firm-level benefits associated with the illegal act might save the firm a large (or small) amount of money; the depicted manager might be promoted, evaluated positively by peers, or by top management for engaging in the illegal act.

In one study that uses the vignette data, my co-authors and I were interested in the interaction of ethics/morality, anticipated informal consequences and legal sanctions with respect to a decision to engage in illegal and unethical conduct (Smith, Simpson and Huang, 2006). Using the business ethics and deterrence literature as a guide, we hypothesized that formal sanctions could have a direct or indirect effect on corporate offending. What we found was that formal sanctions operated primarily through the perceived consequences of engaging in the violation (outcome expectancies) and moral evaluations (see Figure 1 for a schematic diagram of our expected relationships) and a description of our findings. Those who perceived formal sanctions to be likely and consequential were also more apt to think that there would be substantial informal consequences for them if the act were discovered within the firm. Similarly, respondents who thought formal sanctions were likely and severe were more apt to judge the illegal behaviours as morally wrong.

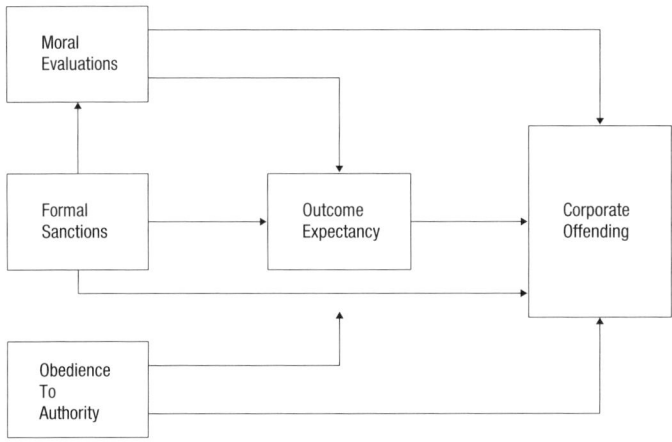

Path 1. Formal Sanctions to Corporate Offending (+, no support for hypothesis)*
Path 2. Formal Sanctions to Outcome Expectancy (+, support hypothesis)
Path 3. Outcome Expectancy to Corporate Offending (-, support hypothesis)
Path 4. Moral Evaluations to Corporate Offending (-, support hypothesis)
Path 5. Formal Sanctions to Moral Evaluations (+, support hypothesis)
Path 6. Obedience to Authority to Corporate Offending (+, support hypothesis)
Path 7. Obedience to Authority to Outcome Expectancy (-, support hypothesis)
Path 8. Moral Evaluations to Outcome Expectancy (+, support hypothesis)

* The direct positive effect of formal sanctions on offending intentions is counter to our research hypothesis, but the cumulative indirect effect of formal sanctions is negative.

Figure 1   Model of Corporate Offending

We also discovered that morality and informal sanctions were directly associated with a lower likelihood of illegal conduct. But, moral evaluations also lowered the offending risk through outcome expectancies (i.e. informal consequences). Respondents who objected to the acts on moral grounds were more apt to view the behaviours as having substantial informal costs which then affected offending considerations. Finally, obedience to authority (ordered to violate the law by a supervisor) increased offending risk directly but also through its association with outcome expectancies (obedience significantly decreased the perceived informal costs of offending).

We found that many of our respondents (most with significant managerial experience) indicated a willingness to offend even though the depicted behaviour directly contradicted their moral code. We were curious as to why this might be the case and speculated that following the dictates of one's superior within an organization would give individuals an excuse to morally disengage (Bandura, 2002) while invoking a *role-based motive* (Kelman and Hamilton,1989: 209). In other words, within an organization, following the direct order of one's supervisor trumps individual moral responsibility. This process allows the actor to claim a duty to obey while denying personal responsibility for the action.

These results are consistent with and build upon an integrated rational choice perspective my co-author Ray Paternoster and I developed and tested (1993), using data from a different vignette survey (1996). We found that legal threats triggered social controls which, in turn, deterred illegality. Our research suggests that the social embeddedness of managers may be a key to crime inhibition. Only respondents who perceived high social costs associated with offending (such as executives and managers in training who have attained high levels of social capital through education, work, and respect of family) were susceptible to the formal sanction trigger. This earlier study also found, however, that offending intentions were increased when managers thought the law was *illegitimate* (Paternoster and Simpson, 1996:577). To the extent that regulatory laws are unreasonable and perceived by managers as harmful, even the morally inhibited may be swayed into committing corporate crime if there is 'some appeal to a higher, more compelling, or more immediate moral principle.'

Several results from the vignette studies relate to the questions asked at the beginning of this chapter, in particular questions about the relative impact of regulation vis-à-vis other mechanisms of social control and the shortcomings of counter-productive regulation.

– How important is regulation compared to other incentives and mechanisms of social control and how does it interact with those mechanisms? Regulation (formal sanctions) will be enhanced when formal sanctions build around moral evaluations and when formal interventions take the potential for informal sanction threats into account (consistent with Braithwaite's enforcement pyramid). Yet, regulatory efforts may be stymied by criminous authority structures (or a rouge supervisor). Managers will obey authority, even when they are ordered to behave in ways that are inconsistent with their own moral values.

– How do the shortcomings of regulation increase the risk of non-compliance? Results indicate that regulatory unreasonableness (i.e. a perceived lack of legitimacy) increases the risk of non-compliance.

The vignette studies focus on what managers think and report about their likely behaviour under a controlled set of conditions. The study reported below, however, focuses on the non-compliance of companies. In the next section, I discuss some preliminary results from this research.

3.3.2.   *Firm characteristics, offending and crime control*

As noted earlier, extant research on the relationship between firm characteristics, illegal behaviour and crime control is flawed and fraught with inconsistent findings. These relationships are revisited in an NIJ-funded project on environmental compliance (Simpson and Garner, 2001). Information about non-compliance is collected from the Environmental Protection Agency using the Permit Compliance System. The study traces a group of U.S. publicly-owned companies in 4 basic manufacturing industries (steel, pulp, paper and oil refining) for a six-year period (for more information about the sample, see Appendix A).

The PCS data contain self-reports of chemical discharges, an independent measure of corporate compliance distinct from more proactive regulatory activity (e.g. inspections). Facilities self-report the level of discharges for the month and the EPA compares the discharges to the permitted levels to determine whether the facility is in violation. In addition to information about discharges over permitted levels, we also have information in the database on 1) technical violations, such as late monthly reports; 2) compliance schedule violations, where upgrades or discharge reductions were not accomplished on time; and 3) single event violations, such as a significant fish kill. PCS also contains information on EPA response to facility non-compliance because it includes enforcement actions, including actions such as phone calls or warning letters from EPA to firms out of compliance (interventions we would classify as informal). Supplementing the PCS data are administrative and judicial case information from EPA's Docket system and criminal case information from EPA's crimdoc (interventions we would classify as formal).

At the firm level, we have collected a series of economic and structural indicators using Mergent's Online and Computat, including total assets, total liabilities, total current assets, total current liabilities, total stockholders equity, pretax income, net income, sales and the number of employees. These data are coded yearly, beginning two years prior to the PCS/OSHA data (1993-2000). We also have a count of the number of facilities (major) that a company owns based on matches to the PCS database.

The preliminary analyses reported here examine whether company characteristics affect firm compliance and, if a firm is subject to sanction, whether: (a) firm characteristics are related to the type of sanction levied (formal versus informal); and (b) firm non-compliance is affected by previous sanctions (by type).

Variable relationships are examined using OLS Panel Models with Fixed Effects. This research design is preferable as it controls for potentially confounding effects of unobserved time-stable sources of corporate offending (Brame, Bushway and Paternoster, 1999) and the fact that observations are not independent of one another (i.e. the same firm is followed over time). Descriptive statistics for all variables of interest are listed in Appendix B. Again, we see that the relationship between firm economic performance indicators and self-reported EPA violation rates is equivocal. In the yearly panels (Appendix C, Table 1), firm level changes in profitability (measured as total stockholders equity) are unrelated to any of the pollution measures (reported levels of BOD, TSS, conventional pollutants, toxic pollutants) while shifts in company return on assets are positively related to offending. However, these results change once the two variables are included in the same models (Appendix C, Table 2). Declines in company profitability are now associated with higher non-compliance rates (consistent with a poverty causes crime explanation) at the same time that increases in firm return on assets are associated with increasing non-compliance rates. Thus, upward shifts in a company's return on investment appear to be positively related to firm non-compliance (perhaps indicating high returns on a relatively dated set of assets) while declines in firm profitability increase EPA non-compliance (across conventional pollutants).

Moving to the relationship between sanction type (formal versus informal; type of legal intervention) and EPA non-compliance, results in Table 3 (see Appendix C) show a consistent positive relationship between informal sanctions (e.g. phone calls and warning levels) and non-compliance (TSS and conventional pollutants). Thus, informal actions by EPA offer little deterrent value and, in effect, appear to increase non-compliance. There is a slight deterrent effect associated with formal sanctions for conventional pollutants (p < .10). Generally, the level of non-compliance is unaffected by who brings the sanction (e.g. regulatory agency, civil or criminal mechanisms).[5]

Finally, in Table 4 (see Appendix C), we report results for a pooled probity model that examines whether sanction type (measured as a dummy variable where informal sanctions are coded as 0 and formal sanctions are coded as 1 is related to firm characteristics. A probity analysis is utilized when the dependent variable (in this case intervention type) takes a discrete number of mutually exclusive (and mutually exhaustive) values and those values are ordered (Borooah, 2002). Here, there is some evidence that the type of intervention used by the EPA varies by firm profitability. Lower levels of firm profit are slightly (p < .10) related to more formal types of regulatory intervention, even after controlling for the number of firm violations (a variable that has a counterintuitive negative relationship with intervention strategy, i.e. more violations predict an increased likelihood of *informal* regulatory interventions).[6] However, additional analyses revealed that none of the other firm-level measures (e.g. return on assets, number of facilities owned, or company size) were related to regulatory strategy (results available on request).

---

5. In only one equation is there a significant relationship for sanction source, but that relationship is positive (civil, p < .01 for BOD).
6. This result may be consistent, however, with a pyramid strategy of enforcement. EPA may rely – at least initially – on informal mechanisms when firms violate the law moving toward formal mechanisms once offending reaches a 'tipping point.'

We must be careful in the conclusions that we draw from this study because our results are preliminary. However, at this point, neither the type (administrative, civil, criminal) nor style (formal versus informal) of regulatory intervention are readily predictable from firm level characteristics and there is no clear relationship between regulatory intervention strategies (informal and formal) and levels of non-compliance. There is a hint that formal sanctions may result in deterrence, but this relationship may depend on other factors that we have not yet included in our analysis. Therefore, we are unwilling at this point to suggest that formal sanctions are a better instrument for producing compliance than informal interventions. However, assuming that regulation quality can be measured by some of our indicators, we have little to offer in support of the regulatory quality-compliance relationship.

4.   CONCLUSIONS

This chapter began with a case study of the recent mining disasters in the USA. We learned from this analysis that inconsistencies in and failed implementation of regulatory strategy increase the risk of non-compliance. Politics and scientific gamesmanship decrease the likelihood that regulatory strategies will be adopted and evaluated in a manner that is apt to produce better regulatory schemes and higher levels of compliance. In response to the West Virginia mining disasters, several pieces of legislation are under consideration. Some focus around improving safety, but others seek higher fines and penalties against violators. The Mine Safety and Health Administration, for instance, wants the authority to impose $220,000 fines (a substantial increase from present maximum of $60,000). The larger fines are sought as a means to 'raise the ante for mine operators to abide by the law' (Frank, *U.S.A. Today*, 19 January 2006). Unfortunately, the politically expedient *get tough on crime* recommendations have relatively little empirical merit at this point in time – especially without consideration and research on how legal sanctions operate in conjunction with other social control mechanisms.

Results from our vignette study indicate that formal sanctions can reduce the likelihood of misconduct indirectly, by acting on outcome expectancies and moral evaluations. Formal sanctions are more likely to be effective if associated with the prospect of loss of respect of business associates, friends and family. Further, formal sanctions are indicative of society's views of the morality of certain conduct, influencing the individual's moral evaluations of the act. The recent public reporting of a doubling of sentences in the U.S. Sentencing Guidelines – and in subsequent court cases – seems likely to support an increase in the perception of these crimes as morally wrong. Consistent with deterrence theory, interventions that better familiarize managers with the law *and* convey the moral opprobrium attached to illegal conduct may effectively inhibit corporate wrongdoing. In such a way, both moral evaluations and outcome expectancies may be influenced by greater awareness of formal sanctions. However, a key element in this determination is whether the law, sanctions and regulatory procedures are understood to be legitimate and fair. Creative compliance or actual defiance, as we saw in the Paternoster and Simpson vignette study (1996), may result if the law and its operation lack normative consensus.

When we shift our focus from managers to companies, we confirm that crime control is a complicated process. Firm characteristics predict monthly non-compliance and regulatory response, but not in a simple or straightforward manner. Firm shifts in profitability downward and return on assets upward are associated with higher levels of self-reported non-compliance (another firm characteristic is not being associated with non-compliance). The companies that are not doing well economically, however, appear to qualify for more formal regulatory interventions. But, ironically, companies with more violations (both in terms of absolute numbers and rates) are handled at a lower level of the enforcement pyramid (informally).

It may be that because EPA generally cares about and reacts in a formal way to cases of *significant non-compliance*, our measurement of violations (by count and rate) has produced this unlikely result. Our measures may overwhelmingly capture less serious cases, which would explain the negative relationship between violations and sanction type. This is something we can explore further in the data. The firm profitability-formal intervention relationship may be due to more efficiency in self-regulation. That is to say, profitable companies are more apt to have working environmental management systems in place that effectively monitor permitted levels of conventional pollutants. If regulators view these firms as good environmental citizens, they are more likely to respond to non-compliance (when it does occur) in a less punitive way. An alternative explanation however, is that profitable firms are also politically powerful entities. As such, they may use their influence to avoid more visible and damaging punishments. From this view, regulation fails because punishments are not certain and the process lacks legitimacy and transparency.

As is typical in these kinds of review chapters, I conclude my remarks with a plea for more and better research. Answers to the important questions around which this chapter has been organized are far from conclusive and require more sophisticated research designs and better data access (companies and agencies).

References

Asch, P. and J.J. Seneca (1975). Characteristics of Collusive Firms. *Journal of Industrial Economics*, 23: pp. 223-247.

Ayres, I. and J. Braithwaite (1992). *Responsive Regulation: Transcending the Deregulation Debate*. New York: Oxford.

Bandura, A. (2002). Selective Moral Disengagement in the Exercise of Moral Agency. *Journal of Moral Education*, 3: pp. 101-119.

Bardach, E. and R.A. Kagan (1982). *Going by the Book: The Problem of Regulatory Unreasonableness*. Philadelphia: Temple University Press.

Becker, G.S. (1968). Crime and Punishment: An economic approach. *Journal of Political Economy*, 76: pp. 169-217.

Borooah, V.K. (2002). *Logit and Probit: Ordered and Multinomial Models*. Thousand Oaks, CA: Sage.

Brame, R., S. Bushway and R. Paternoster (1999). On the Use of Panel Research Designs and Random Effects Models to Investigate Static and Dynamic Theories of Criminal Offending. *Criminology*, 37: pp. 599-641.

Braithwaite, J. (1985). *To Punish or Persuade*. Albany, NY: SUNY Press.

– (1989). *Crime, Shame and Reintegration*. Cambridge: Cambridge University Press.

Cahill, L.B. and R.W. Kane (1994). Corporate Environmental Performance Expectations in the 1990s. *Total Quality Environmental Management*, 3: pp. 409-420.

Clinard, M.B. and P. Yeager (1980). *Corporate Crime*. New York: The Free Press.

Coffee, J. Collins (1981/2). No Soul to Damn: No Body to Kick: An Unscandalized Inquiry into the Problem of Corporate Punishment. *Michigan Law Review*, 79: pp. 386-459.

Cohen, M.A. and S.S. Simpson (1997). The Origins of Corporate Criminality: Rational Individual and Organizational Actors. In: *Debating Corporate Crime*, W.S. Lofquist, M.A. Cohen and G.A. Rabe (eds). Cincinnati, Ohio: Anderson Publishing Co.

Conklin, J.E. (1977). *Illegal but not Criminal: Business Crime in America*. Englewood Cliffs, NJ: Prentice-Hall.

Cornish, D.B. and R.V. Clarke (1987). Understanding Crime Displacement: An Application of Rational Choice Theory. *Criminology*, 25: pp. 933-947.

Dowling, P. and J. Kimball (1981). Enforcing Pollution Control Laws in the United States. *Policy Studies Journal*, 11: No. 1.

Ermann, M.D. and G.A. Rabe (1997). Organizational Processes (Not Rational Choices). In: *Debating Corporate Crime*, W.S. Lofquist, M.A. Cohen and G.A. Rabe (eds.). Cincinnati: Anderson Publishing Co.

Geis, G. and L.S. Salinger (1998). Antitrust and Organizational Deviance. In: *Research in the Sociology of Organizations*, P.A. Bamberger and W.J. Sonnenstruhl (eds). Stamford, CT: JAI Press, Vol. 15.

Grasmick, H.G. and R.J. Bursik jr. (1990). Conscience, Significant Others and Rational Choice: Extending the Deterrence Model. *Law & Society Review*, 24: pp. 837-862.

Grasmick, H.G. and D.E. Green (1980). Legal Punishment, Social Disapproval, and Internationalization as Inhibitors of Illegal Behavior. *Journal of Criminal Law and Criminology*, 71: pp. 325-335.

Harrington, W. (1988). Enforcement Leverage when Penalties are Restricted. *Journal of Public Economics*, 37: pp. 29-53.

Jamieson, K.M. (1994). *Organization of Corporate Crime*. Thousand Oaks, CA: Sage.

Jenkins, A. and J. Braithwaite (1993). Profits, pressure and corporate lawbreaking. *Crime, Law and Social Change*, 20: pp. 221-232.

Joseph, M.E. (1998). Organizational Sentencing. *American Criminal Law Review*, 35: pp. 1017-1034.

Kelman, H.C. and V.L. Hamilton (1988). *Crimes of Obedience*. New Haven: Yale University Press.

Laufer, W.S. (1994). Corporate Bodies and Guilty Minds. *Emory Law Journal*, 43: pp. 647-730.

–   (1999). Corporate Liability, Risk Shifting, and the Paradox of Compliance. *Vanderbilt Law Review*, 52: pp. 1343-1420.

Magat, W.A. and W.K. Viscusi (1990). Effectiveness of the EPA's Regulatory Enforcement. *Journal of Law and Economics*, 33: pp. 331-360.

Makkai, T. and J. Braithwaite (1994). The Dialectics of Corporate Deterrence. *Journal of Research in Crime and Delinquency*, 31: pp. 347-373.

McBarnett, D. (2004). After Enron: Corporate Governance, Creative Compliance and the Uses of Corporate Social Responsibility. Conference Paper, *Governing the Corporation* (Queens University, Belfast)

Mine Safety and Health Administration (MSHA) (2006). Fact Sheet, Mine Safety and Health at a Glance. www.msha.gov/MSHAINFO/FactSheets/MSHAFCT10.HTM

–   (2006). Fact sheet 95-1, Mine Safety and Health. www.msha.gov/MSHAINFO/FactSheets/MSHAFCT1.HTM

–   (2006). Sago Mine Information-Citation and Order Explanations. www.msha.gov/sagomine/citationsandorders.asp

Paternoster, R. and S.S. Simpson (1993). A Rational Choice Theory of Corporate Crime. In: 5 *Advances in Criminological Theory: Routine Activity and Rational Choice*, R.V. Clarke and M. Felson (eds.). New Brunswick, NJ: Transaction Books.

–   (1996). Sanction Threats and Appeals to Morality: Testing a Rational Choice Model of Corporate Crime. *Law & Society Review*, 30: pp. 549-583.

Portney, P.R. (2000). EPA and the Evolution of Federal Regulation. In: *Public Policies for Environmental Protection* (second edition), P.R. Portney and R.N. Stavins (eds.). Washington DC: Resources for the Future Press.

Public Management Service (1995). Organization for Economic Cooperation and Development. Recommendation of the Council of the OECD on Improving the Quality of Government Regulation.

Sherman, L.W. (1993). Defiance, Deterrence, and Irrelevance: A Theory of the Criminal Sanction. *Journal of Research in Crime and Delinquency*, 30: pp. 445-537.

Silver, H.J. (2006). Science and Politics: The Uneasy Relationship. 34 (2) *Footnotes*. Washington DC: American Sociological Association.

Simpson, S.S. (1986). The Decomposition of Antitrust. *American Sociological Review*, 51: pp. 859-875.

–   (1987). Cycles of Illegality: Antitrust Violations in Corporate America. *Social Forces*, 64: pp. 943-963.

Simpson, S.S. and J. Garner (2001). Why do Corporations Obey Environmental Law? NIJ Grant (2001-IJ-CX-0020), U.S. Department of Justice: Washington DC.

USAToday.com (2006). T. Frank, Mining Agency: Increase Top Fine. 19 January (A1).

Wells, C. (1993). *Corporations and Criminal Responsibility.* Oxford, UK: Oxford University Press.

Williams, K.R. and R. Hawkins (1989). The Meaning of Arrest for Wife Assault. *Criminology,* 27: pp. 163-181.

Simpson, S.S. and N.M. Schell (2006). Corporate Performance and Occupational Safety and Health Act Violations. Working Paper, Department of Criminology and Criminal Justice, University of Maryland, College Park.

Smith, N.C., S.S. Simpson and C.-Y. Huang (2006). Why Managers Fail to do the Right Thing: An Empirical Study of Unethical and Illegal Conduct. Working Paper, London Business School.

Sparrow, M.K. (2000). *The Regulatory Craft: Controlling Risks, Solving Problems, and Managing Compliance.* Council for Excellence in Government. Washington DC: Brookings Institution Press.

Staw, B.N. and E. Szawajkowski (1975). The Scarcity-Munificence Component of Organizational Acts. *Administrative Science Quarterly,* 20: pp. 345-354.

Vaughn, D. (1996). *The Challenger Launch Decision: Risky Technology, Culture, and Deviance at NASA.* Chicago: University of Chicago Press.

Washingtonpost.com (www.washingtonpost.com) (2006). J. Warrick, Sago Puts Spotlight on Safety Strategy: U.S. Mine Agency Issues Citations, but Penalties are Light. 8 January (A03).

– (2006). L. Messina and N. Zuckerbrod, 2 Missing Men Found Dead after Fire in W.V. Mine. 22 January (A03).

– (2006). Bloomberg News, Senators Say Budget Cuts have Left Mines Unsafe. 24 January (A06).

– (2006). J. Warrick, Federal Mine Agency Considers New Rules to Improve Safety. 31 January (A03).

– (2006). C. Skrzycki, Fuming over Mining Rule. 14 February (D01).

– (2006). Associated Press, W.Va. Mines Cited for More Violations. 16 February.

Appendix A

Data collection began by identifying four industrial sectors – iron and steel (SIC code 3312), pulp mills (SIC Code 2621), paper mills (SIC Code 2621), and oil refining (SIC Code 2911) that are designated as major water users by the EPA and are subject to the provisions of the Clean Water Act (see, EPA Office of Compliance Sector Notebook Projects). Relying on the Ward's Business Directory, Standard and Poor's Industrial Compustat, and Mergent Online, we created a universe of all U.S. based, publicly traded companies operating in 1995 that had their primary business in one of these four sectors. We then searched for all facilities (plants, mills, refineries etc.) owned by these companies that also operated in our SIC codes of interest, drawing on the Directory of Corporate Affiliations, the Environmental Protection Agency's (EPA) Toxic Release Inventory (TRI), and the EPA's Permit Compliance System (PCS). This process yielded 147 unique names that then were cleaned and reduced to a company specific sample (N-61). Next, we matched those facilities pulled from other sources to PCS permit numbers using the EPA's Facility Registry System (FRS). We retained companies for our sample if they were matched to major facilities with permits in the PCS system as of 1995. Major industrial facilities are distinguished from minor dischargers based on specific ratings criteria developed by EPA/State.

Appendix B

Descriptive Statistics, EPA study

EPA Variables	nT	Range	Mean (Std. Dev.)	Interquartile Range
Non-compliance Rate				
BOD	289	0% – 60%	2.09 (5.95)	1.68
TSS	367	0% – 25%	1.53 (3.17)	1.69
Conventional Poll.	378	0% – 26%	1.10 (1.91)	1.39
Toxic Poll.	361	0% – 22%	0.95 (2.35)	0.89
Financial Performance				
Total Stockholders Equity	358	-$1,838,428,928.00 – $70,756,999,168.00	$3,033,541,670.75 ($7,991,302,506.2)	2,021,462,032
Return on Assets	352	-0.32 – 0.18	0.03 (0.06)	0.06
Corporate Structure				
Complexity (Number of Facilities Owned)	378	1 – 23	3.43 (2.96)	3.00
Size (Number of Employees)	336	291 – 112,900	15,419 (19,666)	17,726.00

EPA Variables	nT	Range	Mean (Std. Dev.)
Sanctions			
Total Sanctions (no cases)	4358	0 – 21	0.16 (0.78)
Total Sanctions (with cases)	4358	0 – 22	0.19 (0.85)
Informal Sanctions	4358	0 – 8	0.08 (0.41)
Formal Sanctions (no cases)	4358	0 – 21	0.07 (0.65)
Formal Sanctions (with cases)	4358	0 – 22	0.10 (0.72)

Appendix C

Table 1 OLS Panel Models with Fixed Effects: EPA Violation Rate on Firm Characteristics (Yearly)

	Model 1a		Model 1b		Model 1c		Model 1d	
	Coefficient	t-value	Coefficient	t-value	Coefficient	t-value	Coefficient	t-value
BOD Vio Rate								
Total stockholders equity	-3.46 e-10	-0.95						
Return on assets			8.62	1.92+				
# of facilities owned					0.16	0.33		
# of employees							0.00	0.74
TSS Vio Rate								
Total stockholders equity	-2.66 e-10	-0.88						
Return on assets			10.82	2.92*				
# of facilities owned					-0.05	-0.13		
# of employees							-0.00	-0.45
Con Pollutant Vio Rate								
Total stockholders equity	-1.55 e-10	-0.87						
Return on assets			4.45	2.92*				
# of facilities owned					-0.01	-0.08		
# of employees							2.88 e-06	0.09
Tox Pollutant Vio Rate								
Total stockholders equity	9.00 e-11	0.44						
Return on assets			4.68	2.48*				
# of facilities owned					-0.23	-0.83		
# of employees							0.00	0.48

+ p < .1 * p < .05 ** p < .01 *** p < .001

Table 2   OLS Panel Models with Fixed Effects: EPA Violation Rate on Firm
              Characteristics (Yearly, by Pollutant Type)

	Model 1a	
	Coefficient	t-value
BOD Vio Rate		
Total stockholders equity	-9.67 e-10	-2.25*
Return on assets	9.56	2.14*
TSS Vio Rate		
Total stockholders equity	-9.25 e-10	-2.33*
Return on assets	11.53	3.13**
Con Pollutant Vio Rate		
Total stockholders equity	-4.14 e-10	-2.44*
Return on assets	4.76	3.14**
Tox Pollutant Vio Rate		
Total stockholders equity	-6.66 e-11	-0.31
Return on assets	4.75	2.49**

$+ p < .1$ * $p < .05$ ** $p < .01$ *** $p < .001$

Table 3   OLS Fixed Effects Panel Models: Violation Rate on Sanctions (Monthly)

	Model 1a		Model 1b		Model 1c	
	Coefficient	t-value	Coefficient	t-value	Coefficient	t-value
BOD Vio Rate nt=3200						
# informal sanctions	0.11	0.30			0.11	0.29
# formal sanctions	-0.25	-0.85				
# formal sanctions with cases					-0.11	-0.44
# administrative cases			-0.30	-0.26		
# civil cases			6.40	2.67**		
# criminal cases			-3.48	-0.67		
TSS Vio Rate nt=4100						
# informal sanctions	0.54	2.05*			0.54	2.06*
# formal sanctions	0.23	1.07				
# formal sanctions with cases					0.14	0.80
# administrative cases			-0.32	-0.41		
# civil cases			-0.17	-0.13		
# criminal cases			-1.67	-0.44		
Con Pollutant Vio Rate nt=4200						
# informal sanctions	0.30	2.47**			0.30	2.47**
# formal sanctions	-0.12	-1.73+				
# formal sanctions with cases					-0.12	-1.82+
# administrative cases			-0.40	-1.20		
# civil cases			0.21	0.34		
# criminal cases			-2.52	-1.43		
Tox Pollutant Vio Rate nt=3900						
# informal sanctions	0.03	0.16			0.31	0.17
# formal sanctions	0.04	0.33				
# formal sanctions with cases					0.00	0.06
# administrative cases			-0.40	-0.76		
# civil cases			-0.39	-0.40		
# criminal cases			-0.77	-0.23		

+ $p < .1$ * $p < .05$ ** $p < .01$ *** $p < .001$

Table 4   Pooled Probit Model: EPA Sanction Type on Firm Characteristics (Monthly)

	Model 1a		Model 1b		Model 1c	
	Coefficient	t-value	Coefficient	t-value	Coefficient	t-value
Sanction Type 1 (no cases)						
Total stockholders equity	-3.35 e-11	-1.64+	-3.75 e-11	-1.78+	-3.97 e-11	-1.80+
Violation Rate			-0.03	-1.60		
Number of Violations					-0.09	-1.89+
Sanction Type 2 (with cases)						
Total stockholders equity	-3.05 e-11	-1.66+	-1.04 e-11	-0.99	-1.09 e-11	-1.06
Violation Rate			-0.03	-2.08*		
Number of Violations					-0.09	-2.02*

+ $p < .1$ * $p < .05$ ** $p < .01$ *** $p < .001$

5 | SELF-REGULATION AND COMPLIANCE

ABOUT LAW, ANIMAL WELFARE, AND CERTIFICATION SCHEMES AS
AN ALTERNATIVE FOR PUBLIC INSPECTIONS

Rob van Gestel[1]

'We are inclined both to oversimplify the nature of law and to exaggerate its power. We envisage law as constituted exclusively of its visible institutional and professional features: as composed of documents (a constitution, statutes, precedents), an apparatus (legislatures, courts, executive, departments), and a personnel (judges, lawyers, administrators, policemen). And we are so overawed by the sovereignty that law exercises in principle that we treat it as omnicompetent in fact: since it voices decisions from which there is no appeal, we regard it as able to decide and affect anything at all. In short, we conceive of law after the manner of Aristotle's Unmoved Mover: we think of it as an autonomous and selfsufficient force upon which the rest of the social order depends but which itself depends upon nothing. But law is very like an iceberg: only one-tenth of its substance appears above the social surface in the explicit form of documents, institutions, and professions, while the nine-tenths of its substance that supports its visible fragment leads a subaquatic existence, living in the habits, attitudes, emotions, and aspirations of men.'*

I. Jenkins, Social order and the limits of law, Princeton 1980.

1.   INTRODUCTION

When I was asked by the Dutch Tax Office to deliver a speech about self-regulation for a conference on compliance management, I must confess that I was, at first, somewhat surprised. I wondered what on earth paying taxes has to do with self-regulation. Is the Dutch government seriously considering abandoning the command and control approach in making tax laws? Are we

---

1. Professor of Theory and Methods of Legislation at the Research School for Legislative Studies of Tilburg University, The Netherlands (e-mail: r.a.j.vanGestel@uvt.nl).

really prepared to leave rulemaking and enforcement in this domain up to private regulatory bodies?

If the latter is the case, I would like to be the first to volunteer to draw up a code of conduct about the raising of income taxes for Dutch academics. The fact that you are probably smiling right now already implies that, in this case, self-regulation could easily generate all kinds of conflicts between private and public interests. More in general, this is confirmed by research in the field of law and economics. People like Anthony Ogus have argued that self-regulation may, for instance, cause serious market failures and result in the establishment of cartels, especially when there is a lack of transparency in a particular branch of industry, for instance caused by an information asymmetry between companies.[2]

Therefore, I believe that it will be highly unlikely that self-regulation has a big future in the field of taxation policies.[3] In the tax law domain there are too many potential conflicts between the public and private interest, voluntary compliance is all but self-evident in many cases, and free rider behaviour will always lie in wait.

Nevertheless, in other areas, self-regulation might be an option. That is why I would like to address the following question:

'To what extent can one predict if a certain type of self-regulation, like private certification schemes, will (not) work properly from a public interest perspective?'

I will try to answer this question by looking at a particular case that reads like a fairy tale, but is based on a true story. Unfortunately, the story has to do with one of the recent plans of the Dutch government to cut red tape and to simplify the existing body of public laws and regulations. The plan I am referring to aims, among other things, at replacing certain laws that serve to protect the health and welfare of domestic animals by a system of negotiated rulemaking and voluntary certification. Personally, I hope that this plan will find its way into a desk drawer of some anonymous civil servant soon, but because one never knows it cannot harm to perform an *ex ante evaluation* to demonstrate the most important flaws of the plan.[4]

---

2. See: A. Freytag and K. Winkler, The economics of self-regulation in telecommunications under sunset legislation, Research Paper Friedrich Schiller Universität Jena 2004. Available at: http://econpapers.repec.org/paper/jenjenasw/2004-17.htm.
3. This does not necessarily mean that tax law couldn't profit from ideas about 'responsive regulation'. Trying to create a good fit between social norms and legal rules in order to counter tax avoidance has proven to be worthwhile in the past. See, for instance: Braithwaite (ed) Taxing Democracy: Understanding Tax Avoidance and Tax Evasion, Ashgate, Aldershot, 2003. However, delegating rulemaking in this field to private parties is, in my opinion, more than a bridge too far.

There are several reasons for choosing animal welfare law as a case study to show why the transplanting of private governance systems to a public context is a complex undertaking. First of all, in this domain relying on self-regulation is not new. The Dutch Ministry for Agriculture, Nature and Food Quality, which is primarily responsible for animal welfare policy, should have been able to learn from previous experiences with quality management, eco-labelling and voluntary certification in this sector.[5] Secondly, ideas about delegating monitoring and inspection activities to private sector organizations seem to match with more general policy concepts of this Ministry about *meta-enforcement* and *public supervision over private monitoring and inspection*.[6] Thirdly, the number of laws and the scope of regulations concerning the welfare of domestic animals are fairly limited so that it was relatively easy to get an overview of the sort and number of interested parties (NGOs, animal shelters, kennels, animal food manufacturers).[7] Fourth, the changes in law and policy concerning alternative ways of organizing compliance have not been finalized yet. That was, of course, a precondition to be able to perform an ex ante evaluation and to try to predict what the possible consequences are going to be if the ideas about voluntary self-regulation will be put in practice.

Before I am going to explain why I feel that the proposals for voluntary certification in the area of the welfare of domestic animals aren't thought-out very well, it might be useful to explain just a little bit more about the current state of affairs concerning regulatory relief in the Netherlands.

4. Ex ante evaluation refers to forward-looking assessment of the likely future effects of law or policy proposals. Equivalents for ex ante evaluations are so-called Regulatory Impact Assessments or RIA's. Somewhat confusing is that at the EU-level the term ex ante evaluation concentrates on the budgetary aspects of policy proposals while RIA's are also focused on other aspects, like enforceability, social and environmental consequences etcetera. See the Communication of the European Commission on Impact Assessments, COM(2002)276 final.
5. See for instance: M.J.W. Smits and M.H.A.J. van Bavel, Mogelijkheden en beperkingen van certificering van natuurbeheer *(Possibilities and Liminations of certification of nature management)*, LEI, The Hague 2004 and M. Verberk, M. Thieme and M. Brander, Certificering en handhaving: Een verkenning van het beleidskader 'Zicht op gezonde teelt' voor handhaving en normnaleving *(Certification and Enforcement: An investigation of the policy framework 'View on healthy cultivation' for enforcement and compliance with norms)*, The Hague 2000.
6. LNV, Beleidskader toezicht op controle *(Policy framework supervision of control)*, The Hague 2005.
7. A special institutional forum for the welfare of domestic animals has been installed (Forum Welzijn Gezelschapsdieren) by the Ministry and there have been a number of conferences and workshops where members of the academic community could meet respresentatives of the industry and NGOs to discuss the plans about privatizing the regulation in this domain.

2.   TOWARDS A PRACTICAL LEGAL SYSTEM

The Dutch Cabinet wants to improve the relationship between government
and society. The current minister of Justice feels that the primary task of the
legislature is not only to make sure that laws are technically correct, but also
to promote a social and legal infrastructure that enables citizens and companies to solve their own problems and settle their disputes outside of court.
Therefore the Justice department designed an ambitious programme to
accomplish regulatory relief, called *towards a practical legal system*.[8] This programme plans to cut red tape and make private parties more responsible
when it comes to regulation, compliance and enforcement.

2.1.   Emerging trends in lawmaking

It is not easy to determine what the theory behind the plans to make our legal
system more practical is all about, because the Dutch government hasn't put
much effort in explaining the empirical basis for the recent shift in its regulatory policy. Nevertheless, what one could say is that there is a trend towards
more inspirational and open-ended rules. As Westerman has pointed out, the
formulation of open-ended and result-prescribing rules is defended by the
Dutch legislature with the argument that it is more effective and efficient to
give private organizations a margin of discretion in order to reach the desired
aims the legislature is trying to pursue.[9]

The formulation of result-prescribing rules is clearly advocated as a regulatory strategy that belongs to a responsive government that prefers to use *car-
rots instead of sticks* in order to make laws work. Other than a command and
control approach, this regulatory strategy mainly aims at convincing people to
obey the law by calling on their judgment to find the most appropriate means
to fill in the goals the legislature has set. In some cases these goals are trans-
lated into specific targets, like a proposed decrease in the emission of substance
X to the amount Y. In other cases, however, the prescribed rules are less specific
and more inspirational. Some so-called duties of care have this character.[10]

---

8.   A practical legal system: On the nature and causes of increasing legislation, its unwanted
     effects and how to tackle them, Dutch Parliamentary Documents II, 2003-2004, 29 279, No. 9.
     Available in English at www.justitie.nl/english.
9.   P. Westerman, The emergence of new types of norms, in: L. Wintgens (eds), Essays in legispru-
     dence, Ashgate 2006 (forthcoming).
10. In the Anglo-Saxon tradition of lawmaking. Duties of care are normally associated with tort
     law and negligence, while positive law in the Netherlands considers 'zorgplichten' (Duties of
     care) are often seen as an alternative for more detailed and technical ways of rulemaking,
     which appeal to ethical values in a certain sector. Compare N.J. McBride, Duties of Care – Do
     they Really Exist?, Oxford Journal of Legal Studies 2004/3, pp. 417-441, with the Dutch report
     by the Commissie Zijlstra, Ruimte voor zorgplichten (*Zijlstra commission, Room for Duties of
     care*), The Hague 2004.

They demand, for example *good housekeeping* for employers in the field of labour conditions, *continuous improvement* in the course of environmental management of corporations, or *responsible care* in the health care sector.

In the words of Lon Fuller, the latter category of rules can be considered to represent a *morality of aspiration* while the first category ask for a *morality of duty*.[11] Some scholars associate the idea of open-ended inspirational rules with a communicative model of lawmaking,[12] but I won't go into this here, while it is rather speculative if the Dutch government has deliberately opted for a new model of lawmaking. Certainly imaginable is that the current shifts in regulation and governance spring from more trivial sources. As far as the propaganda for self-monitoring and certification is concerned, the popularity of less hierarchical steering mechanisms could very well have something to do with the call for governmental risk reduction in society and the public protests against failing inspection and enforcement regimes. The growing quest for control gave rise to the idea to bring in private organizations and delegate some monitoring and inspection tasks to non-governmental bodies.[13]

2.2. Consequences for compliance monitoring

Stimulating self-regulation is considered to be one of the possibilities to reduce the burdens of legislation. But the problem is that the point where rules are experienced as a burden is influenced by many different factors. Apart from the number of rules, these factors include:
- The scope for alternative conduct offered by the rules;
- the transparency of rules and how recognizable they are;
- consistency with other legal rules in force;
- the manner in which they are implemented;[14]
- the information that is required to monitor compliance;
- the way in which compliance is ensured (for example governmental supervision or pressure from society).

---

11. L. Fuller, The Morality of Law, New Haven 1968, pp. 5-6.
12. For more about this model: W. Witteveen, Turning to communication in the study of legislation, in N. Zeegers, W. Witteveen and B. van Klink (eds.), Social and Symbolic Effects of Legislation under the Rule of Law, Edwin Mellen Press, Lewinston/Queenston/Lampeter 2005, pp. 17-44.
13. This also includes the use of so-called 'supply side' pressures and trying to encourage front runner corporations to go beyond compliance. See N. Gunningham and P. Grabosky, Smart regulation. Designing Environmental Policy, Clarendon Press, Oxford 1998. See for Dutch examples of using stakeholder influence in compliance strategies: WRR-rapport, De borging van het publiek belang (*Advisory Council on Government Policy-report, the safeguarding of public interest*), The Hague 2000.
14. Laws that use programme-type provisions and consist of open texture could also lead to a shift in regulatory burdens from the public to the private domain.

One of the most interesting statements in the programme *Towards a practical legal system* concerns enforcement and sanctioning. In that respect it is argued that better use could be made of self-regulation together with alternative supervision tools. By using the *watchful eyes* of non-governmental agents, private parties could be made jointly responsible for monitoring compliance of private codes of conduct and negotiated agreements.[15] Thus, enforcement agencies should be able to limit themselves to monitoring the quality of self-monitoring. This corresponds closely with the concept of responsive regulation. One of the basic thoughts behind this concept is that law enforcers should be responsive to how effectively citizens or corporations are regulating themselves before deciding whether to escalate intervention. A distinctive part of the theory of responsive law lies in the application of the so-called regulatory pyramid. The idea of this pyramid is that regulators should always start at the bottom of the pyramid in terms of regulatory interventions. The point of departure in stimulating compliance is normally a strategy of persuasion. Only when dialogue fails should regulators move up the pyramid towards more punitive approaches, like warning letters, civil penalties, criminal penalties and license suspension or, ultimately, license revocation.[16]

The general idea behind *meta-enforcement* is to shift the burden of proof for compliance with laws and regulations. Public inspection agencies should no longer be held solely responsible for the detection of violations. Instead, private companies must be asked to check on a regular basis if they are still in compliance through the use of self-care systems and other quality control mechanisms. For that purpose, companies could hire an independent third party, like a certification body, to double check the proper working of these self-care systems on a regular basis.[17] The assumption behind this idea is that public inspection agencies will then have to pay less attention to companies with a valid certificate. This should create some elbowroom for them in order to be able to focus more on the compliance behaviour of notorious violators and free riders.

---

15. Dutch Ministry of Justice, Watchful eyes: A fresh look at supervision arrangements, The Hague, Dutch Parliamentary Documents II, 2003–2004, 29 279, No. 13.
16. J. Braithwaite, Restorative Justice and Responsive Regulation, Oxford University Press 2002, pp. 29-42.
17. See about certification in relation to enforcement programmes in general E. Meidinger, Environmental Certification Programs and U.S. Environmental Law: Closer Than You May Think, Environmental Law Reporter 2001, pp. 10162-10179.

3.　　　SELF-REGULATION AND COMPLIANCE

The core elements of the quest for self-regulation and alternative supervision systems are all but new in the Netherlands. In the early 1990s, there had already been a plan to improve the quality of legislation, called: A View of Legislation. In this document, a passionate plea was held for legally structured and conditioned self-regulation. As a result the Dutch government introduced the so-called *General guidelines for the drafting of legislation*.[18] Section 8 of these guidelines determines that the government shall refrain from lawmaking if self-regulation or co-regulation could solve the policy problem at hand.

More recently the European Commission, together with the Council and Parliament came up with an inter-institutional agreement, called *Better lawmaking*. This document also underlines the importance of self-regulation to enhance the acceptance of rules and regulations for economic operators. Hence self-regulation is defined as:

> 'the possibility for economic operators, the social partners, non-governmental organizations or associations to adopt amongst themselves and for themselves common guidelines at European level (particularly codes of practice or sectoral agreements).'[19]

In the report of the Working Group *Better Regulation*, the idea and approach of co-regulation is considered to be an implementation mechanism,[20] which implies increased use of framework legislation to lay down the basic rights and obligations, but also the arrangements for secondary legislation and self-regulation on the national level to fill in the details.[21] This approach that combines hard law instruments, like directives, with soft law regulations such as voluntary agreements or certification schemes, is very similar to what the Dutch legislature appears to have in mind.

---

18. These guidelines are available (only in Dutch) at: http://www.justitie.nl/images/ Aanwijzingen_tcm34-2447.pdf.
19. European Parliament, Council, Commission, Interinstitutional Agreement on better law-making, Official Journal of the European Union PbL EG 2003, C 321/01.
20. In the Interinstitutional agreement co-regulation is defined as 'the mechanism whereby a Community legislative act entrusts the attainment of the objectives defined by the legislative authority to parties which are recognised in the field (such as economic operators, the social partners, non-governmental organisations, or associations).'
21. White Paper on European Governance, Work Area No. 2, Handling the Process of Producing and Implementing Community Rules, Group 2c, May 2001. See also Ph. Eijlander, Possibilities and constraints in the use of self-regulation and co-regulation in legislative policy: experiences in the Netherlands – lessons to be learned for the EU?, Electronic Journal of Comparative Law 2005/1.

Unfortunately, none of the aforementioned documents are very clear about when to use self-regulatory codes and negotiated agreements. This is remarkable because self-regulation does not only have advantages, such as: a high level of commitment of firms and associations to *their own* rules; a better connection with the expertise inside the industry;[22] a greater comprehensiveness towards and acceptance by the addressees;[23] more flexibility when it comes to adjusting the rules to changing circumstances; lower costs for the administration etcetera.[24]

As we al know, self-regulation may also cause concern. Non-state rules are often legally not binding. Therefore it is often uncertain whether they will hold in a court of law as soon as conflicts arise in relation to the interpretation or implementation of these private rules. Another disadvantage could be that the public might not trust self-regulatory bodies to apply the rules in the public's or the consumer's interest.[25] Like the history of the former guilds has shown, private rulemaking will sometimes stifle competition. Particularly in markets with one or more dominant players, self-regulation might be used to keep newcomers out of business, by setting standards which are especially hard to meet.

Many also question the adequacy of enforcement in self-regulatory regimes.[26] Industry may be unwilling to commit the resources needed for vigorous self-enforcement or there may be a lack of power or commitment inside a certain private sector to enforce adequate sanctions. Sometimes, the ultimate sanction is nothing more than expulsion. Whether this will be an effective deterrent, largely depends upon the benefits of the membership of the organization and the chance that non-compliance will be detected and cause serious harm to a particular company's reputation.[27] As a result *bad*

22. I. Ayres and J. Braithwaite, Responsive regulation: Transcending the Deregulation debate, 1992, p. 103.
23. T. Tyler, Why people obey the Law, New Haven: Yale University Press, 1990.
24. R. Baldwin and M. Cave, Understanding regulation: Theory, strategy, and Practice, Oxford University Press, Oxford 1999, p. 40.
25. Peter P. Swire, Markets, Self-Regulation, and Government Enforcement in then Protection of Personal Information, in, L. Irving, Privacy and Self-regulation in the information age, available at: http://www.ntia.doc.gov/reports/privacy/privacy_rpt.htm.
26. Rather sceptical about self-regulation in the environmental arena is, for instance, R.A. van de Peppel, Naleving van milieurecht: Toepassing van beleidsinstrumenten op de Nederlandse verfindustrie *(Compliance with environmental law: Application of policy instruments to the Dutch paint industry)*, Kluwer, Deventer 1995. More positive in this respect is J.M. Verschuuren, EC Environmental Law and Self-Regulation in the Member States: in Search of a Legislative Framework, in: H. Somsen (ed.), Yearbook of European Environmental Law, Oxford University Press 2000, pp. 103-121.
27. An interesting and extensive empirical study in the Netherlands about the background factors of regulatory compliance and violation by corporations, which includes the influence of self-regulatory incentives on the internalization and enforcement of legal rules is done by W. Huisman, Tussen winst en moraal: Achtergronden van regelnaleving en regelovertreding door ondernemingen, Boom Juridische uitgevers, The Hague 2001 (This extensive study on compliance behaviour of corporations 'Between profit and morality. Background factors of regulatory compliance and violation by corporations' has a summary in English).

actors will sometimes be unlikely to comply, and *good actors* will be placed at a competitive disadvantage.[28]

It is my opinion that lawmakers who consider the introduction of a certain self-regulatory mechanism will have to study the following carefully: 1) how that particular system works, 2) to what extent government regulation is needed to provide a framework for private rulemaking and 3) what the specific characteristics are of the sector in which the instrument will be applied. Whenever these questions are neglected, trouble is waiting just around the corner. The best way to show what I mean is probably to return to the plans of making animal welfare laws more responsive and enforceable.

4.   WELFARE OF DOMESTIC ANIMALS

Our current legislation regarding animal welfare is considered to be far too complicated and detailed (for instance rules about the necessary professional skills of the holder; obligatory rules about identification and vaccination and reporting; rules about cleaning and decontamination of animal shelters up to rules about the minimum number of hours a day dogs should be allowed to be run outside). A number of rules have given rise to unnecessary burdens on commerce, and the poor compliance with existing rules is believed to undermine the effectiveness of even the more important parts of the animal health and welfare laws. As a consequence, the Minister responsible for this policy area has set out a plan to diminish and simplify the legislation concerning domestic animals, to make more use of duties of care, and last but not least to develop a more prominent role for other types of supervision, partly by the sector itself.

The overall idea is to create a shift in governance structures and, to a certain extent, replace legislation and public inspections by a system of voluntary self-regulation.[29]

4.1.   PETTY PROBLEMS?

Dutch people apparently like pets. Our country has close to 16.000.000 inhabitants. Together they have about 1.8 million dogs, 3.3 million cats, 1 million rabbits, 0.8 million rodents, 19 million fish, and about 0.25 million reptiles and amphibians. In practice this means that in about 55% of all Dutch house-

28. A.J. Campbell, Self-regulation and the media, Federal Communications Law Journal 1999, p. 718.
29. Ministerie van Justitie, Naar een effectieve borging van dierenwelzijn (*Dutch Ministry of Justice, Towards and effective safeguarding of animal welfare*), The Hague 2004.

holds there are one or more pets.[30] Considering these numbers, it is not hard to imagine that there are also problems in the sector when it comes to the breeding, buying, selling and keeping of domestic animals. The most well known are:
- incompetence in relation to the breeding of animals;
- illegal trading on black markets;
- keeping animals with insufficient knowledge as to the animals' needs and behaviour;
- people buying animals on impulse, leading to the holding of pets in unsuitable accommodations, neglect, animal abuse and mistreatment more in general.

In the Netherlands we have quite a vast amount of laws and regulations about animal welfare. The most important law in this area is without a doubt the Animal Health and Welfare Act of 1992 (AHWA). This act applies to vertebrate animals kept by people, ranging from production animals (like cows and horses) to circus animals, and pets. The AHWA lays down general provisions, which prohibit, for example:
- inflicting unnecessary pain or injury, or endangering an animal's health or welfare;
- withholding essential care;
- awarding animals as a prize, reward or gift etcetera.

Sections 36 and 37 of the AHWA contain some so-called duties of care. These sections function as a safety net in the prevention of animal abuse and the withholding of essential care towards animals when no specific rules or regulations applicable for the situation are at hand. Nevertheless, convictions for breaking these rules are rather rare. In practice it is hard to prove that someone is guilty of animal abuse or withholding essential care because this will often occur behind closed doors. Another determining factor seems to be the burden of proof in case of a violation of a duty of care. In practice it is often hard for enforcement agents to prove that someone has been withholding essential care. The AHWA does not offer criteria to establish what *essential care* actually means and courts will often leave a margin of discretion to the addressees of the rules before deciding that a violation has occurred.[31] Fur-

---

30. See for a specification of facts and figures: Raad voor Dierenaangelegenheden, Forum welzijn gezelschapsdieren, Gedeelde zorg: Feiten en cijfers (*Council on Animal Affairs, Forum for welfare of domestic animals, Shared care: Facts and figures*), The Hague 2006. Also available at: http://www9.minlnv.nl/pls/portal30/docs/FOLDER/MINLNV/LNV/STAF/STAF_DV/KAMER-CORRESPONDENTIE/2006/05/20060515_DL_2006_995_BIJLAGE2.PDF.
31. About this in relation to Article 6 of the AHWA: F.H. de Jonge en B.M. Spruijt, Kennis over dierenwelzijn; toepassing in recht en regelgeving, Justitiële Verkenningen (*Knowledge on welfare of domestic animals; application in law and regulation, Judicial Investigations*) 2001/9, p. 62.

thermore, the number of public inspectors is rather limited, which means that the rate of inspections is low and enforcement actions depend heavily on tips about possible abuse by animal protection societies and private citizens.[32]

4.2.   *Towards a new system of safeguarding the welfare of domestic animals?*

A while ago, a working group of policymakers from different ministries presented a new plan to safeguard the health and welfare of domestic animals. Some of the most important elements in this plan are:

– the policy objectives concerning animal welfare have often changed in the past and are still rather vague;
– there is a structural lack of manpower for the inspection of current laws and regulations in the field of animal health and welfare;
– the responsibility of the holder of domestic animals has to be stressed. He has to be informed better about the best ways to keep and breed animals;
– the domestic animal industry itself has to internalize that safeguarding the health and well-being of animals is its core business. This has to be embedded in management standards and quality control systems;
– the Dutch Cabinet is aiming for a considerable reduction of current laws and regulations and a significant decrease in administrative burdens for the industry. Therefore, replacing ineffective administrative rules and regulations by new ones, and increasing the capacity for public inspections is not an option;
– therefore the introduction of voluntary certification schemes that encourage self-monitoring and self-enforcement by the industry should be promoted.

At first sight, one of the main problems of the report is, at least in my opinion, that it shows signs of *tunnel vision*. Starting point of the argumentation by the working group is that less administrative regulations and fewer public inspections are desirable in any case. Therefore, the option of using private certification schemes as a lighter and perhaps cheaper alternative for public inspections has been welcomed too easily. The report *Towards effective safeguarding of animal welfare*, written by the commission, repeatedly argues that the point of departure is to diminish regulatory burdens. Because government-based certification models are usually accompanied by extra rules, these models are immediately put aside without an explanation why voluntary certification is the best option to achieve the goals of the AHWA. At the

---

32. S. van der Wouw, Procederen tegen dierenleed, Justitiële Verkenningen (*Legal proceedings against animal suffering, Judicial Investigations*) 2001/9, p. 68.

same time the report rightfully acknowledges that voluntary certification can only be effective if there is a strong preference on the side of consumers for buying certified *products*.[33] No research whatsoever has been done to discover if this consumer preference is more than *wishful thinking*.

I personally believe that the assignment of the commission, which did not have any members representing the various interests of the animal welfare sector, has blurred the vision of policymakers. The primary task of the commission was to look for ways to reduce regulatory burdens, not to solve problems in the sector in the most effective and efficient manner. There is no doubt in my mind that the commission has: 1) failed to take a critical look at the self-regulatory potential of the domestic animal industry, and 2) neglected a number of fundamental differences between private certification and public inspections.

4.3.   The self-regulatory potential in the sector

One of the suggestions in the report from the official working group has been to revoke the Royal decree on cats and dogs,[34] and to resolve the current problems by means of self-regulation. This is an interesting thought, because if you look at the history of this rather recent piece of legislation, one of the first things to stand out is the next sentence on the first page of the explanatory memorandum of this decree:

> 'The motive for this decree lies primarily in the wish of the permanent commission for agriculture, nature conservation and fishery of the Dutch Parliament (as stated in parliamentary proceeding 1995/1996, 24 140, nr. 18) to establish exhaustive legislation for animal welfare by means of a Royal decree instead of relying on self-regulation. [translation RvG]'[35]

Parliamentary hearings have brought to light that the domestic animal industry has been unwilling or incapable to guarantee a proper level of animal health and welfare on a voluntary basis. Some of the problems in the industry are:
- that the degree of organization is low;
- that many companies in the sector are not susceptible to social persuasion to comply with existing laws and regulations;
- that it is unlikely that the sector is prepared to go beyond compliance and;

33. Rapport, Naar een effectieve borging van dierenwelzijn *(Dutch report, towards an effective safeguarding of animal welfare)*, The Hague 2004, amongst others pp. 64 and 89.
34. Besluit van 11 januari 1999, houdende regelen inzake bedrijfsmatige verkoop, aflevering en inbewaringneming van honden en katten (Honden- en kattenbesluit 1999) *(Decision of 11 January 1999, providing regulations concerning commercial selling, delivery and taking into custody of dogs and cats (dogs and cats decision of 1999)*, Staatsblad *(Bulletin of Acts and Decrees)* 1999, 36.
35. Staatsblad *(Bulletin of Acts and Decrees)* 1999, 36, p. 12.

– that consumers are not willing to carry the costs that come along with voluntary quality management and self-monitoring.[36]

Less than ten years ago most members of parliament argued that a change of attitude in the sector would not appear if the responsible minister kept on speaking softly without carrying a big stick in terms of enforcement.[37] Because self-regulation is back on the political agenda so prominently, one wonders to what extent the sector has changed in the meantime. This suspicion is strengthened by the fact that the report of the working group argues that the sector could be characterized as *highly emotional*. There are persistent conflicts of interest between industry, animal protection societies, and consumers' organizations etcetera. Furthermore, the market for domestic animals is anything but transparent.[38] There are, for instance, lots of illegal kennels, and black marketeers, who are willing to sell animals to anyone against much lower prices than legitimate pet shops.[39]

Perhaps the most interesting thing is that since 1996 a private certification body does already exist in the sector. This organization is known as the: *Stichting dierbaar* (Pet foundation). The organization certifies pet shops, animal shelters, trimming parlours, dog kennels, etcetera.[40] The criteria to qualify for certification have to do with topics like: professional skills, animal care, veterinary control and quality management. Until now, however, only a limited number of organizations have applied for certification by the foundation. Unfortunately, the working group did not attempt to find out why. A few phone calls to the foundation and a number of potential clients would have been enough to get the answer to this question. After all, the reasons are quite simple. Certification is not free of charge and there is no legal obligation to apply for a certificate. Accordingly, most parties do not require a certificate as long as customers do not demand it, and there is no legal obligation whatsoever to be certified.

So much for the idea of voluntary certification as an alternative for public inspections, one is inclined to say. Nonetheless, it might be worthwhile to take a deeper look at the policy presumptions behind the plea for self-monitoring and certification. What exactly do policymakers expect from certification and to what extent are these expectations realistic?

---

36. See the report, Naar een effectieve borging van dierenwelzijn, The Hague 2004.
37. Dutch Parliamentary Documents II 1995-1996, 24 140, No. 18, p. 2.
38. For self-regulation to work it is of the utmost importance that different interests are represented in the rule-making process and are willing to work together. Furhtermore, transparency of decision-making should be guaranteed. See: S.E. Gaines and C. Kimber, Redirecting Self-regulation, Journal of Environmental Law 2001/2, pp. 157-184.
39. Nederlandse Vereniging tot Bescherming van Dieren, Zwartboek malafide hondenhandel *(Dutch society for the Protection of Animals, black book malafide dog trade)*, The Hague 2004.
40. See www.stichtingdierbaar.nl.

5.   FALSE EXPECTATIONS ABOUT CERTIFICATION

Although the working group does not say it out loud in the report on animal welfare, it is quite clear that the makers believe that the introduction of private certification schemes will diminish the need to monitor compliance of certified organizations by public inspection agencies. For a number of reasons this is a dangerous thought.

First of all, this thought rests on the idea that responsible consumers will seek high quality certificates to make sure that the pet they, for instance, are going to buy has been treated well, and is perfectly healthy. Therefore the requirements to get a certificate should be strict. Of course, that may be true, but there are no guarantees that this will be the case. As long as Dutch consumers stay cheap, they are probably going to buy the most inexpensive animals. That could mean: 1) not buying pets from a certified shop, or 2) a race to the bottom in the certification of quality management systems, because of competitive behaviour amongst different certification bodies operating on the same market for domestic animals. After all, it is not unlikely that companies driven by external stakeholder pressure are going to look for the most *flexible* certification body.[41]

5.1.   *What is certification?*[42]

Policymakers sometimes seem to forget that certification is in principle a commercial activity, developed to ensure that a certain product, person, or system conforms to specified requirements. While in business-to-business relations, certification is often used to guarantee a certain (standard) quality of production activities, it can also be used by companies to offer externally validated information to consumers and other stakeholders. Certification of the production of tropical red wood, for instance, serves to provide consum-

---

41. To learn more about this phenomenon, see also G.J.M. Evers, Experiences with certification: Reconsidering the use of a communicative instrument for the purpose of enforcing legislation, Tilburg Foreign Law Review 2003/10. Available at: http://www.tilburguniversity.nl/tilec/events/seminars/051203/TFLR02.pdf.
42. The next paragraphs are largely based on extensive research performed by Ph. Eijlander, G.J.M. Evers, R.A.J. van Gestel, De inkadering van certificatie en accreditatie in beleid en wetgeving, *(The incorporation of certification and accreditation in policy and legislation)* Tilburg 2003; G.J.M. Evers, Blind vertrouwen? Een onderzoek naar de toepassing van certificatie ten dienste van de handhaving van wettelijke voorschriften, Dissertatie *(Blind trust? A study into the application of certification for the purpose of the enforcement of legal stipulations, Dissertation)*, The Hague 2002; R.A.J. van Gestel, Certificatie als alternatief voor toezicht op de naleving van milieuwetten? Over transplantatie van private kwaliteitssystemen naar een publieke context, Preadvies Vereniging voor Wetgeving en Wetgevingsbeleid *(Certification as an alternative to supervision of compliance of environmental law? On the transplantation of private quality systems to a public context, Pre-advise Institution for Legislation and Legislation policy)*, The Hague 2002.

ers with reliable information about the origin of a particular product in order to make them aware about what they are buying. Indirectly this can also benefit public goals, like the protection of rain forests.[43]

For a number of reasons, however, one should be very careful when copying certification systems directly onto a public law context. First of all, the requirements on which a certification assessment takes place are the product of a negotiating process between stakeholders. Although it may appear as if this process is conducted in the same way that laws and (other) public regulations are made, there are important differences. To name just one, there is normally no guarantee of government involvement in the rulemaking process and democratic principles do not apply to certification and standardization.

Above all certification is a management and communication tool.[44] Therefore the advantages of the improvement of the image of the organization under certification must (at least) counterbalance the costs of certification. Although a certification body has a responsibility to all interested parties, according to the European standards for the accreditation of certification bodies, it remains a commercial organization that provides services to its clients. Because of this, the impartial and independent status of certification bodies cannot be interpreted the same way as the legal requirements of impartiality that apply to enforcement agencies. For certification bodies, the requirement of independence is closely connected with the absence of institutional connections with supervised organizations, or with market activities that could influence the judgment of the certification body, like counselling.

These requirements resemble the idea of independence for public supervisors. Yet, the commercial connection between the certification body and the certified organization, as well as the existence of competition between certification bodies, are considered to be normal, while these characteristics would be inconceivable as far as the activities of public authorities were concerned.

5.2. *Certification must not be confused with supervision and enforcement*

The divergent character of certification compared to enforcement is clearly exposed when it comes to the question to what extent a certification body should measure the actual compliance of the certified organization or the question if the certification body should report violations of public regula-

---

43. See for instance: E. Rehbinder, Forest certification and environmental law, in: E. Meidinger, C. Elliott, G. Oesten (eds.), Social and political dimensions of forest certification, Forstbuch, Remagen-Oberwinter 2003 and S. Bernstein and B. Cashore, Non-state Global Governance: Is Forest Certification a Legitimate Alternative to a Global forest Convention?, in: J.T. Kirton and M. J. Trebilcock, Hard Choices, Soft Law: Voluntary Standards in Global Trade, Environment and Social Governance, Ashgate 2004, pp. 33-63.
44. See V.C. De Graaff, Private certification in a governance context, Eburon publishers, Delft 1995, p. 5, who distinguishes between public and private certification.

tions discovered during an audit to the public authorities. Mostly the business community strongly opposes such suggestions, because they would result in the use of *their* instrument in a way that can lead to self-incrimination.[45] Certified organizations will probably feel that their willingness to provide for self-surveillance is going to be used against them. Furthermore, there are some important differences between private certification and public inspections. Let me summarize a few of the most important:

– Audits of the working of a self-care system by a certification body are a service asked for and paid for by the inspectee. There is no legal duty to cooperate with assessments performed by auditors. In case of public inspections, the law states that not cooperating is considered to be a separate offence.
– Certification audits are systematically executed in a way that is equal for all similar clients. They show regular intervals and are always announced beforehand. Because voluntary certification is a normal commercial service in which the auditor gives an advice to the management of an organization, there is no reason to adopt a vigilant attitude towards the person or company under supervision.
– Certification bodies will, according to their contract, not share information about the compliance behaviour of their clients, with government officials. Of course the legislature could make rules that force them to do so, but that would probably lead to a transparency paradox. If companies know that there is a serious risk that auditors are going to pass on confidential information about non-compliance, they are probably going to lose their willingness to adopt an open and responsive attitude towards the certification body.
– A certification body has no means to force its clients to comply with laws and regulations. The only *sanctions* it has are the suspension, or, in case non-conformities are constantly repeated, withdrawal of a certificate. Ultimately the client can always decide to discontinue his contract and move on to another certification body, which will perhaps show a more flexible attitude.

Naturally some safeguards are built into the system of certification. One of them is the fact that the Dutch Accreditation Board (DAC) acknowledges and monitors certification bodies on the basis of European and international stan-

45. Also the danger of a 'transparency paradox' plays a role in this context. This paradox concerns the link between the preparedness of corporations to provide reliable information about compliance behaviour. The willingness to be open about non-compliance will often disappear as soon as this information is going to be used against them. See C. Waling, 'Bedrijfsinterne milieuzorg. De keerzijde van transparantie', Justitiële Verkenningen (*'Internal company environmental management. The other side of transparency'*, *Judicial investigations*) 1999 2, p. 48 and M. Kidd, 'Environmental Audits and Self-Incrimination, The Comparative and International Law Journal of Southern Africa 37 2004/1, pp. 84-95.

dards for the operation of certification activities.[46] However, one must not confuse accreditation with a public supervision over certification bodies. The DAC is still a private foundation that performs a service that could be seen as a sort of *certification of certification bodies*. Apart from the quite vague criteria for the assessment of these bodies according to international standards, the council itself has been criticized in the past for concentrating too much on the formal aspects of certification and not paying enough attention on the skills of auditors and the way audits are actually carried out.[47]

6.   LESSONS TO BE LEARNED

Perhaps the overall lesson to be learned is that legislators and policymakers have to be aware of the danger of developing a tunnel vision while looking for regulatory relief. In the vast majority of circumstances, neither pure self-regulation nor strict command and control regulation will be a preferable solution. A cunning blend of voluntary and incentive driven ways of rule-making is often the best option.[48] Yet, the challenge of course is how to combine these incentives in a way that the overall effectiveness and efficiency of regulation will improve.

I am inclined to believe that the plan of the Dutch government to use certification in animal welfare policy focuses too much on simpler rules and cutting red tape per se. This has led to an emphasis on the advantages of self-enforcement without having an open eye for possible deficiencies and side effects.[49] In the taskforce for better regulation nobody seems to worry, for instance, about the risk of a mere shift of regulatory burdens from public authorities to private organizations. Moreover, the specific characteristics that discern certification audits from public inspections should not be overlooked. As Sparrow has argued:

'If complete consensus was possible on any regulatory issue – that is, if a solution existed that served the interests of every private party – the issue would probably not warrant regulatory attention. Because regulation and enforcement, by their

---

46. For more information about the DAC: www.rva.nl.
47. See: W. Hoogers and H.J. De Vries, Toezicht op certificatie-instellingen kan beter (*Supervision of certification institutions can be better*), SIGMA 1998/1, pp. 8-12 and H.J.H.L. Kortes, Een te grijs gebied: Accreditatie in het bestuursrecht (*A too grey area: Accreditation in administrative law*), RegelMaat 2002/4, pp. 113-122.
48. R. Baldwin, Is better regulation, smarter regulation?, Public Law 2005, pp. 485-511.
49. In the report, Towards a practical legal system, certification as an alternative for public inspections is introduced as a new policy initiative, but in proposals for deregulation a few years before nearly the same suggestion came up. See: MDW-rapport, Normalisatie en certificatie (*Market Forces, Deregulation and Legislative Quality Project report, Normalization and certification*), The Hague 1996.

nature, elevate broad public purposes above the interests of private parties, one should expect regulatory practice to carry with it irreducible conflicts.'[50]

Before putting too much trust in self-regulation, there should have been a thorough investigation to determine whether there is enough self-regulatory potential inside the animal welfare sector. A look at the current practice should at least have led to a certain amount of scepticism about that potential, because the sector is badly organized, highly emotional and divided. The certification body, which is already active in this domain, has not been able to guarantee a level playing field of quality management in the domestic animal industry. Moreover, a closer look at the characteristics of voluntary certification as an instrument to facilitate compliance monitoring would have learned that assessments performed by auditors on behalf of private certification bodies could be an excellent tool to filter out unintended compliance failures. However, it is not a full alternative for public inspections and law enforcement.

Finally policymakers should be aware of the dangers that go along with a transplantation of self-regulatory mechanisms into a public law context. Self-regulation will sometimes be more effective than governmental regulations, because the rules have been made by people with more commitment and technical expertise, according to less formalized procedures, and with more possibilities to react on sudden technical, social or economic changes in society. On the other hand, if self-regulatory mechanisms, like certification, are being transformed into public policy instruments they are bound to lose some of these characteristics. In case of certification one cannot expect that companies are willing to be open and honest about their performance towards auditors if this information will later be used against them and result in punitive sanctions.

One has to bear in mind that the only task of inspection agencies is not to offer compliance assistance. They should, from time to time, double-check the results of monitoring reports and investigate by themselves whether a facility complies with the relevant laws and regulations. Public authorities may never totally rely on the results of audits performed by certification bodies. By using a method of paying surprise visits and performing spot checks, public inspectors can keep private auditors and verifiers alert, thereby also lifting their level of investigation. After all, one may assume that the management of a facility will not be pleased when it is confronted with the discovery of non-compliance by the authorities that could have been prevented by an adequately performed external audit.

---

50. M. Sparrow, The regulatory craft: Controlling risks, solving problems and managing compliance, The Brookings Institution, Washington 2000, p. 17.

6 | IS REINTEGRATIVE SHAMING RELEVANT TO TAX EVASION AND AVOIDANCE?

Valerie Braithwaite[1]

When individuals engage in tax evasion and avoidance, they act against a legal obligation they have to obey the law. If their actions are detected by an authority, and/or by others in their social network, they are likely to be negatively sanctioned and this may happen at a number of levels in a number of different ways. The sanctions may be imposed by a formal authority (for example, a revenue authority, court) or may be delivered through an informal network (for example, tax adviser, employer, partner, employee, family member). The sanctioning may inflict an economic, social or psychological cost on the individual (Grasmick and Bursik, 1990). The target of the sanctioning may be the individual or the act, in other words, sanctioning may be directed toward *a tax cheat* or toward *an act of cheating*. Whatever the path of the sanctioning process, all have one thing in common: Sanctioning for cheating communicates disapproval.

These different paths to sanctioning are rarely mutually exclusive. In the case of tax evasion and avoidance, disapproval is most commonly communicated formally through the revenue authority imposing financial costs of fines and penalties. If the evasion or avoidance is serious enough, it may be made public, perhaps through media exposure of a court case. Then the sanctioning process incorporates the loss of a good reputation when associated with being charged with cheating on tax. On a quite different level, sanctioning may come about through formal or informal counselling and dialogue that explains and persuades as to the irresponsibility of evasion or avoidance. Sanctioning does not disappear simply because the revenue authority does

1. Regulatory Institutions Network, Research School of Social Sciences, Australian National University, Canberra ACT 0200, Australia (e-mail: Valerie.Braithwaite@anu.edu.au).

not know or chooses not to hold the individual accountable. Tax advisers, family and friends, if they find out about the activity, may either condemn or caution the person for what they have done. And even if no-one knows, individuals must reconcile breaking the law with the image of being a law-abiding citizen, if not in their own eyes, at least in the eyes of someone close to them.

When tax evasion or avoidance leads individuals to feel uncomfortable about their own identity or how others see their identity, they are grappling with feelings of shame. The purpose of this paper is to analyse feelings of shame, identify causal pathways involving shame, and discuss the implications of this approach for the design of the tax system and its future sustainability. The paper has four objectives: (1) to draw a distinction between socially adaptive and socially non-adaptive forms of shame; (2) to examine how adaptive and non-adaptive shame management is associated with taxpaying enforcement practices; (3) to use reintegrative shaming theory to explain how a sanctioning system can facilitate or undermine adaptive shame management by taxpayers and thereby affect voluntary compliance; and (4) to draw on Australian data involving a sample of taxpayers sanctioned for their involvement in mass marketed schemes to demonstrate that revenue authorities have options for pursuing courses of action that enable taxpayers to manage shame adaptively or non-adaptively. Where the option chosen increases the likelihood of adaptive shame management, two desirable outcomes should occur: the moral obligation of the taxpaying community to pay their tax in the future should strengthen and the tax authority is provided with opportunity to build greater integrity into the tax system.

1.   SOCIALLY ADAPTIVE AND NON-ADAPTIVE SHAME

1.1.   *Defining shame*

Shame is an emotion that generally makes most of us feel like disappearing: We commonly associate it with public disgrace after being caught or exposed for acting in ways that society deems unacceptable. We may even feel some sense of resentment that anyone should have the right to judge us and force us to feel shame. But this is a populist understanding that ignores much of what we know about the shame emotions and the part they play in human behaviour.

Researchers who have followed Tomkin's (1987) affect theory argue that the family of shame emotions (embarrassment, shame and guilt) are always in play either as something we are anticipating, avoiding or managing. As such, they are primary regulators of our behaviour, sometimes without our even being aware of it. When we are forced to confront shame in a *shame showdown*, we feel the emotion acutely and no-one questions the unpleasantness of the state of shame. It's little wonder that we don't like to think about it. But these shame showdowns are not necessarily public events, and they are not always full-blown personal debacles. We feel shame regularly and privately, when we reflect on our failure to achieve valued goals or when we realize we have behaved in ways that are inappropriate. Sometimes it's a niggling feeling that something is wrong, sometimes it is combined with other emotions such as sadness and disappointment, and sometimes it beds down in us with anger.

In the work of our research group on shame, distinctions between shame and guilt do not unlock analytic insight. We follow Nathan Harris (2001, 2003, forthcoming) who brings shame and guilt together as intertwined, powerful and mutually reinforcing emotions that are tied to our self-worth, and as such are distinct from the milder emotion of embarrassment. Harris debunks old distinctions between shame as an emotion that others *impose* upon us for breaking social norms and guilt as an emotion that we *generate* ourselves because we know we did not live up to our own standards.

Drawing on the work of philosopher Bernard Williams (1993) and psychologists Henri Tajfel (1978) and John Turner (Turner, Hogg, Oakes, Reicher and Wetherell, 1987), Harris points out that the evaluations we hold of ourselves and the evaluations that our significant others and reference groups hold of us are inextricably intertwined. Our values and standards are not peculiar to us, they are shared with our group; indeed they are acquired through our interactions with our group, and reinforced by them through our social exchanges. When we fail to live up to these values and standards, we need others to help us make sense of what we have done. 'Did I really do that?' 'Was it as bad as I think – or as bad as you think?' This social validation process is something that we all do, even if the other we are talking to is an imaginary figure in our head. In the process of deciding whether we have or have not done wrong, we need others to affirm our standards ('Yes, you do hold that value, as do we.') and validate our behaviour ('Yes, you did act in a way that breached that standard.'). If in the process we decide we fall short as the person that we and others think we are, we feel bad about ourselves, and we do so because we have failed in our own eyes (what many call guilt) and in the eyes of our reference group (what many call shame). Our eyes and our group's eyes are interconnected. If they are not, as Bernard Williams put it, we are left with no alternative but to believe we are living in the midst of cranks!

The shame-guilt that is felt when we fail to live up to a standard of competence or moral conduct that we have internalized and that others expect of us is theorized by Harris as an emotional response to the perception that our ethical identity is under threat. Ethical identity, according to Harris, is the link between us and the group, between shame and guilt. Our ethical identity is that part of us that sets standards for how we should behave and what we should be able to do, and as such is shaped both by ourselves and significant others. One reinforces the other. Feeling we have let ourselves down is validated by seeing that others think so too. Seeing others disapprove of us makes us consider the possibility that we have failed to live up to our ethical identity. When we become aware that we have not lived up to our ethical identity, we experience shame. Shame is the signal for us to confront and acknowledge our failing; and if possible do something about it.

Shame is therefore our moral and competence sensor. It tells us when we are going off-course in that we are not behaving in accordance with our ethical identity; although the circumstances have to be such that we are prepared to listen to our sensor and reflect on our behaviour so that we understand how we have failed ourselves. This is not always easy, because shame is such a personally threatening emotion and we are such self-protective creatures. But there is little doubt that we can learn to manage shame well, if we have the role models (see Bandura, 1986 on social learning), and if we have the kind of environment where we can learn from acknowledging our mistakes (see Braithwaite, 2002 on restorative justice and responsive regulation).

1.2.   Managing shame well

Most times we deal with shame responsively and adaptively by recognizing our mistakes, backtracking to make things right, perhaps smoothing things over with a joke against ourselves, or if another is involved and has been hurt by our action, apologizing for any offence we may have caused. We learn to recognize the shame signal and move quickly to deal with it and put it behind us. Some may see this as the use of high-level social skills. So it is. But they are social skills that come into play in a particular situation – a situation where our personal identity, the person whom we know ourselves to be, or at least, whom we like to think of ourselves as being, comes into question. More is needed than social skills; we need the courage to take stock of our intentions and behaviour, and deal with our identity threatening experiences.

When we do, we may face up to some things that we can do better or that we should not have done. Having taken a good look at ourselves and worked through our failings, we are then in a position to engage with the world more openly and honestly, to do things better next time, unhindered by the weight of our parcel of identity threats. It is neither desirable nor necessary to drown in a sense of personal failing or inadequacy. Shadd Maruna's (2001) empirical work on how criminals *make good* after serving their sentences demonstrates the benefits of moving past shame in a way that is not personally destructive.

Instead of dwelling endlessly on their parcel of identity threats, they come to identify a *real self*, a self that did not make the mistakes of the past, and that can become the new dominant identity that dictates the path of the future. In this way, they can separate themselves from the old identity that got them into trouble with the law. Either way, whether the parcel of identity threats has been undone and examined in detail, or fleetingly examined and boxed as a remnant of the past, the individual has at some level come to terms with his or her demons. There is no pretence that nothing happened.

1.3.   *Managing shame badly*

The 'nothing happened', 'I'm not at fault', 'it doesn't matter' response is the most damaging when we experience a threat to our identity. Intuitively, we know we must protect ourselves from these identity threats because they make us feel so ill at ease with our lot in the world. Our energy is directed toward self-protection – we need to stay clear of reminders of our failings and of people who might expose us for who we are. It does not occur to us that we need to do something constructive to deal directly with that parcel of identity threats that we live with inside us, tightly wrapped, ready to explode as one threat piles on top of another. Instead we become intent on buttressing reasons for not dealing with them: the problem belongs to others, not to us, or it didn't happen. By not being prepared to admit that the problems exist and by not entertaining the possibility that we are part of these problems, we are denied the opportunity to learn from our mistakes. Our chances of getting it right next time are reduced because we don't fully understand why we got it wrong last time. Our defensiveness about our shame becomes a handicap. And we miss the opportunity of learning the art of adaptive shame management.

1.4.   *Shame acknowledgment and shame displacement*

Eliza Ahmed (2001), who has been responsible for the development of shame management theory, summarizes our responses to the challenge of unwrapping our parcel of threatened identities in terms of two separate dimensions. The first is a dimension of shame acknowledgment where we recognize that we have caused harm, we feel sorry for what we have done, accept responsibility, and try to make amends. The second dimension is shame displacement. When we become overwhelmed by the horribleness of our actions, we re-seal our parcel of identity threats and look elsewhere, outside ourselves. We blame the person we hurt, the place where it happened, the onlookers, anything to move the focus away from ourselves.

2.   MANAGING SHAME WELL – NOT JUST ABOUT US, BUT OUR SOCIAL
            INFRASTRUCTURE

While courage is one element in managing our shame well, it would be a mistake to place all the responsibility on the individual. Kurt Lewin (1951), one
of the founding fathers of social psychology, introduced the idea that what
we do and who we are at any point in time cannot be understood by focusing
on the individual alone, we must also examine that person's *life space*. Life
space is psychological in the sense that it captures all the forces that converge
on a person in a particular situation with the potential for shaping thoughts,
feelings and actions.

The importance of this way of thinking for psychologists in the 1930s and
1940s was profound. Instead of viewing an individual as the product of a
long developmental history that made them a unique individual ready to
choose one path and shun another, Lewin (1951) demonstrated that we are
what our situation tells us we should be. Importantly, Lewin placed the spotlight on social interaction, demonstrating to us that while individuals may
have a unique history, they are also social beings, who are responsive to the
social expectations, social truths and social rewards in their environment.
Modern social psychology rests on these principles of definition of self in
terms of group membership and group processes, with behaviour understood as part of how we perceive and make sense of our life space at any particular time.

The work of Lewin (1951) when placed alongside that of micro-sociolo-
gists such as Goffman (1969) raises the question of what kind of social infrastructure enables us to adopt a *self* that can manage shame well. The simple
answer is a 'safe' space (see Ahmed et al., 2001 for discussion of this concept),
one that removes the threat to our ethical identity. Such an option is institu-
tionally challenging when the law has been broken or when harm is done.
The act that has already occurred cannot be *taken back*. The social infrastructure must allow for the harm to be recognized by self and other so that an
outcome can be achieved that involves *making good*. As is seen below, authorities often fail in their mission to provide social infrastructure that is both cen-
sorious of wrongdoing and that enables opportunities for *making good*.

2.1.   How regulation can undermine adaptive shame management

Authorities, with the best of intentions for regulating unlawful behaviours,
often are leaders in the creation of life space that is counterproductive for
adaptive shame management. Ian Ayres and John Braithwaite (1992) have
been critics of overly intrusive regulatory measures, pointing out that it can
be counterproductive to 'use a sledgehammer to swat a fly'. If a person is pre-

pared to admit to a mistake and make amends, why introduce punitive tactics that make them psychologically close down? The field of taxation is replete with examples of how tax authorities have used overly punitive responses to tax non-compliance and abused their powers. For the purposes of this paper, consideration of two of the flow-on effects of the many complaints and horror stories will suffice, made more remarkable because they are not unique to any particular tax jurisdiction but are relevant to all. The point being made through these examples is that while the moral high ground is held by critics of the tax authority and while the public see the tax authority as acting like a bully, the social infrastructure is beautifully positioned, not for shame acknowledgment as is desirable, but rather for shame displacement by individual taxpayers.

First, in most fields of regulation, it is accepted that people fail to comply, sometimes because they don't want to, but sometimes because they don't know how to, or they misunderstand what is being asked of them (Kagan and Scholz, 1984). Tax authorities have been particularly slow to incorporate this into their regulatory thinking. A substantial body of research in the tax field has been necessary to prove that tax law is so complex that people make mistakes in tax payments by accident (Long and Swingen, 1991). Indeed, the term non-compliance is preferred by many in preference to evasion (Webley, Robben, Elffers and Hessing, 1991) to impress upon tax authorities that mistakes do happen and taxpayers who make innocent mistakes should not be sanctioned with the same level of severity as those who are deliberate and persistent law breakers. In other words, this research has been conducted to show that every non-compliant taxpayer is not a tax cheat and that taxpayers may need help in order to understand complex demands from tax authorities in order to comply with their expectations.

The second example is a more direct indicator of a tax culture of poor shame management. Tax authorities across the democratic world have been scrutinized by government committees for their heavy handed and unreasonable style in dealings with taxpayers (Joint Committee of Public Accounts Report, 1993; National Commission on Restructuring the Internal Revenue Service, 1997; Senate Economics References Committee, 2002). The introduction of Taxpayers' Bills of Rights and Charters, supported by the United Nations (Organisation for Economic Co-operation and Development, 2001), is the upshot of widespread discontent about the way in which tax authorities have gone about the collection of taxes from the general population. While tax authorities have tried and continue to try to moderate their style to be more client-focused (Job, this volume), the public pressure is ongoing. Most governments have set up special purpose advocacy units with powers to investigate the decisions and actions of tax authorities on behalf of taxpayers who feel unfairly treated.

These criticisms of punitiveness and heavy-handedness as a hindrance to building a culture of shame acknowledgment do not imply that rules are unnecessary and that disapproval is inappropriate in the regulatory context. Organizational rules and sanctions serve the important function of communicating seriousness of unacceptable behaviour. The rule is not the problem, rather the way it is enforced, that is, either through imposing overly harsh penalties or applying penalties in circumstances that are destructive of the likelihood of future compliance. There is limited social value in rules being enforced in ways that make it very difficult for people to deal with their shortcomings and learn to regulate themselves effectively. By taking control of the situation through inflicting outside punishment, we can take away the individual's capacity to search their soul and judge for themselves how their behaviour may have been at odds with theirs and others' expectations. Bruno Frey (1997) refers to this as using regulation to *crowd out* our moral self. I would say that regulation can frighten us into making sure that our parcel of threatened identities is wrapped more tightly than ever before. Otherwise, our shame may increase to the point of being unbearable.

If some environments can be hostile to shame acknowledgment and increase the prospects of shame displacement, what kind of environment can reverse this process and make it easier for us to face up to what we have done? And is that possible in a regulatory situation where authority's disapproval needs to be built into the social infrastructure?

2.2.   Reintegrative shaming environments

Reintegrative shaming theory (Braithwaite, 1989) spells out for us the characteristics of a regulatory environment that facilitates adaptive shame management. One element is interdependence. Individuals who are dependent on each other for the exchange of goods or for accomplishing a goal through the execution of a chain of tasks have good reasons for making it easier for one of their number to face up to their threatened identities. This is not likely to happen, however, unless the psychological space is right, that is, people feel assured that they are a valued member of the group, and they, in turn, value other members of the group.

Interdependence, therefore, is not always going to make its presence felt so that individuals feel accountable. Moreover, with multiple identities and segregated networks, we can hide an *unacceptable* identity, share it only with tolerant others, and assume quite another more socially appropriate identity as our social infrastructure changes its form. Not infrequently, these are the circumstances in which law is used, evidence collected, and individuals are held accountable for their actions. According to reintegrative shaming theory, in order for shame to be acknowledged and resolved in these situations, those who have been caught behaving illegally need to not only face their accusers and the evidence against them, but also be given the support necessary to repair the damage and change their future behaviour.

John Braithwaite (1989) describes sanctioning systems that recognize the need to offer hope for a better future while re-affirming normative principles of right and wrong as systems of reintegrative shaming. This means that we don't refrain from disapproval, but that we put clear boundaries around it, and as the person unravels their parcel of threatened identities, we go the extra mile to reaffirm the value of the person and the hope we have for the future. We assure them that they need not face this shame again, they can connect with another identity of which they can be proud, and that we will be there to help them realize their ambitions. Reintegrative shaming is contrasted with stigmatizing shaming which condemns the whole person and offers little hope for being accepted into the community in the future. When we brand people as *evil* or as *cheats*, we are communicating disrespect and rejection of the whole person. The door is not left open for anyone – either the labeller or the labelled – to manage shame well.

The use of reintegrative shaming in the taxation context is not far-fetched and is not too large a step forward from the kind of dialogue that occurs now, particularly with tax practitioners and advisers. The next section begins with an account taken from Braithwaite and Braithwaite (2007) of how such an encounter might proceed.

3.   WHAT DOES REINTEGRATIVE SHAMING THEORY HAVE TO OFFER?

3.1.   *A possible restorative justice response to a real tax event*

A major partner in a accounting firm got one of their wealthy clients into a lot of trouble for tax non-compliance. A more senior partner then visited the senior ATO (Australian Tax Office) officer handling the matter and said: 'This is a rogue partner and we are going to get rid of him. We would hate the ATO to think that other partners condone what he did.' Such an encounter creates the opportunity the tax authority needs to tackle the ethical climate in the major accounting firms and investment banks. The senior ATO officers *could* have replied:

'That's good that your other partners do not condone this and I'm pleased to hear it, because we at the ATO were disturbed by the non-compliance that occurred here and are always concerned with something of this gravity that it might reflect a culture of non-compliance in your firm. Could we have a meeting to discuss this with all your partners?'

When they agree to this, as regulatory experience with restorative justice elsewhere suggests they would, a request would be made for a restorative justice practitioner to facilitate the meeting. This facilitator would insist that the *rogue* partner who was about to be moved out also attend. He would be the first person asked to speak by the facilitator. He would be asked to tell in his own words how the incident that had got him into hot water had occurred. It might turn out that the *rogue* partner was not a rogue partner at all, but a fall-guy who was actually following the culture of the firm. The conversation would conclude by focusing on the harm done by the incident, with everyone being asked to contribute ideas for preventive action to ensure the problem did not arise again. If the suggestion had not already been made, the Tax Officer could propose an audit of the firm's systems for compliance with ethical standards. An independent evaluation of compliance systems would be conducted by an external consultant whose independence enjoyed the confidence of both the firm and the Tax Office. Its recommendations would be reported back to a reconvened meeting of the group, which would discuss whether they went far enough. A year later the group might meet again to receive a report from the accounting firm and the independent consultant on how thoroughly the reforms to the compliance culture had been implemented.

3.2.   *What does adaptive and non-adaptive shame management mean for ordinary taxpayers?*

At this point, the more practically minded might ask: how can this be applied to tax jurisdictions which incorporate millions of taxpayers, many of whom are cheating the system of tax dollars in different ways and to different degrees? Obviously, automated procedures are essential for processing the volumes of documents and data that flow into such systems, identifying cases requiring investigation, and initiating procedures to amend tax assessments. In such cases, the principles of reintegrative shaming cannot be practiced routinely one-on-one but need to be abstracted and implemented in a fashion that engages with the masses.

This is already occurring to a limited extent and I will use the Australian Taxation Office's Compliance Model (Job, this volume) as an example. In order to ensure that the processes of disapproval or shaming are reasonable, the Compliance Model recommends a series of *probes* to ascertain the likely risk to revenue that non-compliance of a particular kind is imposing. Taxpayers are encouraged to volunteer corrections and amendments. This is not to say that penalties won't be imposed, but penalties are monitored for their appropriateness and it is not unheard of for fines to be waived with only an interest charge when taxpayers are cooperative. The objective is to settle most problems with the minimum level of intrusiveness. If cooperation is not forthcoming from the taxpayer, enforcement activity increases in its intrusiveness in graduated steps until the matter is settled.

Reintegration comes into the use of the Model on a mass scale at two levels. First, when a taxpayer signals a willingness to be cooperative, the tax authority responds positively and de-escalates intrusiveness (but does not lose interest in the outcome!). If the cooperative posturing by the taxpayer proves not to be genuine, escalation, at a more accelerated pace than before, is the immediate response. Second, reintegration has two components: (1) respecting the person (while disapproving of the act of wrongdoing); and (2) finding a path of repair and restoration of relationships. The first component has already been institutionalized on a mass scale in many tax jurisdictions through Taxpayers' Bills of Rights and Charters. Admittedly the intellectual framework behind these developments has been that of human rights. But part of the reason why rights are so important in the tax context is the belief that tax authorities should not have the power to shame inappropriately. Rights discourse may not explicitly refer to reintegrative processes, but it places limits on the damage that can be inflicted on individuals in the name of law and order. Respecting the individual, respecting their right to privacy and confidentiality, providing taxpayers with explanations for tax authority decisions, and opportunities to contest assessments and reach agreements are therefore ways in which improvements have been made in the direction of recognizing the importance of reintegration in the context of law breaking behaviour.

Admittedly these are only baby steps in working out how reintegrative shaming can be implemented on a grand scale in tax jurisdictions. Much needs to be done in learning how to implement such processes, and undoubtedly many mistakes will be made before we get it right. If it is so difficult, a good question to ask is, should we bother? I will conclude this paper by giving reasons why we should persevere with this challenge.

First, it should be noted that interdependence between taxpayers and revenue authorities is high in democratic societies, particularly in those with a tax system that relies heavily on self-assessment. Tax authorities need the cooperation of taxpayers and usually taxpayers are keen to hear back from tax authorities, particularly if the tax authority owes them money. Voluntary taxpaying is at the heart of effective tax systems in many countries and has been explained through a number of different lenses, sometimes separately, sometimes in combination. Willingness to pay tax has been linked to perceived benefits, a desire to conform to social norms, lack of other options (or coercion), fear and obligation or duty. Of these, arguably the most consistent predictor of tax evasion among individuals and across countries has been obligation (see reviews by Andreoni et al., 1998, Richardson and Sawyer, 2001 and Webley et al., 1991) or what is commonly referred to as *tax morale* (Feld and Frey, 2002, 2005; Frey, 2003; Frey and Feld, 2001).

Tax morale is not to be taken for granted. Building and protecting tax morale needs to be a purposeful activity of tax authorities, and implementing principles of reintegrative shaming is one way of ensuring this outcome is achieved (for another, see the work on direct democracy by Feld and Frey, 2005 and Frey and Feld, 2001). To explain how this occurs, we turn to motivational posturing theory (Braithwaite, Braithwaite, Gibson and Makkai, 1994; Braithwaite 1995, 2003).

Individual taxpayers control the social distance they place between themselves and the tax authority. When tax morale is high, the social distance that taxpayers place between themselves and the authority should be relatively low. In contrast, when tax morale is low and taxpayers feel uncomfortable, they will move away from the authority to avoid engagement and to protect themselves from any threat that the authority might direct their way. Socially distant postures include (1) resistance, or opposing the position taken by the authority, (2) disengagement, or cutting oneself off from the authority psychologically, and (3) game playing, or contesting the power of the authority through finding loopholes in the law. The more cooperative postures that enable the tax authority to influence and persuade taxpayers to do the right thing are believing in the system (commitment) and accepting that the authority knows what is best (capitulation).

Motivational posturing theory offers three important insights to tax officials. First, taxpayers choose how distant they want to be from an authority. Second, the greater the distance, the less control the authority has to influence behaviour. Third, the psychological basis of social distance can be of two kinds. The first aspect of distancing is related to disliking or being unsympathetic to the authority, and is best represented by the resistance posture. The second aspect has little to do with how favourably one regards authority, and more to do with how seriously one takes authority. This second dimension, defined by disengagement and game playing, has been called dismissiveness. It amounts to lacking respect for authority, possibly regarding the authority as weak. Resistance and dismissiveness are two different forms of defiance that require different responses from authorities. It follows from these three propositions that if tax authorities want to continue relying on a voluntary taxpaying culture, they must manage postures, containing the defiant postures and building the cooperative postures.

The necessity of managing motivational postures explains why tax administrations need to make reintegrative shaming a standard in their enforcement strategies, ethically based disapproval as well as reintegration. Ethically based disapproval is considered particularly important for curbing dismissiveness, reintegration is particularly important for curbing resistance.

Through disapproving or creating shame over tax evasion, tax authorities are able to legitimate the ethical identity of being an honest taxpayer and affirm the value they place on high tax morale. This is not necessarily an easy task, particularly when dealing with those who reject a moral base for taxpaying on ideological grounds. Dismissiveness is just such a posture. It has been associated with the choice of not valuing public benefits, not accepting the government's view of justice, and rejecting a moral obligation to pay tax. Regulating dismissiveness of this kind presents a challenge for authorities in a democratic society because the legitimacy of the system, the effectiveness of the law and the capability to enforce the law are all brought into question.

While recognizing the threat this poses to the tax system, it is important to acknowledge that dismissiveness serves an important function in a democracy. Dismissive defiance signals that for at least a proportion of the population, well-entrenched institutions are not necessarily considered valuable or necessary. The principles of taxation and the design of the tax system need to be debated, not swept under the carpet. And opposition should certainly not be blindly crushed out of existence. This is where reintegrative shaming has a role. Reintegrative shaming offers prospects of deliberation and dialogue about what is *right*. Success at managing dismissiveness in a sustainable way involves openness, dialogue, persuasion, listening to different points of view, and perhaps even changing the tax system.

Reintegration, on the other hand, is important for curbing the displacement of shame and the resistance that taxpayers express when they are forced to confront their wrongdoing. It is concern about the stress and strain in the relationship with the authority that pushes people toward resistant defiance. Reintegration or taking steps to treat the person with respect and communicate hope and expectation for a law-abiding future provides the means for repairing damaged relationships and re-invigorating voluntary compliance. This latter process overlaps substantially with the work of Tyler (1990) on procedural justice. In keeping with the work of Tyler (1990), resistant defiance among taxpayers who have felt the ire of the Australian Taxation Office responds favourably to procedural fairness and to evidence that the tax authority can be trusted to serve the public interest (Murphy, 2004; 2005). But procedural justice alone is not enough when objectives and rules are contentious. Reintegrative shaming offers prospects of addressing both processes and ends.

Reintegrative shaming provides a framework for both those involved in evasion and avoidance and those involved in enforcing tax law to have their say, to exchange their views on the harms that each creates in the society, and ultimately to identify points of difference and points of agreement. There is no suggestion here that the tax authority should compromise on its enforcement activities. But it has a responsibility to explain why tax laws take the form they do, why enforcement is important and why it is done a certain way. Through listening and learning, taxpayers may come to appreciate the tax system more, and tax officials may come to understand how they might improve the integrity of their own system so that it gains greater respect from taxpayers.

4.   A CASE STUDY OF THE PSYCHOLOGY OF THE SANCTIONED
          TAXPAYER

In presenting an argument for how reintegrative shaming can benefit tax authorities, an issue that lingers and remains unaddressed is why would taxpayers accused of evasion or avoidance feel ashamed? If they object to taxation in principle, they may feel proud of their defiance. While this is undoubtedly true for some, our data suggest that for most disapproval from a legitimate authority is threatening, even if the taxpayer has the lowest regard for the institution that the authority oversees.

Between 2000 and 2002, the Centre for Tax System Integrity collected data from taxpayers from the general population (N = 3,253 from two random samples) and from a random sample of 2,292 taxpayers who had been involved in mass marketed aggressive tax planning schemes that the Australian Taxation Office had ruled as tax avoidance schemes (see Murphy, 2003). The ruling covered the last 6 years of tax lodgements in some cases. Many taxpayers had large repayments to make to the tax authority, as well as fines and penalties. Taxpayers claimed that promoters had assured them that the schemes were legal and that the actions of the tax authority were unfair. The tensions erupted in a very public conflict between this group of taxpayers and the Australian Taxation Office, resulting in a government enquiry (Murphy, 2003; Senate Economics References Committee, 2002). The episode ended with the tax authority making considerable compromises to reach a settlement and end the dispute. Penalties and interest were waived and generous terms of payment for back tax were offered to those who were unknowing consumers of the schemes.

A study comparing the attitudes of the general population sample and the investor sample just after settlement produced some interesting results (Braithwaite, Murphy and Reinhart, 2007). The investor group showed higher levels of resistant defiance than the general population group, but they showed lower levels of dismissive defiance. In other words, they expressed adversarial attitudes toward the tax authority and much antipathy. They were angry that the Tax Office would not approve their investments and had treated them as if they were tax cheats. At the same time, these investors were disinclined to dismiss the office's authority as irrelevant. The tax authority's enforcement action made it unpopular, but it also placed constraints on what taxpayers felt they could do without any adverse consequences.

In addition to measuring motivational postures and the degree to which taxpayers were resistant and dismissive, the general population and investor groups were compared on how they coped with taxation as a threat to material wellbeing. Coping responses were conceptualized in three ways. Individuals could *feel oppressed* by the taxation experience, or they could *take control*, challenging the tax authority's decisions, or they could *think morally*, accepting that they had a duty or obligation to pay tax. All three reactions were much stronger in the investor group than in the general population group. The investors who had been in conflict with the Tax Office felt more oppressed overall; they also favoured actions to take control of their situation to challenge the tax authority and surprisingly, they also thought morally about themselves as having an honest taxpaying identity. This mixture of heightened coping reactions to the tax threat creates a highly volatile population for the tax authority to manage, particularly considering that the group regarded the procedural justice they were afforded as poor (Murphy, 2005).

Australia's mass marketed schemes episode did not show the tax authority in the best possible light. The hope for resolving this conflict without jeopardizing the integrity of the Tax Office in the public eye arguably lay in a different direction to that taken in the heat of the contest. Firming up investors' pride in being an honest taxpayer so that they would not want to become involved in such schemes in the future should have been the prime objective, while simultaneously sending a message that involvement in mass marketed schemes of these kinds was not acceptable. Australia's tax administrators deemed the investors' actions dishonest, and they were not about to change their decision on this point. But they failed in finding a way of leading taxpayers through what was a very unpleasant and unacceptable tax situation. The emphasis was on punishing people who were depicted as foolhardy and should have known better. It was not until the public enquiry that attention turned to clarifying the law and warning taxpayers early of ATO concerns. These practices have now been adopted by the Australian Taxation Office. This change provides a positive message to the community that says: 'We will work with you to prevent this situation from occurring again.' It expresses confidence that the ATO expects far fewer Australians to venture down the mass marketed scheme path, once they have been informed that such schemes are under investigation as possibly unlawful.

What the Australian Taxation Office had failed to do in dealing with the scheme investors early on was to recognize that when confronted with the full force of the law, most people don't want to be labelled as tax cheats, and are looking for ways to restore their reputation in their own eyes, if not in others. Australia's mass marketed schemes debacle involved the management of shame on all sides, with far more displacement being aired than acknowledgment. It is possible that it could have been managed much better if the institutional infrastructure for the resolution of the conflict had provided opportunities for respectful dialogue at an early stage. It should be possible for taxpayers and tax officials to share their views and move conflict more quickly to a fair and reasonable resolution within a restorative justice and responsive regulation framework (Braithwaite, 2002).

5.   CONCLUSION

When we consider the power of shame and our attempts to manage it adaptively, particularly when authority deems it necessary to punish us, it is important to recognize that people's narratives about themselves are complex. There is no blanket treatment from a regulator that can effectively cast these narratives out of existence. But narratives can be reconstructed (Maruna, 2001). Tax authorities would be wise to broaden their remit of law enforcement. They need to understand the narratives of their regulatory communities, put down their big sticks, roll up their sleeves and engage in dialogue about what tax law means and whose interests it serves. Persuade people that while it is a nuisance to pay, it is fair. Understanding that the principles of reintegrative shaming is a first step to embarking on this road of discovery.

References

Ahmed, E. (2001). Shame management: Regulating bullying. In: *Shame management through reintegration*, E. Ahmed, N. Harris, J. Braithwaite and V. Braithwaite. Cambridge, UK: Cambridge University Press, pp. 211-314.

Ahmed, E., N. Harris, J. Braithwaite and V. Braithwaite (2001). *Shame management through reintegration.* Cambridge, UK: Cambridge University Press.

Andreoni, J., B. Erard and J. Feinstein (1998). Tax compliance. *Journal of Economic Literature* 36, pp. 818-860.

Ayres, I. and J. Braithwaite (1992). *Responsive Regulation: Transcending the Deregulation Debate.* Oxford: Oxford University Press.

Bandura, A. (1986). *Social Foundations of Thought and Action: A Social Cognitive Theory.* Englewood Cliffs, NJ: Prentice Hall.

Braithwaite, J. (1989). *Crime, Shame and Reintegration.* Cambridge: Cambridge University Press.

– (2002). *Restorative Justice and Responsive Regulation.* New York: Oxford University Press.

– (2005). *Markets in Vice, Markets in Virtue.* New York and Sydney: Oxford University Press and Federation Press.

Braithwaite, V. (1995). Games of engagement: postures within the regulatory community. *Law and Policy* 17, pp. 225-255.

– (2003). Dancing with tax authorities: motivational postures and non-compliant actions. In: *Taxing Democracy: Understanding Tax Avoidance and Evasion*, V. Braithwaite (ed). Aldershot, UK: Ashgate, pp. 15-39.

Braithwaite, V. and J. Braithwaite (2007). Democratic sentiment and cyclical markets in vice. *British Journal of Criminology.* (Forthcoming.)

Braithwaite, V., J. Braithwaite, D. Gibson and T. Makkai (1994). Regulatory styles, motivational postures and nursing home compliance. *Law and Policy* 16, pp. 363-394.

Braithwaite, V., K. Murphy and M. Reinhart (2007). Taxation threat, motivational postures, and responsive regulation. *Law and Policy.* (Forthcoming.)

Feld, L. and B. Frey (2002). Trust breeds trust: How taxpayers are treated. *Economics of Governance* 3, pp. 87-99.

– (2005). *Tax compliance as the result of a psychological contract: The role of incentives and responsive regulation.* Centre for Tax System Integrity Working Paper 76, Australian National University, Canberra.

Frey, B. (1997). *Not Just for the Money: An Economic Theory of Personal Motivation.* Cheltenham, UK: Edward Elgar.

– (2003). The Role of Deterrence and Tax Morale in Taxation in the European Union. Jelle Zijlstra Lecture, Netherlands Institute for Advanced Study in the Humanities and Social Sciences (NIAS).

Frey, B. and L. Feld (2001). The Tax Authority and the Taxpayer: An Exploratory Analysis. Paper presented at the Second International Conference on Taxation, Centre for Tax System Integrity, Australian National University, Canberra, 10-11 December.

Goffman, E. (1969). *Where the Action Is: Three Essays*. London: Penguin Press.

Grasmick, H.G. and R.J. Bursik jr, (1990). Conscience, significant others, and rational choice: Extending the deterrence model. *Law and Society Review* 24, pp. 837-861.

Harris, N. (2001). Shaming and shame: Regulating drink-driving. In: *Shame management through reintegration,* E. Ahmed, N. Harris, J. Braithwaite and V. Braithwaite. Cambridge, UK: Cambridge University Press, pp. 73-210.

 - (2003). Reassessing the dimensionality of the moral emotions. *British Journal of Psychology* 94, pp. 457-473.

 - Shame, ethical identity and justice interventions: Lessons from research on the psychology of influence. In: *Emotions, Crime and Justice*, S. Karstedt, I. Loader and H. Strang (eds.). Hart Publishing. (Forthcoming.)

Job, J. and D. Honaker (2003). Short-term experience with responsive regulation in the Australian Taxation Office. In: *Taxing Democracy: Understanding Tax Avoidance and Evasion*, V. Braithwaite (ed.). Ashgate, Aldershot, pp. 111-130.

Job, J., A. Stout and R. Smith (2006). Culture change in regulatory institutions: From command-and-control to responsive regulation in taxation administration. In: *Managing and maintaining compliance*. The Hague: Boom Legal publishers.

Joint Committee of Public Accounts (1993). *An Assessment of Tax. A Report on an Enquiry into the Australian Taxation Office*. JCPA Report No. 326. Canberra: Australian Government Publishing Service.

Kagan, R. and J.T. Scholz (1984). The criminology of the corporation and regulatory enforcement strategies. In: *Enforcing Regulation*, K. Hawkins and J. Thomas (eds.). Boston: Kluwer-Nijhoff.

Lewin, K. (1951). *Field Theory in Social Science: Selected Theoretical Papers*, D. Cartwright (ed.). New York: Harper and Row.

Maruna, S. (2001). *Making Good: How Ex-convicts Reform and Rebuild their Lives*. Washington, DC: American Psychological Association.

Murphy, K. (2003). An examination of taxpayers' attitudes towards the Australian tax system. Findings from a survey of tax scheme investors. *Australian Tax Forum* 18, pp. 209-242.

 - (2004). The role of trust in nurturing compliance. A study of accused tax avoiders. *Law and Human Behavior* 28, pp. 187-209.

 - (2005). Regulating more effectively. The relationship between procedural justice, legitimacy and tax non-compliance. *Journal of Law Society* 32, pp. 562-589.

National Commission on Restructuring the Internal Revenue Service (1997). *A Vision for a New IRS*. Washington DC: National Commission on Restructuring the Internal Revenue Service.

Organisation for Economic Co-operation and Development (2001). *Taxpayer rights and obligations – practice note GAP002*. Centre for Tax Policy and Administration.

Richardson, M. and A.J. Sawyer (2001). A taxonomy of the tax compliance literature. Further findings, problems and prospects. *Australian Taxation Forum* 16, pp. 137-320.

Senate Economics References Committee (2002). *Inquiry into Mass Marketed Tax Effective Schemes and Investor Protection. Final Report*. Canberra: Parliament of Australia.

Tajfel, H. (ed.) (1978). *Differentiation Between Social Groups: Studies in the Social Psychology of Intergroup Relations*. London: Academic Press.

Tomkins, S.S. (1987). Shame. In: *The Many Faces of Shame*, D.L. Nathanson (ed.). New York: Guilford, pp. 133-161

Turner, J.C., M.A. Hogg, P.J. Oakes, S.J. Reicher and M.S. Wetherell (1987). *Rediscovering the Social Group. A self-categorization Theory.* Oxford: Blackwell.

Tyler, T. (1990). *Why People Obey the Law.* New Haven, CT: Yale University Press.

Webley, P., H. Robben, H. Elffers and D. Hessing (1991). *Tax Evasion. An Experimental Approach.* Cambridge: Cambridge University Press.

Williams, B. (1993). *Shame and Necessity.* Berkely, CA: University of California Press.

7 | BETWEEN PERSUASION AND DETERRENCE

SOME LEGAL ASPECTS OF COMPLIANCE IN TAXATION

Richard Happé[1]

1.   INTRODUCTION

Why is taxation justified? In his *The Roaring Nineties*, Joseph Stiglitz makes this clear: 'Every tax system is an expression of a country's basic values – and its politics. It translates into hard cash what might otherwise be simple high-flown rhetoric'.[2] However, it is also clear that it may be expected from every taxpayer that he contributes his fair share. The tax authorities undeniably fulfil an important role in this. In this paper, I will discuss the way the Dutch Tax Administration (hereafter DTA) tries to ensure that taxpayers properly fulfil their tax obligations.

Times have changed in this regard. Twenty-five years ago, the world of taxation was simple. It could be characterized as a black and white situation. In the eyes of the DTA, taxpayers were law-abiding people or they were not. It was the time in which every citizen was supposed to know the law. The tax inspector's philosophy was the so-called 'one hundred percent philosophy': when he checked the tax returns, every deviation from the law had to be corrected. In many cases, this automatically resulted in imposing a fine, a so-called heightening. The General Taxes Act (hereafter GTA) prescribed a heightening of 100% of the tax amount. Then the tax inspector had the discretion to partially remit this fine.[3]

At the end of the 1980s, it became clear: the 'one hundred percent philosophy' proved to be an illusion and the DTA had to abandon it. Since the DTA clearly needed a different philosophy, it embraced the compliance strategy in the early 1990s. Compliance refers to the willingness of the taxpayers to fulfil

---

1.   Professor of Tax Law, University of Tilburg, The Netherlands, e-mail: r.h.happe@uvt.nl.
2.   Joseph Stiglitz, The Roaring Nineties, New York, 2003, p. 177.
3.   This system of automatic heightening was abolished in 1994.

their legal obligations and compliance strategy to the policy of the DTA to maintain and reinforce this compliance.[4] One of the elements of this strategy is that different kinds of taxpayers need different kinds of approaches. In this respect, the Australian Taxation Office states: '[I]t [is] necessary to show fairness and reasonableness to those who [are] willing to cooperate, and focus enforcement capacity on those flagrantly ignoring their tax obligations'.[5]

It will be shown that publicity plays a dominant role in this compliance approach in two different ways. On the one hand, all the information the DTA receives from taxpayers and others and which it uses to levy an assessment, must be kept secret. That is, the DTA is obliged to preserve the confidentiality of all information supplied by the taxpayers.

On the other hand, the DTA has opted for the strategy of communication with the taxpayers and handles publicity in an instrumental way: it increasingly uses the media to improve the results of its actions. Against the background of its duty of secrecy, the DTA employs the instrument of media publicity to deal with non-compliant behaviour of taxpayers. In some situations it uses publicity to persuade the taxpayers to be more compliant, in others it uses media publicity as a means of deterrence.[6] If the DTA applies its full enforcement capacity to a particular taxpayer, it aims to achieve a general preventive effect at the same time.[7] In terms of shame management, it uses stigmatization of the wrongdoer to deter other taxpayers from committing tax fraud in the future.

I will focus on some practical, legal applications of the strategy. I will discuss three types of situations from the perspective of the compliance strategy with regard to taxpayers who commit tax fraud. Firstly, taxpayers who wish to correct mistakes they made in the past can choose to disclose voluntarily. They prefer reintegrating just in time to being stigmatized later. Secondly, people who persevere in their fraudulent behaviour should expect a different reaction from the DTA. The normal reaction is a sanction imposed by the DTA or the criminal judge. It will appear that especially fraudulent VIPs and tax advisers can expect a severe approach of the authorities in order to achieve a strong general deterrent effect. Finally, I will pay attention to the possibility of restoring compliant behaviour by means of settlements. Sometimes the DTA and the Public Prosecution Service can separate the people

---

4. Cash Economy Task Force, Improving Tax Compliance in the Cash Economy, Australian Taxation Office, Canberra, 1998, p. 25.
5. Valerie Braithwaite, A New Approach to Tax Compliance. In: Valerie Braithwaite (ed.), Taxing Democracy, Aldershot, 2003, p. 2.
6. On the role of persuasion and deterrence in tax enforcement, see Valerie Braithwaite and John Braithwaite, An Evolving Compliance Model for Tax Enforcement. In: Neal Shover and John Paul Wright (eds.), Crimes of Privilege, Readings in White-Collar Crime, Oxford, 2001, p. 406.
7. Valerie Braithwaite, Tax System Integrity and Compliance. The Democratic Management of the Tax System. In: Valerie Braithwaite (ed.). Taxing Democracy. Aldershot, 2003, p. 272.

who committed serious tax fraud from the company or firm to which they belong. In my opinion, it is possible to give a company legal opportunities to reintegrate and to structurally improve its compliance.

2.   VOLUNTARY DISCLOSURE

2.1.   Legal framework

Many countries have regulations for voluntary disclosure. The core of most of these regulations is the opportunity it offers people who want to make a clean slate. They can disclose information to the authorities in order to bring their underreported tax returns in compliance. In the Netherlands, just as in other countries, the regulation is part of statutory law. By contrast, in the US, voluntary disclosure is a matter of internal practice of the IRS, though the US practice has been published.[8] The difference is evident: in the Netherlands, people have a right to invoke a statutory provision; in the US, voluntary disclosure is more of a favour. Dutch taxpayers who disclose correctly will not be fined or sanctioned. In the US, a voluntary disclosure does not automatically guarantee immunity from prosecution. The IRS can only give a recommendation to the Public Prosecutor Service. In the UK, the Inland Revenue cannot grant immunity but it can allow a maximum abatement of the penalty of 30% in case of voluntary disclosure; 10% abatement can be added if there is full cooperation.[9]

Voluntary disclosure is an exception to the penalization of a punishable act after the event has been completed. If people commit an offence, it is impossible to undo it, but it is possible in tax law. The reason for this is that a taxpayer, who once started to commit tax fraud and thus underreported his tax return, is forced to continue the fraud in his subsequent tax returns for fear of the fraud being discovered by the tax inspector. If he does not persist but reports his correct taxable income in the next year, the tax inspector will probably notice the difference between the two tax returns and will discover the fraud.[10] As a result of this mechanism, many tax offenders become 'repeat players' or 'repeat offenders'. Voluntary disclosure offers a way out of this vicious circle. In a way these regulations involve a legal instrument of shame management by enabling tax offenders to acknowledge and discharge shame. It makes it possible for tax offenders to reintegrate.[11]

8.   See IR-2002-135, 11 December 2002 at <www.irs.gov.com>.
9.   See IHTM36183 at <www.hmrc.gov.uk.com>.
10. See e.g. the Dutch Parliamentary Documents: Kamerstukken II 1954/55, 4080, No. 3, p. 28.
11. See John Braithwaite and Valerie Braithwaite (2001). Shame, Shame Management and Regulation. In: Eliza Ahmed, Nathan Harris, John Braithwaite and Valerie Braithwaite, Shame Management Through Reintegration. Cambridge, pp. 19-69.

Of course, voluntary disclosure has a number of additional advantages for the tax authorities. First of all, people pay their taxes after all, so it is good for the treasury and it contributes to equal treatment of all taxpayers. Secondly, it saves the tax authorities a great deal of audit energy, which can then be spent on other cases. In addition, in many cases, it is rather doubtful whether the tax inspector would have discovered the tax fraud at all. The most important point is, however, that it turns non-compliant taxpayers into compliant tax-payers.

In the past decade, tax authorities have changed their attitude towards voluntary disclosure. Before then, the tax authorities generally adopted a passive attitude. It was up to the taxpayer to make use of the voluntary disclosure regulation. If a taxpayer informed the tax inspector he wanted to disclose underpaid tax, the basic reaction of the tax inspector was to check whether the case of the taxpayer fell under the regulation. In short, it was a matter of interpretation. This passive attitude has now been dropped and the voluntary disclosure regulation has become a management tool. Many countries use it to persuade their taxpayers to correct their underreported tax returns. For example, in 2002, the IRS republished its Voluntary Disclosure Practice. The language was modernized to help clarify particular issues and some examples were added. It also stated explicitly that publicity or media coverage regarding enforcement and compliance efforts would not bar a tax-payer from making a voluntary disclosure.[12] The tax authorities increasingly use media publicity as a management tool in order to influence taxpayers.

Especially in the field of international tax fraud, many countries apply voluntary disclosure in this way. An important factor is that tax authorities cooperate on a much larger scale than before and exchange more information with each other in the battle against international tax evasion. A current Dutch example, the 'bank accounts' project, illustrates this.

2.2.   Tools of persuasion

It is a well-known fact that many citizens of the countries surrounding Luxembourg held and hold secret bank accounts at Luxembourg banks because of the rather lenient fiscal climate and the strict banking secrecy laws of Luxembourg.[13] At the end of 2001, the DTA spontaneously received a great deal

---

12. David B. Palmer, Chief of IRS Criminal Investigation, 'Back to Tax!' A Mid-Year Overview of IRS Criminal Investigation, Journal of Tax Practice and Procedure/August-September 2003, p. 46. Also at: <www.irs.gov.com>.
13. The EU has tried to counter this practice with a directive concerning taxation of savings income (Council Directive 2003/48/EC). Compare also Council Directive 2003/49/EC concerning a common system of taxation applicable to interest and royalty payments made between associated companies of different Member States. See also Ben J.M. Terra and Peter J. Wattel (2005). European Tax Law. Deventer, p. 614.

of information from the Belgian Tax Administration. The information had been stolen by some employees of the Kredietbank Luxembourg, who wanted to blackmail the bank. The information concerned the data of approximately ten thousand bank accounts of Dutch taxpayers. Before concrete action was taken against particular Dutch taxpayers, some newspapers brought the news about the bank accounts and the impending actions of the DTA. Shortly after that, the DTA opted for the strategy of communication with the taxpayers and opened a website on this subject.[14] The most important item on the site was a description of the voluntary disclosure regulation in rather inviting wording. The message communicated by the DTA was clear: what can you do to make use of the regulation before the tax inspector knocks on your door? Because then it will be too late.

The DTA said it is very satisfied about this 'bank accounts' project. It levied more than three thousand additional assessments: 30% of these assessments concerned taxpayers who had voluntarily disclosed their under-reported tax returns. The total extra amount of tax collected was €170 million. In the follow-up, the DTA organized an international conference to share its experience in this project with other tax authorities. It resulted in more exchange of information with several other countries.[15]

It is worth mentioning that the DTA also investigated the motives of the people who had disclosed voluntarily. On the ground of the results of this psychological investigation, the DTA refined the use of the publicity tool. In the next project, concerning hidden foreign-source income, this was brought into practice. The DTA website was improved and newspapers brought the news about the new project, including the possibility of voluntary disclosure and the availability of an information leaflet. Thereupon, the DTA published an advertisement in all the national and regional newspapers, telling the readers about the possibility of voluntary disclosure. As a result of this advertisement, hundreds of taxpayers made a voluntary disclosure.[16] The DTA rather explicitly plays on the taxpayer's fear of being discovered.

What can be learnt from the Dutch 'bank account' project? First, I think it is a good example of compliance strategy. It is a good thing to inform the taxpayers actively about the disclosure rules and to use psychological and communicative methods to improve the efficacy of publicity. People become more aware of the choice they have to make: either to continue their fraudulent behaviour or to come forward and disclose. It is perfectly legitimate to strongly appeal to people's conscience, even if this involves deliberately

---

14. <www.belastingdienst.nl>.
15. Beheersverslag Belastingdienst 2003 *(Management report Tax Administration)*, The Hague, 2004, p. 31.
16. Beheersverslag Belastingdienst 2004 *(Management report Tax Administration)*, The Hague, 2005, pp. 22/23.

exploiting their fear of being found out. The emphasis that was put on the damage to society by tax fraud is also a good thing. The legal provisions and the publicity make it possible for fraudulent taxpayers to become compliant taxpayers again. The project proves that the use of persuasive methods can be very effective in achieving this goal.

A second evaluative remark is that it is doubtful whether the concrete *bank accounts* project was as successful as the DTA claims it was. Given the more serious cases, namely the people who had large bank accounts and who did not disclose voluntarily, there is less reason for being so enthusiastic. In accordance with the policy of the DTA and the Public Prosecution Service these people were prosecuted for tax fraud. By the end of 2005, all these cases had been abandoned by the Public Prosecution Service. According to several judgments of the criminal courts the evidence of fraud was not convincing enough. As a result, the Public Prosecution Service dropped all charges.[17] This part of the story was not successful at all.

Problems have also arisen about cases in which additional assessments were levied together with large fines. In an important case, in which the taxpayer had remained silent, the DTA refused to give all the information it had at its disposal. For this reason, the Tax Division of the Dutch Court set aside both the additional assessments and the fines.[18] The case is now pending a decision by the Supreme Court.

The risk of this development is that, in the perception of both compliant taxpayers and also of those who disclosed voluntarily, the people who denied the existence of their bank accounts or kept silent about them are now better off. In this respect, the publicity campaign of the DTA has also had negative consequences. It raises the unwelcome question of whether crime does pay after all. From the point of view of improving the compliance behaviour of these taxpayers and also of other taxpayers who read about it in the newspapers, this is a bad development. The DTA possibly underestimated this backfire effect. It is recommended that, next time, the DTA and the Public Prosecution Service make an ex ante evaluation. They must investigate thoroughly which difficulties they may encounter with regard to the burden of proof. Special attention must also be paid to the difference between the burden of proof in tax and in criminal trials. In my opinion, these points are underestimated. It would also be a good thing if experts from outside the DTA, like outstanding tax lawyers or criminal lawyers, were to be asked to give a second opinion beforehand. An objective opinion, in time, can help to prevent tunnel vision. Projects such as the *bank accounts* project must be strong cases in the legal sense.

17. E.g. Court of Amsterdam, 12 October 2005, V-N 2006/14.12.
18. Court of 's-Hertogenbosch, 22 September 2005, V-N 2005/51.1.

Finally, in my opinion voluntary disclosure can be a valuable instrument to improve the taxpayer's compliance. Publicity can also support this instrument, provided that the tax authorities have strong evidence. In this respect, people sometimes argue for a general tax amnesty.[19] The core of such proposals is that, if taxpayers disclose their underreported income, the DTA will not levy tax about the then reported income or, another possibility, will levy tax at a substantially reduced tax rate. Undoubtedly such an amnesty will be a financial success in the short term but, in the long term, the disadvantages will be greater. Since it insinuates that tax fraud pays and it violates the principle of equality, it will erode the taxpayer's willingness to comply.[20] Voluntary disclosure rules restore the balance in an ethically acceptable way between people who disclose and the compliant taxpayers in terms of taxation.

3.   ADMINISTRATIVE FINE OR CRIMINAL SANCTION

3.1.   Legal framework

Everything that happens in relation to taxation must be kept secret.[21] Confidentiality is essential for the willingness of taxpayers to give all the necessary information. It is very important for the DTA that taxpayers know that the information they give to the tax inspector will not be used for other government ends.[22] In many countries, the tax authorities have a legal obligation of confidentiality.[23] Tax Divisions of the Dutch courts have the same legal obligation as the DTA.

However, legal proceedings take place in open court. According to Article 6 of the European Convention on Human Rights (ECHR) everyone is entitled to a public hearing before a court and, in addition, the court must deliver its ruling in public. Especially in criminal trials, the role of the press is very important. Newspapers are informed automatically about cases which are brought to court. In this way, the press can select the cases which they want to pay attention to. However, the right to privacy imposes a limitation. If decisions are published, on the web for example, they are anonymous to a certain

---

19. See e.g. K.L.M. van Mens and R. Steenman, Naar een generaal pardon voor zwartspaarders? *(Towards a general pardon for undeclared savers?)*, NJB 2003, p. 2.
20. An example is the Belgian fiscal amnesty of 2004. The justifiability of this 'One Time Voluntary Tax Return' (De Eenmalige Bevrijdende Aangifte), law of 31 December 2003, caused a lot of discussion. People could disclose their underreported income at a rate between 6 and 9%. They also received criminal immunity.
21. See Art. 67 GTA.
22. Exceptions need a legal basis.
23. See, for example, the UK Official Secrets Act 1989. In general, Duncan Bentley (ed.), Taxpayers' Rights, An International Perspective, Adelaide, Australia, 1998.

extent. Because the hearings are public and the press is informed which trial is going on, however, those who are interested will be aware of the suspect's identity.

How does this right to a public hearing and the role of publicity relate to the obligation of secrecy for the Tax Divisions? In accordance with Article 6 ECHR, Article 121 of the Dutch Constitution states that trials shall be held in public and that judgments shall be pronounced in public. In this context, the General Administrative Law Act (hereafter GALA) contains a similar provision for all administrative judgments.[24] Normal fiscal cases and fiscal fine cases are in principle always public, but the fiscal secrecy provision imposes limitations.[25] In practice, other people than the taxpayer and the tax inspector do not know which fiscal trials take place, who is involved in them, and when the hearings will be held. In addition, it is the general impression that judges in tax cases do not even pronounce their verdicts publicly. The reason is simple: no audience. Only the tax inspector and the taxpayer involved can be present, but normally they are informed in another way, by phone or mail. Only if the press was informed beforehand about the date of pronunciation of the judgment, a journalist present can hear the conclusion of the court and the name of the taxpayer, but that is hardly ever the case.[26]

Concluding, although Article 6 ECHR contains the right to a public hearing and the public pronunciation of the judgment in fiscal fines cases, both actually happen in complete secrecy and are inaccessible for other persons. The public nature of taxation cases is completely different from criminal cases. From the perspective of compliance, no publication has the same effect as the inspector's obligation of confidentiality: it contributes to the willingness of the taxpayers to cooperate with the tax inspector. The opposite is the case where criminal law is involved. Publication about a criminal case will strengthen the public prosecutor's position in the eyes of the public and increase the general preventive effect. In terms of shame management, it could be said that criminal law is aimed at shaming and at damaging someone's reputation, while tax law is intended for the reverse situation, namely, avoiding public shaming and damage to a person's reputation.

---

24. Art. 8:67 and Art. 8:78 GALA.
25. Art. 67 GTA.
26. See also M.W.C. Feteris, Taxpayer Protection and Tax Fines, in: Dirk Albregtse and Henk van Arendonk (eds.), Taxpayer Protection in the European Union, Deventer, 1998, p. 71; also M.W.C. Feteris, Fiscale bestuurlijke boetes en het recht op een behoorlijk proces *(Fiscal administrative fines and the right to a fair and due process)*, Deventer, 2002, p. 410.

3.2. *Improving general compliance by punishing VIPs and tax advisers*

As shown above, the DTA has become aware of the importance of the tool of media publicity in recent years. This does not mean that the DTA exercises less restraint regarding its secrecy obligation than before. However, in the latest Dutch *Report, Settlement and Prosecution guidelines* (*Aanmeldings-, Transactie- en Vervolgingsrichtlijnen*, hence RSP guidelines), the DTA has created a situation in which it can benefit from the different approach of the Public Prosecution Service to publicity.[27] The guidelines contain the report, settlement and prosecution rules, agreed between the DTA and the Public Prosecution Service. In case of serious tax fraud, the tax inspector will transfer the case to the public prosecutor instead of imposing a fine himself. This also implies a transition from secrecy to publicity. The most recent version of the RSP guidelines explicitly refers to the compliance approach. On one hand, the guidelines mention the approach to compliant taxpayers: to help them meet their tax obligations as much as possible. On the other hand, and this is the real subject of the guidelines, they define how the DTA and the Public Prosecution Service should deal with non-compliant taxpayers. The most important reason for changing the guidelines was the wish to concentrate the use of criminal law on criminal cases with a serious social impact. The purpose is to obtain a strong, generally preventive effect: to deter other persons from committing tax fraud. Therefore, the current RSP guidelines express the willingness to follow through on non-compliance: to prosecute severe fraud cases and, consequently, bring them to the attention of the media. It is evident that publicity is an indispensable weapon to achieve this goal of shame management.[28] It is also clear that stigmatization of the wrongdoer plays a pivotal role here.[29]

An important question is whether the strong, generally preventive or deterrent effect can be obtained. According to John Braithwaite and Gilbert Geis, 'general deterrence refers to the consequences of a conviction for those who are not caught, but who through observing the penalties imposed on others decide not to violate the law'.[30] In their opinion, this deterrent effect is doubtful with traditional crime, but may well be strong with corporate crime.

---

27. Aanmeldings-, Transactie- en Vervolgingsrichtlijnen voor fiscale delicten en douanedelicten (*Notifications-, Transaction-, and Prosecution guidelines for fiscal offences and customs offences*) 2006, DGB2005/6956M, Netherlands Government Gazette (Stcrt.) No. 247.
28. See also John Braithwaite, Markets in Vice, Markets in Virtue, Oxford, 2005, p. 181.
29. About stigmatization, see John Braithwaite and Valerie Braithwaite, Shame, Shame Management and Regulation, in: Eliza Ahmed, Nathan Harris, John Braithwaite, and Valerie Braithwaite, Shame Management through Reintegration, Cambridge, 2001, pp. 4 and 39.
30. John Braithwaite and Gilbert Geis, On Theory and Action for Corporate Crime Control, in: Neal Shover and John Paul Wright (eds.), Crimes of Privilege, Readings in White-Collar Crime, Oxford, 2001, p. 371.

They report that the consensus among scholars is overwhelmingly optimistic as regards general deterrence concerning corporate crime. In my opinion, tax fraud can be seen as a variety of corporate crime.

The RSP guidelines indicate that especially VIPs who commit tax fraud must be prosecuted. Soccer-players and pop musicians must therefore be careful. This is also the case with people who play an important role in politics, like Mayors or Members of Parliament. Such people have a greater chance to be prosecuted for tax fraud than ordinary people who have committed a similar tax fraud. In the current guidelines, the status of the taxpayer unmistakably plays a far more prominent role than before. It is probably not an exaggeration to presume this is an important element of the compliance strategy of the DTA.[31] If well-known people are convicted of tax fraud and the media bring the news, this will greatly damage their reputation. According to the DTA and the Public Prosecution Service, this will strengthen the voluntary compliance of the majority of taxpayers and increase the deterrent effect to those taxpayers who feel more or less attracted to tax fraud.

However, the aspect of being a VIP must be dealt with carefully. The principles of equality and proportionality must especially be taken into account. In my opinion, being a well-known or important person is an insufficient reason to prosecute someone if ordinary people in otherwise similar situations would not have been prosecuted. That would be like going back to the Middle Ages: putting someone in the pillory. The quality of being a VIP is not specific enough. Particularly, it is important whether the VIP possesses a position of trust in society, such as Members of Parliament or high officials. By committing tax fraud, these people betray the citizens' trust. The citizens are the stakeholders and their interest is impaired by the tax fraud of such VIPs. In such serious cases, it can be justified to damage someone's reputation in light of the relevant legal principles.

The RSP guidelines also mention tax advisers as a category of people to prosecute. In my opinion, this has to do with the functioning of the DTA directly. Tax advisers are not only important to their clients, but also to the DTA itself. For the DTA, reliability of tax advisers is crucial. They fill in the tax returns for their clients and develop tax planning ideas for them. Nowadays, this has become even more important, because tax law is so complicated and detailed that, very often, taxpayers rely completely on their tax adviser for their tax affairs.[32] If a tax adviser disappoints the DTA's trust by committing fraud or by advising his clients how to commit fraud, this is a very serious matter. He breaks the law and violates the confidence of the DTA. Besides, he does not only damage the interests of the DTA, but at the

---

31. This is, of course, also the case for the Public Prosecution Service.
32. See about this subject John Braithwaite, Markets in Vice, Markets in Virtue, Oxford, 2005, p. 52.

same time he damages the interests, prestige and reputation of the fiscal profession as well.[33] In a certain way, prosecution of a tax adviser who committed tax fraud or advised others how to do it, is in a direct line with the disciplinary committees of the organizations of tax advisers. It is out of the question that a fraudulent tax adviser also violates the professional standards of his organization. It should be made legally possible for a court to publish its judgment as an additional punishment as well.[34]

It would go too far to *automatically* publish fiscal criminal judgments, let alone judgments concerning fines imposed by the DTA, as is more or less the case in Ireland.[35] In my opinion, such an approach is too simple and too rough: it is not appropriate in every case. The principle of proportionality demands a more detailed scrutiny of the specific circumstances of the case. Besides, the method of the pillory must not be revived in this way. A compliance strategy also offers more refined methods to achieve its goal. In her contribution, Valerie Braithwaite has pointed out that punishment can be counterproductive in certain situations.

4.   SETTLEMENTS

4.1.   An example

The fate of Arthur Andersen, once the biggest accounting firm in the world, is well-known. It collapsed in 2002 in the wake of the Enron scandal. Last year, KPMG US escaped this fate in the nick of time. At the end of August 2005, it reached a settlement with Attorney General Alberto Gonzales. The firm admitted to wrongdoing, thus sidestepping a criminal indictment that might have put it out of business.[36] Gonzales remarked:

> 'KPMG – one of the largest accounting firms in the country – has admitted to criminal wrongdoing in the largest-ever tax shelter fraud. Over a six-year period, KPMG and allegedly nine defendants deliberately perpetrated a scheme that generated more than 11 billion of phoney tax losses. That scheme enabled wealthy KPMG clients to evade billions of dollars in taxes they owed on income and capital gains. While the firm was earning at least 115 million dollars in fees by defrauding government tax collectors, ordinary citizens were stuck with the bill. KPMG has been charged with conspiracy to defraud the IRS. However, the Justice Depart-

---

33. In a different sense, see B.J.G.L. Jaeger, *Een kleine stille revolutie in het fiscaal strafrecht (A small and quiet revolution in tax criminal law)*, WFR 2006/6661, p. 241.
34. See Art. 27 Dutch Criminal Code.
35. See Section 1086 of the Irish Taxes Consolidation Act 1997.
36. New York Times, 29 August 2005.

ment has agreed to defer prosecution on that charge, provided that KPMG meets a series of stringent conditions. KPMG will pay fines, restitution, and penalties that add up to 456 million dollars, cooperate fully with the Government's investigation and – perhaps most important – they will establish a compliance and ethics program to help prevent such wrongdoing in the future. In addition, nine individuals who participated in this scheme by allegedly creating fraudulent tax shelters, preparing false tax returns, and hiding their actions from the IRS have been indicted. They will be prosecuted to the fullest extent of the law.'

He continued:

'Today's announcement reflects the reality that the conviction of an organization can affect innocent workers and others associated with the organization, and can even have an impact on the national economy. The Department's longstanding principles take account of such collateral consequences of prosecuting an organization.'[37]

KPMG US was relieved and expressed regret about its past tax practices. It announced that it would also implement elevated standards for its tax business.[38] KPMG US thus escaped the fate of Arthur Andersen.[39] It was given the opportunity to get rid of its old image as an aggressive tax planner and can make a contribution to effectively implementing the ethical taxation standards.[40] In terms of shame management, it was given the opportunity to reintegrate.[41] In this context, it is noteworthy that, in 2004, KPMG US had published a discussion paper called *Tax in the Boardroom*. The role of the compliance strategy of tax authorities is prominent in the paper. Besides, it suggests that managing directors are responsible for setting out the philosophical and ethical principles and concludes that 'being *tax compliant* is a state to which companies should aspire and [which] boards should seek to achieve'.[42] Both documents, the settlement with Attorney General Gonzales and that discussion paper, not only illustrate an important development in thinking of one of the big firms, but also the broader, current discussion about the ethical aspects of taxation.

---

37. Prepared remarks of Attorney General Alberto R. Gonzales at the Press Conference Regarding KPMG Corporate Fraud Case, at <http://www.usdoj.gov/ag/speeches/2005/082905agkpgm corpfraud.htm>.
38. <www.us.kpmg.com>.
39. This incident only concerns KPMG US.
40. See John Braithwaite, Markets in Vice, Markets in Virtue, Oxford, 2005, p. 189, who discusses the Arthur Andersen case in a comparable way.
41. See John Braithwaite and Valerie Braithwaite, Shame, Shame Management and Regulation, in: Eliza Ahmed, Nathan Harris, John Braithwaite and Valerie Braithwaite, Shame Management through Reintegration, Cambridge, 2001, p. 39.
42. Tax in the Boardroom, A Discussion Paper, <www.us.kpmg.com>.

4.2. *Legal instruments for restoring tax compliance*

In the KPMG US case, the authorities distinguished between the real offenders and the company they belonged to. While the offenders were prosecuted, the company was given the opportunity to reintegrate. Would such an approach of integration also be possible in the Netherlands? Are there legal instruments available to the DTA and the Public Prosecution to restore compliant behaviour as the IRS and the Attorney General did in the KPMG case? The discussion of these instruments must be seen against the background that all that happens in the sphere of fiscal fines remains secret, in any case practically, in contrast to criminal cases, where the press has access to hearings and judgments.

4.2.1. *Compromise between tax inspector and taxpayer*

If the tax inspector wants to impose a fine, he is allowed to reach a compromise with the taxpayer about the amount of the fine. According to the case law of the Dutch Supreme Court, the taxpayer is also bound by the compromise.[43] In my opinion, it is also allowed to agree to other conditions, such as to file the tax return correctly, or to improve the bookkeeping. These two examples have a strictly legal character. They are legal obligations, laid down in the tax law (GTA).[44] However, I think it is also possible to create other conditions, which are related to the aim of promoting compliance. For example, the taxpayer entrepreneur has to take an integrity course. Another condition could be to hire an expert in business ethics and tax compliance to introduce and establish a best practice in the company. A model of a fiscal corporate governance code could be very useful in such situations.

Such conditions could be linked to the condition that, if such compliance conditions are not met, an additional fine will have to be paid.[45] This could be done by giving extension of payment for a part of the total amount of the fine. After a period of good behaviour, this part of the fine could be remitted.

If the DTA should consider introducing such integrity elements, coordination is a prerequisite, in my opinion. It must be dealt with under the supervision of the management of the DTA, not of an individual tax inspector. On the basis of experiences with such compromises, guidelines would have to be developed in order to handle subsequent cases. In that way, the DTA could strike the proper balance between rules and discretion.[46]

---

43. HR 9 October 1996, BNB 1997/53.
44. See also P.J. Wattel's annotation of BNB 1997/53.
45. An important advantage for the taxpayer is that after a compromise has been agreed on and the inspector has executed his part of the compromise, i.e. has imposed the agreed fine, the prosecutor cannot start a new case, because of the 'una via' principle (Art. 69a GTA). About this subject, see also W.E.C.A Valkenburg, Fiscaal straf- en strafprocesrecht, Deventer, 2001, pp. 250-252.
46. Kenneth Culp Davis, Discretionary Justice, Baton Rouge, 1969, p. 44.

4.2.2. *Transaction offered by the management of the DTA*

In more serious cases which meet the requirements of the RSP guidelines, the DTA management could be of the opinion that it is not fitting to prosecute a taxpayer. If that is the case, the DTA management can offer the taxpayer a *transaction*. In Article 76 of the GTA, the various conditions are enumerated.[47] The most important conditions are the payment of an amount of money to the maximum amount of the fine, and the fulfilment of a tax obligation which has not yet been fulfilled. The RSP guidelines explicitly indicate that the DTA management must strive to impose a higher fine than would have been imposed by the tax inspector.

Principally, the taxpayer has the freedom to accept or to reject the transaction. The European Court of Human Rights (ECHR) decided: 'absence of constraint is at all events one of the conditions to be satisfied; this much is dictated by an international instrument founded on freedom and the rule of law'.[48] In practice, the taxpayer has to make his decision under the threat that he will probably be prosecuted if he rejects the transaction. It is clear that the element of a public criminal trial will play an important role in his deliberations. The transaction is a matter between the taxpayer and the DTA alone, whereas prosecution is a public affair. This means it is his last chance to prevent being shamed in public.

On the other hand, there is also a limitation for the DTA. Article 76 GTA enumerates all conditions which the DTA management is permitted to make. It is a closed system, so it is not allowed to agree to things that further the compliance of the taxpayer, as is the case with a compromise. For example, the DTA cannot demand that the taxpayer takes measures to enhance the ethical behaviour of himself and of his enterprise in tax matters, but the transaction can still be very useful in a compliance strategy. It makes it possible to distinguish between the people who committed the tax fraud and the organization to which they belong. The KPMG case can partly serve as an example. KPMG agreed to a settlement with the authorities and paid USD 456 million. In this way, KPMG was given the opportunity to restore its reputation, not only to the authorities but also to the public.[49]

4.2.3. *Conditional decision not to prosecute*

Although the public prosecutor is not allowed to make a fiscal settlement, he can do something similar: the conditional decision not to prosecute (*voorwaardelijk sepot*). The public prosecutor promises not to prosecute, provided

---

47. See also Art. 74 Dutch Criminal Code. The provision of the fiscal transaction of Art. 76 GTA excludes the general transaction of Art. 74 Dutch Criminal Code.
48. ECHR 27 February 1980, No. 6903/75, NJ 1980, 561.
49. KPMG also reached a $225 million settlement with approximately 275 former clients who had used its tax shelters.

the suspect fulfils certain conditions. He is not bound to the legal conditions laid down in Article 76 of the GTA or Article 74 of the Dutch Criminal Code. He can also impose other conditions. In practice, this conditional decision has been used to give instructions concerning the suspect's behaviour.[50] A well-known example is a course to be followed by drivers who are addicted to alcohol, in order to kick the habit.

This provides opportunities for use in fiscal fraud cases. For example, the public prosecutor could demand that the enterprise establish a compliance and ethics programme to help prevent such wrongdoing in the future, as happened in the KPMG case. The conditional decision has an additional value in terms of a compliance strategy over and above the settlement mentioned before.

4.2.4. Punishment order

Finally, in the near future, the legal provisions in the GTA and the Criminal Code concerning the transaction will be changed. Instead of *transaction* the law will refer to *punishment order*.[51] In general, the public prosecutor will have a better grip on the fiscal transaction.[52] If, for example, the taxpayer does not consent to the punishment order imposed by the DTA management, he can lodge an appeal with the public prosecutor. In this framework, two remarks have to be made. First, it is important that the bill proposes the same conditions as Article 76 GTA does now. This is in contrast with the proposed provision in the Criminal Code in the same bill.[53] The latter provision will be extended with the possibility to give instructions concerning the suspect's behaviour. In this respect, the practice of 'the conditional decision not to prosecute' will be codified in the Criminal Code, but this possibility will not be laid down in Article 76 GTA.[54]

In my opinion, from the perspective of a tax compliance strategy, omitting this possibility from the fiscal provision would be a shame. It is therefore recommended to amend the proposed fiscal provision in order to make it possible for the DTA management to make such behavioural conditions.

A second recommendation concerns publicity. Both the criminal and the fiscal provision contain an article regarding publicity (Art. 257h). On request, the public prosecutor and the management of the DTA give a copy of the punishment order to anyone who asks for it. A copy can be refused to protect the interests of the suspect or other persons mentioned in the punishment

---

50. See Dutch Parliamentary Documents 2004/05, 29 849, No. 3, p. 25.
51. So-called 'strafbeschikking' *(Punishment order)*.
52. See further G.J.M.E. de Bont, De fiscale strafbeschikking: een ongewenste nouveauté?! *(The tax punishment order: an undesired nouveauté?!)*, WFR 2005/6648, p. 1553.
53. Art. 257a Dutch Criminal Code.
54. Dutch Parliamentary Documents 2004/05, 29 849, No. 3, p. 24.

order. This is at the discretion of officials of both organizations. If the management refuses to give a copy, the applicant can lodge a complaint with the public prosecutor. In this respect, the DTA is obliged to adjust its policy to that of the public prosecutor. Additionally, it underlines that the fiscal punishment order also belongs to the sphere of prosecution and not of taxation. It does not belong to the realm of secrecy of taxation, but to that of publicity of prosecution.

In this line of action, it would also be appropriate if the DTA management or the public prosecutor were to publish press releases about important fiscal punishment orders of their own accord.[55] To make this possible for fiscal orders the relevant guidelines would have to be changed.[56] It could be regulated in the same way as in the case of orders made by the Public Prosecution Service.

In conclusion, both the DTA and the Public Prosecution Service in the Netherlands have legal means at their disposal to take steps similar to those taken in the KPMG case. If the DTA and the Public Prosecution Service put these means into practice, this will support the DTA's compliance strategy.

5.   CONCLUSION

Since the early 1990s, the DTA has embraced the compliance strategy. Among other things, it implies that different kinds of taxpayers need different kinds of approaches. This is also the case within the category of non-compliant taxpayers. With regard to this category, the DTA has differentiated its approach. Sometimes the DTA uses the tool of persuasion, sometimes of deterrence, and sometimes a combination of the two. In these situations, media publicity plays an important role. Against the background of its legal obligation of secrecy, the DTA applies media publicity as an instrument to cope with the non-compliant behaviour of taxpayers. It can be qualified as an example of shame management.

As for voluntary disclosure, which is a legal right for taxpayers in the Netherlands, the DTA uses the strategy of communication with the taxpayers in a general way. It actively informs taxpayers about the disclosure rules through the media. In the 'bank accounts' project hundreds of wealthy taxpayers voluntarily disclosed, bringing in an additional tax revenue amounting to €170 million. The publicity campaign unmistakably contributed to this

---

55. See the proposed Art. 257h of the Criminal Code and the Guidelines High Transactions and Transaction in Special Cases (*Aanwijzing hoge transacties en transacties in bijzondere zaken*), Stcrt. 2002, 39.
56. This concerns both the RSP guidelines and the Guidelines High Transactions and Transaction in Special Cases.

result in a substantial way. As a result of the campaign, non-compliant tax-payers became more aware of the choice either to persevere in their behaviour or to come forward to disclose.

The same project also shows that the DTA must operate very carefully on the legal level. For example, because of a lack of evidence, all more serious cases of tax fraud in the 'bank account' project had to be dropped by the Public Prosecution Service. This raised the unwelcome question of whether crime does pay after all. The DTA should avoid such a backfire effect in the future, for example, by making a thorough ex ante evaluation of the legal aspects of a case.

The second situation is where the DTA and the Public Prosecution Service have to choose between either imposing a fine on the taxpayer or prosecuting him. The duty of secrecy in taxation also plays an important role in this situation. If the tax inspector imposes a fine, he is not allowed to make this public. If the taxpayer lodges an appeal, there is only a theoretical possibility that the judgment will become public. The opposite is the case when criminal law is involved: in that sphere publicity is very important. Article 6 ECHR demands a public hearing and the public pronunciation of the judgment. Besides, public prosecutors use the media to strengthen their case.

According to DTA guidelines and guidelines of the Public Prosecution Service the tax inspector will transfer cases of serious tax fraud to the public prosecutor. In this context, the most recent version of the guidelines aims at a general deterrent effect. Among scholars it is believed that this effect is strong in case of white-collar crime. In this context, the guidelines indicate that especially VIPs and tax advisers have a larger chance to be prosecuted for tax fraud. In terms of shame management, it uses stigmatization of VIPs now in order to deter other taxpayers from committing tax fraud in the future.

This policy must be dealt with carefully. Being a VIP, for example, is too vague a reason to prosecute someone. It is crucial whether a VIP possesses a position of trust in society, for example, such as Members of Parliament or high officials. If such a person betrays this trust by committing tax fraud, it could be justified to do some damage to his reputation.

The third and final situation concerns the case in which there are reasons for distinguishing between the people who committed the serious tax fraud and the company or firm to which they belong. The KPMG US case is an example of this situation. The authorities could consider offering the organization the possibility to reintegrate and to restore compliant behaviour. In the framework of a compromise, the tax inspector and the organization could agree on both the amount of the fine and on establishing a fiscal corporate governance code.

In more serious cases which meet the requirements of the RSP guidelines, the Dutch public prosecutor could make a similar proposal as an essential element of his conditional decision not to prosecute. In the future, the public prosecutor will have the legal ability to do this in the form of a punishment order. At the moment, the DTA management has no legal means to make such a proposal in serious criminal cases. According to the pending bill concerning the punishment order, this will not change in the future. It would be a good thing if the Dutch legislator decides to amend the bill in order to make this possible.

In conclusion, in dealing with tax offenders, the DTA and the Public Prosecution Service have legal and other means at their disposal. The compliance strategy offers an appropriate framework to apply these means in a responsible way. In the case of tax offenders, the strategy makes it possible to distinguish between different kinds of offenders and to employ deterrence or persuasion to reach its goal. It is never too late to become a compliant taxpayer again.

8 | Culture change in regulatory institutions: from command-and-control to responsive regulation in taxation administration

Jenny Job, Andrew Stout and Rachael Smith[1]

1. Introduction

Scholars of taxation tend to focus on the translation of policy into law, the interpretation of the law, and what taxation means for the economic wellbeing of the country and its citizens. Less examined is a more practical aspect of taxation law and policy – its administration. One largely overlooked and poorly understood part of taxation administration is regulatory and organizational culture, an aspect of the implementation of law and policy highlighted by Meidinger (1987). Knowledge of regulatory and organizational cultures assists understanding of how law and policy work in practice (Meidinger 1987).

This article focuses on the implementation of taxation law and policy by the taxation administrations of Australia, New Zealand and East Timor. We choose these three countries because they are currently implementing responsive regulation – a move away from the 'traditional' command-and-control style of regulating taxation law and policy. While we examine taxa-

1. Centre for Tax System Integrity, Research School of Social Sciences, Australian National University, Canberra ACT 0200, Australia (e-mail: jenny.job@anu.edu.au). We are grateful to the reviewers for their helpful comments and suggestions on a previous draft of this chapter. The views contained in this article are representative of the authors only. The publishing of this article does not constitute an endorsement of or any other expression of opinion by the Australian Taxation Office, New Zealand Inland Revenue or the East Timor Revenue Service.

tion administration in three different nations, the focus is on regulatory and organizational culture. This chapter is not an examination of the advantages and disadvantages of responsive regulation, or a judgment of its worth. Also, we will not discuss the impact of this change on compliance with tax law and policy. We start from the position that two taxation administrations have already decided to adopt a responsive regulatory approach, and another is considering whether to adopt this approach.

The aim of this article is to examine Meidinger's views on the importance of culture in social change within regulatory institutions. To do this we will use taxation administration to explore organizational culture and the introduction of new ideas into organizations by translation rather than diffusion, as Latour (1986) and Sinclair (1991) suggest. We highlight that regulatory and bureaucratic cultures are different to those in private enterprise, but that success in the adoption of new ways of working necessitates acknowledgement of different occupational cultures within an organizational culture. In explaining the shift to a responsive regulatory style in these taxation administrations, we will explore: what is meant by culture; why these taxation administrations chose to adopt a responsive regulatory approach; the circumstances which necessitated a change in the way they had traditionally regulated; how they made the change; and the challenges they have faced in trying to implement a responsive regulatory approach to taxation administration.[2] We conclude by agreeing with Meidinger that consideration of culture is important in making social change in regulatory organizations, and suggest that organizational cultures which encourage translation of new ideas are those which most successfully effect culture change.

2.   CULTURE: THE WAY WE SEE THINGS

Culture is 'a way of looking at things' (Meidinger 1987:356), but it also comprises behaviour – 'it is what they enact in their daily lives' (Meidinger 1987:361). Culture serves a purpose, providing 'a necessary medium for social interaction that both constrains group behaviour and creates possibilities for new forms of social interaction' (Meidinger 1987:363). There are many

---

2.   As taxation administrators, we have been personally involved in a range of ways in implementing the change to responsive regulation in not only the three taxation administrations being examined in this paper, but have also supported staff in taxation administrations in two additional countries in understanding, adapting and adopting responsive regulation to their specific needs. Our work has involved development of a tax-specific model of responsive regulation in 1997, development of training programmes for revenue administration staff, conducting information and training sessions about responsive regulation for revenue administration staff, surveying tax employees on their perceptions of and attitudes towards responsive regulation and its impact on their work, and analysis of the results of these surveys.

types of culture – national, organizational and occupational cultures – which are different in terms of values and practices (Hofstede 1994), and which merge and compete in regulatory domains (Meidinger 1987). The focus in this paper is on organizational culture which sits within the national culture and includes occupational cultures.

While the public and newcomers to an organization are aware of its 'look and feel', organizational culture goes far deeper than this symbolic outer layer (Hofstede 1994; Schein 2004; Sinclair 1991). Hofstede (1994: 183) maintains it is the *'shared perceptions of daily practices … [which are] the core of an organization's culture…'*. It also includes patterns of behaviour which staff regard as normal and meaningful, and which reflect a deeper value system (Schein 2004). The implementation of law is affected by the beliefs people have about the way things are done in an organization (Deal and Kennedy 1988; Schein 2004; Sinclair 1991).

Organizational culture is affected by many factors including the function of the organization, occupational identities, and, in this case, the demands of bureaucracy. The normal patterns of behaviour within an organization are based on assumptions or values and beliefs about the purpose of the organization, with which staff identify (Schein 2004; Sinclair 1991). The distinct nature of its function – it 'takes' from the community so that other government organizations can 'give' – means that a taxation administration's view of the world is different from most other government organizations. The focus is on the revenue.

Many public servants bring with them their own professional or occupational identity, which holds its own values (Sinclair 1991). Taxation administrations comprise a wide range of occupations, such as those who identify as auditors, lawyers, economists, information technology and human resources specialists, and so on.

Despite its different function, many practices of a taxation administration are similar to other government organizations. The way regulators of tax law and policy look at the world is in part determined by their role as public or civil servants, whose attitudes towards their work are different to those in private enterprise (Sinclair 1991). Major behavioural drivers of public servants are their strong identification with the public interest and belief that their work is for the public benefit (Sinclair 1991).

The public service, whether it is being developed (as it is in East Timor), or is long established (as in Australia and New Zealand), emerges from Weber's nineteenth century innovation of rational bureaucracy (Hughes 1994). Bureaucracy demands certain behaviours from the official: *reliability, strict devotion to regulations, discipline, methodical performance of routine activities, conformity* and *literal adherence to rules* (Merton 1939).

Trained to work within the rigidity of bureaucracy, officials with regulatory responsibilities have favoured a similarly rigid style of regulation. Traditionally, the dominant strategy in compliance management is deterrence (Aalders and Wilthagen 1997; Dodd and Hutter 2000; Parker and Braithwaite 2003:130; Shover, Clelland and Lynxwiler 1986). The deterrence approach assumes that taxpayers are self-interested rational actors who take advantage of opportunities to maximize their own outcomes. Based on deterrence theory, command-and-control regulation advocates precise and narrowly drawn rules, threatened penalties for non-compliance, punishment for violators, and takes a one-size-fits-all approach (Bardach and Kagan 1982; Dodd and Hutter 2000; Grabosky 1995; Job and Honaker 2003:113; Reiss 1984). It has its advantages in large bureaucracies as Sparrow (2000:37) points out:

'A strong defence against litigation, a strong base from which to pull back, external support, a strong sense of mission, internal cohesion, and an effective mechanism for producing consistency …, it helps to prevent corruption …[and] lessens or eliminates the competitive advantage gained through non-compliance, by imposing financial penalties and requiring corrective actions.'

Alongside these attractions are substantial drawbacks, exacerbated in circumstances where the limits to both the law and rules become apparent (Sparrow 2000:36). The capacity to oversee and monitor the population is closely scrutinized from a cost perspective in new public management philosophy (Hughes 1994). Effectiveness may also be questionable because government has a limited capacity for *sustained oversight*, and deterrence effects are short-term (Braithwaite 2005; Braithwaite 2003b; Braithwaite and Braithwaite 2001:483; Parker and Braithwaite 2003; Scott 2004:483). Some have questioned whether a traditional deterrence approach in taxation actually deters at all (Grasmick and Bursik 1990; Klepper and Nagin 1989). There is also doubt about its ability to either improve compliance or to 'rehabilitate'. For example, prosecutions and fines for non-lodgement of tax returns in Australia only had a short-term effect, with reduced lodgement rates being noted in subsequent years (Williams 2001). Rather than rehabilitating, a deterrence approach may de-legitimize government authority, with perceived breaches of procedural justice and heavy-handed treatment encouraging resistance (Murphy 2003; Wenzel 2005). Regulatory culture may produce community perceptions of inconsistent, unfair or overly harsh administration (Sparrow 2000). For example, there were complaints about Australian Taxation Office (ATO) inconsistency in making and implementing tax rulings resulting in businesses *shop[ping] around* ATO offices for a preferred ruling (Kavanagh 1997).

3.   SEEING THINGS DIFFERENTLY

During the 1980s, a shift began in the public service in the western world from administration to management, with the expectation that results would be achieved in a fast, efficient and innovative manner (Hughes 1994). These public sector reforms occurred at the same time as challenges to regulatory style. Disillusionment with a command-and-control style of regulation promoted interest in cooperative compliance, a style of regulation that relied less on coercion and obedience and more on education and persuasion. Cooperative compliance was regarded with scepticism by regulators who were operating at the coalface where intransigent non-compliance was frequently encountered, but it became popular rhetoric among the advocates of deregulation.

To move beyond the long-term intellectual debate about *strong state regulation* versus *deregulation*, Ayres and Braithwaite (1992) offered the notion of responsive regulation. This was based on the idea that government regulation should choose when to intervene and when not to intervene, adopting a philosophy of being responsive to *industry structure, the differing motivations of regulated actors* and *industry conduct* (Ayres and Braithwaite 1992:3-4). Responsive regulation focuses on the behaviour of those being regulated and the behaviour of the regulator. Being responsive means altering one's own behaviour to respond to different circumstances. To some extent, street-level bureaucrats are responsive as they use their discretion to make 'policy' when the law they are given to implement is unclear (Lipsky 1980).

The coordinated shifts from administration to management and from command-and-control regulation to responsive regulation both represent change in behaviour and culture, transforming the public sector and its relationship with government and society (Hughes 1994:66). While many think of regulation as ensuring the following of rules, in its broadest sense, 'regulation means influencing the flow of events ... [and] ... means much the same thing as governance' (Parker & Braithwaite, 2003:119). This distinction is important because the behaviour and practices of those who follow rules are different from the behaviour and practices of those who influence events.

In the next two sections we will describe the circumstances which challenged the taxation administrations of Australia, New Zealand and East Timor and encouraged them to consider changing their normal patterns of behaviour.

4.   REFORMING THE 'TRADITIONAL' BY ADOPTING RESPONSIVE
      REGULATION

Australia and New Zealand made the shift to responsive regulation because
of community complaint and government investigation into their taxation
administrations. East Timor wanted a fresh approach to its management of
government systems, and is exploring the appropriateness of responsive regulation in the setting up of the country's new taxation system.

Responsive regulation has usually been applied in small regulatory communities where encounters with inspectors occur face-to-face, as in regulation of the environment, nursing homes and occupational health and safety
standards (Braithwaite 2002; Braithwaite and Grabosky 1985; Gunningham
and Grabosky 1998). So why would you use responsive regulation in a large-
scale regulatory setting like taxation where the number of people regulated
may go up to a few million, making face-to-face interaction the exception
rather than the norm?

Responsive regulation is very useful when compliance is not automatic,
simple and straightforward (Braithwaite 2006 forthcoming). This is very
much the case with taxation law and policy. Responsive regulation provides
the means by which positive reinforcement, through providing support,
acknowledging achievements and recognizing effort, can be blended with
enforcement practices. This is not necessarily the way taxation administrations have regulated taxation law and policy. However, there were valid reasons why these three taxation administrations considered changing their
'traditional' regulatory culture as we will explain below.

5.   ORGANIZATIONAL CULTURES UNDER SIEGE

During the last thirty years, citizens of several countries have voiced their
discontent with their taxation systems (Aaron and Slemrod 2004; Job and
Honaker 2003). Taxation administrations in the English-speaking democra-
cies have been plagued by community challenges to their legitimacy. For
years, the Internal Revenue Service in the United States was accused of being
'rude, abusive, or unhelpful' and of offering a poor and deteriorating service
(Job and Honaker 2003:2). More recently, accusations have been made about
the overuse and abuse of powers, and lack of integrity of the Australian Taxation Office (ATO) and New Zealand Inland Revenue (NZIR) (Evening Post
1999; Job and Honaker 2003; The New Zealand Herald 1999; The Press 1999).
For example, in Australia:

'[a]ccusations of excessive and unfair use of power ... were balanced with
claims that the Tax Office was "out of touch" and "lacked understanding" of

"commercial reality"…There were suggestions that the Tax Office's actions were "morally wrong"… and that poor Tax office use of penalties "threatened the integrity of the tax system". (Job & Honaker, 2003:112).

From the 1970s, challenges to the legitimacy of taxation law and policy in Australia gained momentum through the use of tax planning arrangements by the wealthy and large firms to avoid tax (Rawlings 2003; 2004). The marketing of tax evasion schemes was encouraged by '[a] literalist High Court [which] ruled in favour of these schemes' (The Parliament of the Commonwealth of Australia 1993:17). ATO staff were frustrated and angry, and left to deal with enormous increases in workload and complexity, but with no corresponding increase in staff (The Parliament of the Commonwealth of Australia 1993:17). The Joint Committee of Public Accounts noted that '[i]t would be reasonable to suggest that the attitude, even culture, of the ATO which emerged from the evasion scheme years was vastly different from that which existed before' (The Parliament of the Commonwealth of Australia 1993:19).

During the 1980s, the ATO began the long journey of cultural reform which included changes such as staff increases, technological upgrades, organizational restructuring, legislation change, simplification of the law, and increased community consultation and assistance (The Parliament of the Commonwealth of Australia 1993). These initial reforms to the 'look and feel' of the organization were followed by changes which went far deeper to include normal patterns of behaviour. Procedural justice (Tyler 1990) was addressed by a Taxpayers' Charter in 1997, supported by legislation, which outlined the relationship the ATO wished to have with the community (Braithwaite and Reinhart 2000). This was followed a year later by the introduction of a model for the responsive regulation of taxation (Australian Taxation Office 1998).

New Zealand faced challenges similar to Australia's in its taxation administration. In the late 1990s, NZIR's traditional deterrence-based approach attracted considerable media attention and public scrutiny. In 1999 the government established the Finance and Expenditure Committee (FEC) to examine NZIR's interactions with the community. Public submissions to the FEC focused on the negative and often prolonged interactions between NZIR, the *callous and bullying, heavy-handed and dictatorial* style of departmental staff and a *surge in complaints* to the Chief Ombudsman (The New Zealand Herald 2000). Perceptions of a lack of integrity led to questions about NZIR use of traditional command-and-control methods. The FEC enquiry condemned NZIR for its culture of fear and punishment, maintained that '[n]othing less than a culture change will do' (The New Zealand Herald 2000).

The situation in East Timor was somewhat different. The tax system was in disarray following many years of reportedly corrupt tax gathering practices, the breakdown in civil society following the independence referendum, and rampant inflation during the two-year period of the UN administration. It seemed appropriate to reinforce the principles of responsive regulation as the new tax administration sought to build new kinds of relationships; developing Meidinger's (1987:372) regulatory traditions in a responsive and restorative way with the small business proprietors of this new nation.

Given the turbulence in the East Timorese environment, and the consequent lack of documentary evidence of change, two of the authors have relied on their observations and inquiries made during a single visit to work with the street-level officials who were charged with implementing the new taxation regime, to report on the systemic changes that were being made. These two authors were told by officials of the East Timor Revenue Service (ETRS) that citizens were demanding accountability, transparency and culturally appropriate treatment. The big issue facing the ETRS is establishing a new organization that is not tainted with the corruption that was reported to two of the authors as endemic in the previous Indonesian administration. The new system is being established so that tax officials never need to physically touch tax revenues. All collections are to be paid into the banking system.

To summarize, in Australia, New Zealand and East Timor, a lack of community tolerance had developed for a blanket approach to enforcement which was harsh, inflexible and bullying. People were demanding accountability, transparency and appropriate treatment. Change had to be made which focused on organizational culture and the way tax office staff interacted with taxpayers. In the next section we describe how each administration went about making change.

6.   HOW THE CHANGE WAS MADE

6.1.   *In Australia: the Compliance Model*

In 1997, the ATO developed a Compliance Model in consultation with its Cash Economy Taskforce (Australian Taxation Office 1998). The model was based on responsive regulation and combined the work of academics on regulatory methods and practices (Ayres and Braithwaite 1992), with the motivations of the people who were regulated (Ayres and Braithwaite 1992; Braithwaite 1995; Braithwaite et al. 1994). This model, advocated that if taxpayers made mistakes through ignorance or poor financial planning and were prepared to come forward and acknowledge their mistakes, they should be helped. If they were prepared to be cooperative when anomalies were spotted, they should be assisted to put things right and move on. Persistent and consistent attention should focus on the difficult cases and the big fish, not the 'low hanging fruit'. The goals of the Compliance Model were to:

(1) understand taxpayer behaviour; (2) build a cooperative relationship with the community; (3) encourage and support compliance; (4) introduce a range of sanctions, escalating in severity and known to taxpayers so that difficulties could be settled before costs became too great for both parties; (5) reduce the time-consuming handling of complaints about procedural injustice; and (6) implement the Taxpayers' Charter (Australian Taxation Office 1998; see also Braithwaite 2003b).

To fulfil these goals, the ATO began a staff training programme which was interactive and included tax specific stories and case studies to demonstrate both poor methods and preferred methods of enforcement. For example, the innovative advanced pricing programme used for national corporations demonstrated how cooperative approaches can gain higher returns than audits (Braithwaite 2003a). As well, the principles of responsive regulation were incorporated into corporate plans, training packages for newcomers to the ATO, staff performance assessments, recruitment selection criteria, and in the day-to-day operations of the field staff.

6.2.   In New Zealand: 'The Way Forward'

In 2001, the New Zealand government appointed a new Commissioner to NZIR who was tasked with changing the way the department interacted with the community. A number of initiatives were introduced to reposition the department, including a move to responsive regulation in two stages: in 2001 through the department's strategic document 'The Way Forward'; and in 2002 with a training programme for operative staff. In the first phase, 'The Way Forward' outlined four strategic strands: (1) streamline and simplify tax processes; (2) create an environment which promotes compliance; (3) enhance staff capability; and (4) enhance the administration of social policy business. A Compliance Model, adapted from the ATO Compliance Model, formalized the department's ideas for moving from a traditional deterrence-based approach to a more responsive regulatory system.

The Compliance Model was used to support key business strategies, including communications and revenue audit strategies. Changes were made to legislation and policy, for example, new debt and hardship provisions were introduced so that staff could take the customer's personal situation into account before negotiating arrangements for tax arrears. Service delivery initiatives, such as Industry Partnership, used a responsive approach to encouraging compliance in cash-economy industries. NZIR's relationship with the community was rebuilt through more community advisory visits; participation in the whole of government approach to the delivery of services for the community; an improved ability to detect and address non-compliance; and addressing tax avoidance schemes (New Zealand Inland Revenue 2003b).

In September 2002, NZIR began a training programme on the practical application of the Compliance Model for all operative staff. NZIR staff visited the ATO to learn from their experiences in applying the Compliance Model to the regulation of tax law and policy. A training package for all service delivery team leaders was developed, based on a case study and story-telling method of learning, which introduced staff to the Compliance Model through tax and social policy case studies. This was enhanced by telling Compliance Model *success stories* from both New Zealand and Australia. The training package also aimed to start changing organizational culture to gain greater acceptance of the principles of responsive regulation.

Staff reaction to the training was mixed, with more service-oriented staff welcoming the change in direction: 'I have been waiting for this type of thing for years. It is so good for us to finally look at what the community is all about and see how we can help them' (New Zealand Inland Revenue 2003a). An internal survey highlighted an improved understanding of the benefits of responsive regulation. As one NZIR staff member said:

'It appears that revisiting the compliance and penalties regime together with IR's focus on the compliance model and Industry Partnership initiatives have made it easy for taxpayers to feel comfortable about approaching the department when they fall into debt,' (New Zealand Inland Revenue 2003a).

6.3.   *In East Timor: comprehensive training*

In East Timor, the United Nations Transitional Administration East Timor (UNTAET) arranged for a comprehensive training package for the new employees. Accounting and legal training was provided by international accounting firms and interactive responsive regulation training was provided by the ATO.

ETRS managers were introduced to responsive regulation in the form of the ATO Compliance Model. They quickly and instinctively accepted the concepts of the model, particularly the need to maximize procedural fairness, which in their eyes would reduce corruption. The responsive regulation and restorative justice principles built into the ATO Compliance Model seemed to fit with the culture of the indigenous East Timorese employees from the ETRS. The skeletal nature of the model, and the encouragement to adapt within the basic principles of the Model, allowed the locals to absorb the principles in a workshop environment and quickly apply them to local problems that were current at the time of the visit. Illustrative of this process was the workshop on developing an escalating set of sanctions for non-compliance. Although the pyramid took the same general form as the Australian and New Zealand models, the steps were distinctive, for example, working through the village hierarchy to recover individual taxpayer debt. Based on this 'local' experience the ETRS employees were readily able to demonstrate an emergent understanding of modern cooperative approaches to tax administration (Hamilton 2003).

The risks to integrity were different in each of these countries. Each focused on staff training to change organizational culture and improve their relationship with the community. In the next section, we examine the challenges these taxation administrations faced in implementing responsive regulation.

7.   CHALLENGES IN MAKING CULTURE CHANGE

While culture represents the patterns of behaviour in an organization, these patterns influence our norms, values and beliefs, and it is these which must be affected for cultural change to occur (Collins 2002:125). It is thought that senior management should influence the basic values, beliefs or assumptions of staff to make changes to organizational culture (Collins 2002: 125; Schein 2004; Sinclair 1991). This has been criticized as assuming that culture change is little more than the mental reprogramming of a receptive audience (Collins 2002: 125-126). While managers do have influence over staff values, the formality of bureaucratic processes, which favour stability rather than adaptability, and the existence of occupational subcultures with their own values and beliefs can mean resistance to top-down change (Sinclair 1991). A preferred approach to culture change within the public service is for senior management to focus on the symbolic layer of culture, and allow the organizational subcultures to focus on the inner layers by identifying existing staff values and ethics, and areas of common commitment (Sinclair 1991).

In the next part of the paper, we will describe challenges faced by these organizations in implementing responsive regulation. The most important challenges were: (1) resistance to the change; (2) meeting the legal principles of consistency and equity; (3) allowing staff discretion while avoiding corruption; (4) recognition of different occupational skill sets; and (5) the language used to present the new ideas.

7.1.   Resistance

Initial reactions to responsive regulation were similar in both the ATO and NZIR. Typical was the view that the model was common sense. However, many were annoyed and claimed that 'we already do that' (Hobson 2003; Job and Honaker 2003), a response that has been observed in other contexts (Sparrow 2000:208). Other staff believed that the use of the Compliance

Model and responsive regulation was the ATO and NZIR 'going soft' on persistent non-compliers.

In voicing their concerns, staff were beginning the translation process of adapting the new ideas about responsive regulation to their own needs – an important step in a change process (Collins 2002). Staff expressed many reasons why responsive regulation would not work in the administration of tax law and policy: a lack of legislative support, an organizational focus on outputs, fear of making mistakes and fear of change. Sparrow (2000) detailed similar reactions in his work with regulatory administrations in the United States and Britain. He highlighted comments such as: it was not legislated, there was *no time for it*, real life is too *complex*, their work is to *respond* not to stop and think about how to solve problems, new strategies were described as an *extra* and there was no *analytic or budgetary support* (Sparrow 2000:208).

Lack of legislative backing for the change was a perceived problem in each of these taxation jurisdictions. As one New Zealand officer said: 'The compliance model is not supported by legislation and therefore cannot be used in the investigations area' (New Zealand Inland Revenue 2003a). Similarly, lack of budgetary support was an issue for managers. It is easier to measure outputs than outcomes. As one New Zealand tax officer highlighted:

'So many people, including area managers, focus only on the output because of our current purchase document, so all the wonderful things like working under the Compliance Model are unachievable' (New Zealand Inland Revenue 2003a).

Sparrow (2000) observed that it is difficult to obtain commitment to a new idea across an organization when 'management fails to understand or support it'. Manager negativity or lack of manager support for the model allowed staff to adopt the same stance (Job and Honaker 2003). Some would not take the Compliance Model at face value and sat back. As one interviewee said: 'People have some resistance to the concept until such time as they personally experience it or see the results' (Hobson 2003:146). Operational staff were sensitized to how others perceived the change, and they were fearful of making mistakes in the eyes of their managers (Hogwood and Gunn 1984). Others resisted through fear of loss of skills and status (Job and Honaker 2003:120) which threatened people's identity and security. As the reality of implementing cultural change was felt, it also became clear that a command-and-control style of regulation can produce a culture of fear inside an organization which stifles innovation and creativity (Kanter 1989). As one ATO respondent said:

'Many staff are scared of change. They are scared of making a mistake. It is safe to keep doing what you have always done because you know you won't make a mistake and you won't get into trouble' (Job and Honaker 2003:121).

A major challenge in implementing culture change in a regulatory organization is to reduce fear and nurture the courage to try new ways of doing things. This requires active, genuine and visible support from the highest levels of the organization. Operational staff knew this and commented that managers had to *walk the talk*, meaning managers had to lead by example (Job and Honaker 2003:123).

It is not surprising that change to the extent described here would create *considerable discomfort for individuals* within these organizations (Meidinger 1987:360) – after all, every practice in the workplace had been marked for change or scrutiny to see if it met with responsive regulation principles.

7.2.   *Consistency and equity*

In applying the law when regulating responsively there are concerns about the observation of 'fundamental legal principles of openness, accountability, consistency, proportionality and procedural fairness' and 'the potential failure of effective and responsive regulation to security certainty, consistency and predictability in legal principles and values' (Parker and Braithwaite 2003:129). Coupled with these tensions is the reality of the large number of individual interactions which occur between taxation administrations and community members and the complexity and diversity of these interactions.

Very early, several tensions of this nature arose for the ATO and NZIR in their implementation of the Compliance Model. These included a lack of clarity about how the Compliance Model applied to different business situations, how to balance the need for consistent decision making and equity with consideration of individual circumstance, and how to develop the capability of less experienced staff in making judgments about how to apply the Model in line with standard operating procedures. Sinclair (1991:327) suggests such tensions reflect value differences between subcultures within an organization. These differences can be accommodated through identifying existing values, developing common ground and commitments which represent professionalism, such as quality service, or sound client relationships, and agreeing on trade-offs (Sinclair 1991:327).

Exploration of the value differences between different national cultures was undertaken in East Timor by two of the authors with fruitful results. ETRS staff told two of the authors, in their own words, that the responsive nature of the regulatory model fitted well for the mixture of village common law and the proposed legislative tax code for their new country. Explicitly adapting practice, within judicial and legislative guidelines, to local conditions together with using persuasion rather than legal coercion were principles that seemed to strike a chord with the local officials. It was encouraging that the fairness principles that were so important in Australia and New Zealand were equally at home in East Timor's less stable conditions.

Inside the ATO it took several years before people could see that procedural fairness (Tyler 1990), at the taxpayer interaction level, was equally important in both relatively simple telephone and letter enquiries and more complex audit or prosecution cases. Pointing out to staff that the Australian law demanded equality of treatment was not enough. People had to experience the different complexity in the human interactions and realize for themselves that procedural equity applied in both *helping* and *enforcement* cases. Readers in other jurisdictions may scoff at the simplicity of these observations, but we found them to be very real in the day-to-day implementation of responsive regulation.

To illustrate, procedural fairness came to the fore in Australia with cases involving mass-marketed tax avoidance schemes in the late 1990s (Murphy 2005). Investigation of cases involving one particular scheme commenced as responsive regulation was being introduced into the ATO. The first interactions were the old style rapid escalation direct to a demand for repayment and threat of legal action if payment was not made.

Many of the thousands of taxpayers involved had obtained professional advice on the legality of their actions and reacted harshly to the ATO's demands. As time passed and indignation levels rose on both sides, the more conciliatory approach suggested by the ATO Compliance Model eventually won through, together with the results of several test cases, to see most taxpayers repaying the tax due. Unfortunately, a minority was so offended by their initial treatment that they defied demands for payment and legal processes became necessary (Murphy 2005).

7.3.   Discretion and corruption

While the problem of discretion in the application of law is central to the design of regulatory systems and their organizations, the high level of context dependency that exists in taxation systems makes this problem particularly acute. With the introduction of responsive regulation in Australia in 1998, which advocated the use of discretion and a flexible approach, staff felt confused, uncomfortable and/or angry. Illustrative is this comment from the study of the first 18 months of responsive regulation in the ATO:

'[After having] developed a friendly relationship with a taxpayer, they can't now get tough. It's like dobbing in a mate. Before the Compliance Model, staff came from a strong position or base when going to a taxpayer's premises to do an audit. There was no personal relationship....' (Job and Honaker 2003:121).

Moving to a more responsive way of regulating challenged core values, which are the most deeply embedded and most difficult aspect of culture to change (Sinclair 1991). The above quote highlights the difficulty some staff were having with an idea which appeared to be challenging the core value that everyone should be subject to the same process. The need for discretion challenged that value and made life uncertain.

The possibility to capture people who are regulated when they become *real people* in the eyes of the regulator, is well documented in the regulatory literature and requires special measures of accountability in daily work practice. The opportunity for corruption, however, may potentially increase when authority is devolved in a system with high levels of discretion. In Australia and New Zealand, institutional and cultural constraints serve a protective function. The moderate levels of discretion required by responsive regulation, and given to tax system employees working within reasonably stable economies, translates to low levels of corruption by world standards.

Australia and New Zealand have relatively low levels of corruption because they both have extensive internal and external controls imposed on them by their traditional Westminster systems of government. Each country has established legislation and systems of internal and external audit of public sector activity that make corrupt practices difficult. Regular parliamentary scrutiny, rolling audit programmes, and a generally free media sector combine to make corrupt practices high risk activities. After more than a century of this kind of scrutiny, Australian and New Zealand civil servants have an entrenched culture of service to the community that works against corrupt practice by more than a desperate few.

East Timor, on the other hand, has a civil service emerging from twenty-five years of reportedly corrupt practice. Both management and staff in the ETRS appeared keen to make a difference and wanted to establish systems that removed the opportunity for corruption in an attempt to build a culture of legitimate and trustworthy service to the community. These standards were in accordance with the value system they had seen during the tenure of the various United Nations administrations in the period leading up to the establishment of their democracy. To increase levels of trust between tax administrators and the community, the East Timorese authorities had set very low levels of discretion for their employees. Whilst this policy decision may seem to conflict with responsive regulation, the East Timorese were able to see the value of the responsive system of tax administration in enhancing compliance with tax law. By separating their tax collection function from their tax education and enforcement functions, as was recommended by the IMF, they felt that they would be able to manage corruption and also build a tax administration that was responsive to the needs of their emerging nation. Most of the 'doing' could still be done responsively by the officials of the tax administration. Only the collection function, where the potential for corruption had been high in the past, was removed to the more legitimate banking system.

7.4.   *Occupational skill sets*

Before responsive regulation was introduced to the ATO, the shift from public administration to public management had seen restructuring of the organization along client groupings rather than revenue bases, the creation of 'key client managers' to work with large corporate firms, and recruitment of staff to 'help and educate' the community, particularly in the area of small business (see Vehorn and Brondolo 1999). By the mid 1990s, this had reinforced occupational cultures, and created distinct identities and hierarchies in the organization as evidenced by the following comment from an auditor:

'Staff can't do both help and audit work ... that's changing hats midstream. Why do I want to distribute pamphlets? I have tertiary qualifications. Half of the help and educate staff don't have tertiary qualifications' (Job and Honaker 2003:122).

This comment highlights that a culture change process has to deal not just with one organizational culture but with multiple cultures within the one organization, defined by occupation values, status and power.

Much of a taxation administrator's work requires an eye for detail and literal interpretations of complex tax law. These occupational skills of accountants, auditors and lawyers become the dominant practices of the organizational culture. These skills do not always sit comfortably alongside a more fluid and dynamic way of working. As one interviewee stated:

'The Compliance Model is on everyone's mind, but there are different perceptions of what it means. There is an element of it not getting through ... the assimilation of help and advice as part of what we do. Staff still compartmentalise activities. The reason is that different skills are required and many staff do not have the skills to do the help and education work' (Job and Honaker 2003:119).

Some staff preferred to translate the script of responsive regulation into a highly prescribed set of responses to meet the requirements of all situations. For example, some looked for scripts that told them what to say and do to the taxpayer. While such manuals might make staff feel more confident about making the change, Waller (2006 forthcoming) highlights that rigid adherence to a checklist of questions by ATO field staff not only can obstruct a responsive style of regulation, but lessens the credibility of field staff with taxpayers. Taxpayers expect field staff to be knowledgeable, perceptive and smart, not automated.

Other staff tried to protect their identity by mapping themselves on the model:

'So at the rank and file level people map themselves on a model – which I suppose is a human tendency to find where I fit. They don't see it as sort of dynamic – that if you fit here, that's where I live and that's where I am staying and that there isn't a role upwards or downwards in it' (Hobson 2003:142).

As Sparrow (2000: 211) highlighted, '… the difficulties seem to run deeper than the absence of systems, to an absence of understanding. [It is] the concept itself – not just the practice – [that] remains elusive'. Understanding can be assisted by acknowledging occupational values through the language used to express new ideas.

7.5.   *Language – connecting sensibilities*

Without dialogue to help in translation of a new idea, unusual forms or explanations can arise. Without 'finding the right language to describe [the change]', reductionism on the part of those required to implement the change becomes more likely (Sparrow 2000). The language in which responsive regulation was first presented to tax officers may have generated resistance to the new idea and to change because it did not connect with the underlying occupational or organizational cultural values or assumptions of taxation regulators. As one ATO auditor commented:

'My first reaction was: "What's this shit?" Not in terms of what the Model was trying to say, it was just the language, it was in academia. It wasn't until after we started using it, when we started playing with some of the ideas, that I started to understand it. So I guess for someone like me the worst thing to do was to try to get me to read something about it. The first thing to do is not telling me there's a model. Just start the process' (Hobson 2003:146).

This highlights not only that operational staff like to learn by doing, but that a new idea is best understood by using their own language to talk about it, and by translating it into stories that come from their own experiences. Instead of thinking about culture change as diffusion of an idea or mental programming, staff need to translate the idea into something which will achieve their own goals and *bend* cultural norms to make them fit the issues they deal with (Collins 2002: 124; Latour 1986). The process of translation and ongoing transformation by shaping the idea to fit different needs is 'essential for the existence and maintenance' of the idea (Latour 1986: 268). Translation into stories which were relevant to different occupational groups within the organizations allowed staff to see that the new ideas were not necessarily contrary to core values (see Sinclair 1991).

Both ATO and NZIR trainers gathered success stories and 'recruited' champions from within the organization, including some from responsive regulation pilot programmes, to provide examples of situations where responsive regulatory practices had worked without compromising core individual and organizational values. Stories helped to translate the concepts of responsive regulation into the language of particular groups (auditors, lawyers, information technology and human resources experts, and so on). For good reasons, interactive training using story telling and case studies from both tax and other regulatory environments emerged as a preferred training approach, together with on-the-job training and practical experience (see Braithwaite and Wirth 2001). This approach worked well in all three taxation administrations.

8.   Conclusion

We set out to explore Meidinger's claim that culture is important in making social change within regulatory organizations. We also wanted to examine the way these administrations implemented responsive regulation by exploring Latour's notion of translation rather than diffusion, and Sinclair's view that different occupations within a public service organization need to be given the space to 'bend' new ideas to encourage ownership. We did this by examining the adoption of responsive regulation in three taxation administrations.

Each administration faced similar challenges in implementing responsive regulation. In particular, the challenges faced in dealing with issues of consistency and equity and discretion and corruption highlighted the importance of organizational culture, and particularly regulatory culture. Consistency and equity are core values in a regulatory organization because they serve the purpose of ensuring fairness and limiting discretion to avoid the problem of corruption. These issues cannot be ignored in a regulatory organization, and needed to be discussed in terms of how they work in a responsive regulatory environment. Similarly, making the change to responsive regulation highlighted the need to acknowledge different occupational cultures. While resistance in the early stages signalled that people were thinking about responsive regulation, it highlighted that opportunities needed to be created for the different occupational cultures to explore responsive regulation in ways that had meaning for them. This was done through the use of champions, workshops, story telling, interactive training, and the use of their own language to help them to understand the new ideas and develop their own ways of working with it. This reduced fear and resentment and supported people within these organizations in the process of making change.

We conclude by agreeing with Meidinger that consideration of culture is important in making social change in regulatory organizations. Rather than diffusion through a top-down approach, a preferred way of making culture change is by allowing different occupational cultures within an organization the freedom and time to translate new ideas into their own language. Staff comments indicate they wanted the opportunity to translate responsive regulation for themselves. Without this, it is difficult for a new idea to be understood well enough to enable its adaptation to fit the needs of different groups within an organization. Instead, the idea may be diminished or reframed in unanticipated ways.

Changing long practiced and long held beliefs about 'the way we do things around here' is not easy. It is perhaps less difficult to accommodate changes such as contracting out, closer scrutiny of budgeting and reporting, performance-based management, or changed criteria for recruitment and promotion. It is far more difficult to make changes to the *tried and true* behaviours the operative staff have used to do their job, which in many ways define their role in the organization, their self esteem, and their sense of identity. The examples in this article highlight the step these organizations have taken in recent years to become more responsive and work with the public to design and administer tax law and policy. This new way of looking at the world walks hand in hand with the shift from administration to management, from having pre-ordained legitimacy to having to earn that legitimacy in the eyes of a skeptical public.

References

Aalders, M. and T. Wilthagen (1997). Moving beyond command-and-control: Reflexivity in the regulation of occupational safety and health and the environment. *Law & Policy*, 13: pp. 415-443.

Aaron, H.J. and J. Slemrod (eds.) (2004). *The crisis in tax administration*. Washington, D.C.: Brookings Institution Press.

Australian Taxation Office (1998). *Improving Tax Compliance in the Cash Economy*. Canberra: Commonwealth of Australia.

Ayres, I. and J. Braithwaite (1992). *Responsive Regulation: Transcending the Deregulation Debate*. New York: Oxford University Press.

Bardach, E. and R.A. Kagan (1982). *Going by the Book: The Problem of Regulatory Unreasonableness*. Philadelphia: Temple University Press.

Braithwaite, J. (2002). *Restorative Justice and Responsive Regulation*. Oxford and New York: Oxford University Press.

– (2003a). Large Business and the Compliance Model. In: *Taxing Democracy: Understanding tax avoidance and evasion*, V. Braithwaite (ed.). Aldershot: Ashgate Publishing Limited, 177-204.

– (2005). *Markets in Vice, Markets in Virtue*. New York: Federation Press, Sydney and Oxford University Press.

Braithwaite, J. and P. Grabosky (1985). *Occupational health and safety enforcement in Australia: A report to the National Occupational Health and Safety Commission*. Canberra: Australian Institute of Criminology.

Braithwaite, J. and A. Wirth (2001). Towards a framework for large business tax compliance. In: *Centre for Tax System Integrity Working Paper Series*, T. Murphy (ed.). Canberra: Australian National University and Australian Taxation Office.

Braithwaite, V. (1995). Games of Engagement: Postures Within the Regulatory Community. *Law & Policy*, 17.

– (ed.) (2003b). *Taxing Democracy: Understanding Tax Avoidance and Evasion*. Aldershot: Ashgate.

– (2006). Introduction to Responsive Regulation and Taxation, Special issue of Law & Policy. *Law & Policy*.

Braithwaite, V. and J. Braithwaite (2001). An evolving compliance model for tax enforcement. In: *Crimes of Privilege*, N. Shover and J.P. Wright (eds.). New York and Oxford: Oxford University Press.

Braithwaite, V., J. Braithwaite, D. Gibson and T. Makkai (1994). Regulatory Styles, Motivational Postures and Nursing Home Compliance. *Law & Policy*, 16.

Braithwaite, V. and M. Reinhart (2000). The Taxpayers' Charter: Does the Australian Tax Office comply and who benefits? In: *Centre for Tax System Integrity Working Paper Series*, T. Murphy (ed.). Canberra: Australian National University and Australian Taxation Office.

Collins, D. (2002). *Organizational Change: Sociological perspectives.* London: Routledge.

Deal, T.E. and A.A. Kennedy (1988). *Corporate cultures: the rites and rituals of corporate life.* London: Penguin Books.

Dodd, N. and B.M. Hutter (2000). Geopolitics and the regulation of economic life. *Law & Policy,* 22: pp. 1-24.

Evening Post (1999). Five more deaths laid at IRD door. In: *Evening Post 28 May 1999.*

Grabosky, P.N. (1995). Regulation by reward: On the use of incentives as regulatory instruments. *Law & Policy,* 17: pp. 257-282.

Grasmick, H.G. and R.J. Bursik (1990). Conscience, Significant Others, and Rational Choice: Extending the Deterrence Model. *Law & Society Review,* 24: pp. 837-861.

Gunningham, N., P. Grabosky and D. Sinclair (1998). *Smart regulation: designing environmental policy.* Oxford: Oxford University Press.

Hamilton, S. (2003). Putting the Client First: The Emerging Copernican Revolution of Tax Administration. *Tax Notes International,* pp. 568-576.

Hobson, K. (2003). Championing the Compliance Model: From Common Sense to Common Action? In: *Taxing Democracy,* V. Braithwaite (ed.). Aldershot: Ashgate Publishing Limited, pp. 131-158.

Hofstede, G. (1994). *Cultures and Organizations.* London: HarperCollinsBusiness.

Hogwood, B.W. and L.A. Gunn (1984). *Policy Analysis for the Real World.* New York: Oxford University Press.

Hughes, O.E. (1994). *Public Management and Administration.* Houndmills: Macmillan Press.

Job, J. and D. Honaker (2003). Short-term Experience with Responsive Regulation in the Australian Taxation Office. In: *Taxing Democracy: Understanding Tax Avoidance and Evasion,* V. Braithwaite (ed.). Aldershot: Ashgate Publishing Limited.

Kanter, R. Moss (1989). *When Giants Learn to Dance.* New York: Simon and Schuster.

Kavanagh, J. (1997). Three-way Bet Taxes Credulity. In: *The Australian 25 September 1997.*

Klepper, S. and D. Nagin (1989). The Criminal Deterrence Literature: Implications for Research on Taxpayer Compliance. In: *Taxpayer Compliance: Social Science Perspectives,* J.A. Roth and J.T. Scholz (ed.). Philadelphia: University of Pennsylvania Press.

Latour, B. (1986). The powers of association. In: *Power, Action and Belief: A New Sociology of Knowledge?* J. Law (ed.). London: Routledge & Kegan Paul.

Lipsky, M. (1980). *Street-level Bureaucracy: dilemmas of the individual in public services.* New York: Russell Sage Foundation.

Meidinger, E. (1987). Regulatory Culture: A Theoretical Outline. *Law & Policy,* 9.

Merton, R. (1939). Bureaucratic Structure and Personality. *Social Forces,* 18: pp. 560-568.

Murphy, K. (2003). An examination of taxpayers' attitudes towards the Australian tax system: Findings from a survey of tax scheme investors. *Australian Tax Forum,* 18: pp. 209-242.

–   (2005). Regulating more effectively: The relationship between procedural justice, legitimacy and tax non-compliance. In: *Centre for Tax System Integrity Working Paper Series.* Canberra: Regulatory Institutions Network, The Australian National University.

New Zealand Inland Revenue (2003a). *Inland Revenue Climate Survey 2003: Report to Senior Management Team.* Wellington.

–   (2003b). *The Way Forward – Achievements and Future Direction 2003 Onwards.* Wellington.

Parker, C. and J. Braithwaite (2003). Regulation. In: *The Oxford Handbook of Legal Studies*, P. Cane and M. Tushnet (ed.). Oxford: Oxford University Press.

Rawlings, G. (2003). Cultural Narratives of Taxation and Citizenship: Fairness, Groups and Globalisation. *Australian Journal of Social Issues*, 38: pp. 269-305.

– (2004). Laws, Liquidity and Eurobonds. *The Journal of Pacific History*, 39: pp. 325-341.

Reiss, A.J. jr. (1984). Selecting strategies of social control over organizational life. In: *Enforcing Regulation*, K. Hawkins and J.M. Thomas (ed.). Boston: Kluwer-Nijhoff.

Schein, E.H. (2004). *Organizational Culture and Leadership*. San Francisco: Jossey-Bass.

Scott, C. (2004). Regulatory Innovation and the Online Consumer. *Law & Policy*, 26: pp. 477-506.

Shover, N., D. Clelland and J Lynxwiler (1986). *Enforcement or negotiation: constructing a regulatory bureaucracy*. Albany, N.Y.: State University of New York Press.

Sinclair, A. (1991). After Excellence: Models of Organizational Culture for the Public Sector. *Australian Journal of Public Administration*, 50: pp. 321-332.

Sparrow, M. (2000). *The Regulatory Craft*. Washington DC: Brookings Institution Press.

The New Zealand Herald (1999). 'No excuse' for IRD meathook cartoon. In: *The New Zealand Herald*, 28 May 1999.

– (2000). Tax collection with a smile. In: *The New Zealand Herald*, 30 June 2000.

The Parliament of the Commonwealth of Australia, Joint Committee of Public Accounts (1993). *An Assessment of Tax: A Report on an Inquiry into the Australian Taxation Office*. Canberra: Australian Government Publishing Service.

The Press (1999). Tax dept blamed for deaths. In: *The Press*, 27 May 1999.

Tyler, T.R. (1990). *Why people obey the law*. New Haven, CT: Yale University.

Vehorn, C.L. and J. Brondolo (1999). Organizational Options for Tax Administration. *Bulletin for International Fiscal Documentation*, 53: pp. 499-512.

Waller, V. (2006). The one that got away: Detecting non-compliance in order to ensure voluntary compliance. *Law & Policy*.

Wenzel, M. (2005). Motivation or rationalisation? Causal relations between ethics, norms and tax compliance. *Journal of Economic Psychology*, 26: pp. 491-508.

Williams, R. (2001). Prosecuting nonlodgers: to persuade or punish? In: *Centre for Tax System Integrity Working Paper Series*, T. Murphy (ed.). Canberra: Australian National University and Australian Taxation Office.